Where We Belong

ADDITIONAL TITLES BY PAUL SHEPARD AVAILABLE FROM
THE UNIVERSITY OF GEORGIA PRESS

Man in the Landscape: A Historic View of the Esthetics of Nature

Nature and Madness

The Tender Carnivore and the Sacred Game

Thinking Animals: Animals and the Development of Human Intelligence

Paul Shepard

Where We Belong

BEYOND

ABSTRACTION

IN

PERCEIVING

NATURE

Edited by Florence Rose Shepard

The University of Georgia Press *Athens & London*

Acknowledgments for the use of previously published material appear
on pages 243–44, which constitute an extension of the copyright page.

Published by the University of Georgia Press
Athens, Georgia 30602
© 2003 by Florence Rose Shepard
All rights reserved
Designed by Kathi Dailey Morgan
Set in Berthold Baskerville
Printed and bound by Thomson-Shore
The paper in this book meets the guidelines for
permanence and durability of the Committee on
Production Guidelines for Book Longevity of the
Council on Library Resources.

Printed in the United States of America

07 06 05 04 03 C 5 4 3 2 1

Library of Congress Cataloging-in-Publication Data

Shepard, Paul, 1925–
Where we belong : beyond abstraction in perceiving nature / Paul Shepard ;
edited by Florence Rose Shepard.
p. cm.
Includes bibliographical references (p.   ) and index.
ISBN 0-8203-2420-5 (hardcover : alk. paper)
1. Human ecology–Philosophy. 2. Nature (Aesthetics) 3. Landscape assessment.
4. Human-animal relationships. I. Shepard, Florence R. II. Title.
GF21 .S524 2003
304.2–dc21   2002152763

British Library Cataloging-in-Publication Data available

CONTENTS

ILLUSTRATIONS

FOREWORD

I DISCOVERED PAUL SHEPARD'S *MAN IN THE LANDSCAPE*
during my education as a landscape architect in the late 1960s.
It was a revelation. Here was work that integrated a vast array of
concerns and made connections that I felt but could not articulate.
At a time when many were groping for a theoretical framework
and a historical perspective with which to address emerging environmental concerns, here was a foundational text, one that was a
model of careful observation, wide research, and insight. *Man in
the Landscape* became a touchstone for my own work. It contains
the germs for much of Shepard's subsequent research in topics
that would occupy him for the remainder of his life: the eye and
sight; artists and the land; the garden; the American West; the
meaning of nature; and, perhaps most important, the relationships between humans and animals. In all of these investigations
his sources, methods, and exposition have been wide ranging and
exploratory, always recognizing the equal power of the material,
the ideological, and the metaphorical.

What is particularly striking about the selections in this anthology, especially the early essays, is Shepard's prescience in anticipating research and practice in art and ecology, cultural landscape studies, tourism studies, the body, environmental history, and the general concern for the intersection between the physical landscape and material world and the realm of ideas. Much of this is now commonplace; but it was not so when he wrote, and his essays are still informative and remarkably current, for they often pose the most essential and difficult questions. A profound ethic that avoids simple and spurious dichotomies between the humanistic and environmental points of view underlies much of his writing. There is a deep concern for others—humans and other species, plant and animal. His is not a romantic sensibility but one embedded in understanding, appreciation, and even wonder at the natural world and its processes. He rejected landscape as a simple pictorial concept, yet he simultaneously addressed the meanings of those pictures, recalling Oscar Wilde's paradox and provocation that the secret of the world is found in the visible, not the invisible.

Shepard's works are at the intersection of discussions of nature and culture. He was one of the first to help us recognize that the nature of culture and the culture of nature both have their basis in biology. He never allows one to forget that humans are a species, and his investigations, speculations, and occasional proscriptions view us as creatures in our diverse habitats. He examines how culture constructs nature, but also how we know it through a set of perceptual filters—from the biological to the virtual. The true practice of ecological thinking lies in the recognition of the interconnectedness of life and of ideas.

Shepard wrote several volumes on animals and their relationship to humans: *The Tender Carnivore and the Sacred Game* (1973), *Thinking Animals: Animals and the Development of Human Intelligence* (1978), *The Sacred Paw: The Bear in Nature, Myth, and Literature* with Barry Sanders (1985), and *The Others: How Animals Made Us Human* (1996). His other grand theme, embodied in this collection, is human interaction with the natural world, particularly in terms of its aesthetic dimension. He delves deep into the roots of cultural and biological preferences for certain landscapes.

His works teach that thinking and seeing are inseparable. Sight is a complex and dynamic process, and he demands an examination of the entire process and experience. He has us look at what is behind our eyes, in the mind's eye; what is before it, in the various fields of vision; and at the eye itself and its evolution. All of the essays in this collection are about seeing, but their points of view shift and change, giving a truly modernist and cubist perspective. "Point of view" has multiple meanings for Shepard. It refers to ideas and even an ideological position, but it also entails recognition of shifts in positions, spatially and, perhaps most important, temporally. As a modern scientist he reminds us not only to look through the lens but to examine the lens itself—its history, assumptions, and biases—with an awareness, as Heisenberg noted, that the process of observation itself transforms the phenomenon.

His explorations took Shepard to diverse places and landscapes. Surely the result of his own preferences, they included the vast space and often sublime landscapes of the American West and the rich variety of New Zealand. The geographical range and comparisons are fascinating, but the spatial range is more impressive—from the most intimate to vast landscapes, from the local and familiar to the distant and exotic. The overriding theme is always the organism and its relationship to its habitat.

Speaking of the temporal dimension Shepard described the "three octaves of the fourth dimension"—actually a more expansive and comprehensive view of history that includes each individual being of any species (ontogeny), the history of the group, and the history of the species (phylogeny). This temporal range combines geological understanding, evolutionary consciousness, and the historic record with up-to-the-minute where-are-we-going-next insights regarding the life cycle and the idiosyncrasies of each individual. His work often investigates the resonance between these octaves, providing an intellectual map of variable spatial and temporal scales.

These scales are combined in several essays that display a particular interest in the visions of those on the move: pioneers, visitors, and travelers. At one extreme is the pioneer, determined to settle in a new territory; at the other is the temporary vision of the tourist, one of the characteristic personalities of contemporary experience. Individuals in each of these groups feel themselves in the unique position of seeing a place for the first time. Shepard turns this insight into his own intellectual approach—seeing with fresh eyes, but with a simultaneous consciousness of what constituted that point of view. Here is a pioneer writing about pioneers, and he often displays that element of wonder that accompanies the discovery of something beyond one's experience.

Shepard's work is distinguished by his rare ability to move between disciplines with extraordinary facility and to apply insights gained in one arena to other realms of thought, knitting together diverse ideas. His contribution lies in the interstices. He pioneered the investigation of the now popular liminal space. With an understanding of ideas and methods in aesthetics, art history, biology, psychology, history, geology, and more, he provided the intellectual mortar for his successors to build new structures of thought. These pieces are assembled in intellectual puzzles as elegant as the complex joinery of a master woodworker. Even more than interdisciplinary studies Shepard's work built bridges between disciplines, both connecting their insights and methods and offering a new vista from the bridge, the place in between.

The broader significance of Shepard's work and its impacts are finally receiving the recognition they deserve. The time is certainly ripe to republish these sometimes hard to find essays as a cohesive collection. It should be noted that Shepard himself was a superb anthologist; *Environ/mental: Essays of the Planet as Home* (1971) and especially *The Subversive Science: Essays towards an Ecology of Man* (1969), with Daniel McKinley, are classics in need of only modest updating. Anyone interested in the landscape will find the selections in this volume stimulating and provocative. Those who address the landscape as a professional concern – environmental design professionals and especially landscape architects and planners – will find a solid basis here for their work. Environmental historians, art historians, cultural theorists, and others will find methodological models that stretch the boundaries of their disciplines. In these selections (and in many others by Shepard) I found germs of insight that acted as catalysts to my own research and teaching – and I know that I am not alone.

Individuals in a remarkable variety of disciplines have found Paul Shepard alternatively a kindred spirit and a foil for their own work. His work always challenges conventional wisdom. His ideas are not always easy to understand or accept, but it is worth the effort required to get at the depth and complexity of his thought. He does not pander to either a humanist or a scientific sensibility, but expects each to know the vocabulary and language of the other. Sometimes he clearly relishes the role of the iconoclastic provocateur. He draws his ideas from an enormous range of sources, but always there is the naturalist's sensibility, the patient observer, the careful eyewitness, and the Darwinian eye for subtle distinction and grand pattern.

Kenneth Helphand

PREFACE

SHORTLY AFTER THE SUN SETS BEHIND THE HOBACK
Mountains each evening, I turn north to face the Gros Ventres
Mountains; their rosy glow brings closure to my day. Blocked
from my view by Clark Butte, the sun's last light, rich in red rays,
finds its way from below the horizon through the cleft of the
Hoback Canyon and, as if by magic, sets fire to the south-facing
wall of these ancient mountains. People see various symbols and
figures etched by nature in the bare base rock. Some see flying
eagles; like the French explorers and trappers who named the
Gros Ventres and the Grand Tetons, I see feminine images.

Paul Shepard cautioned us about this human proclivity to
project our own meanings on landscapes according to our ken.
Although before his death in 1996 he shared these sunsets with
me from our cabin in Wyoming, he never forsook the grounding
of our perceptions, the landforms carved by time and weather
over eons. He appreciated the aesthetics of the face of the mountain, but its beauty never clouded the love he felt for the earth —

the ordinary dirt, rock, and creatures locked in this evolutionary game. He would not be led astray by mere beauty or appearance, by the notion of landscape.

Following Paul's death, the University of Georgia Press in 1998 reissued his books: *The Tender Carnivore and the Sacred Game* (1973), *Thinking Animals* (1977), and *Nature and Madness* (1980). With the reissue of *Man in the Landscape* (1967) and the publication of *Where We Belong,* his most important work is now accessible to the public. I am deeply grateful to Barbara Ras and the University of Georgia Press for their continued commitment to Paul's writings. As we began this project, Kenny Helphand read the manuscript and offered extremely helpful advice; I thank him as well for his insightful introduction to this volume. And I thank Melba Wheatcroft Shepard, Paul's wife in the years of his landscape research and writing – beginning at Yale University in 1951–54 – for her generosity in talking to me and providing insights into Paul's motivations at the time he wrote these essays.

Those who have followed Paul's thoughtful critique of the genesis of our perception and attitudes toward nature in the United States and new readers alike will welcome *Where We Belong;* it represents the major intellectual commitment of Paul Shepard's early life. Some of the essays are extensions of the research he conducted for his master's thesis, "A Study in Landscape Interpretation" (1952), an analysis of the Hudson River School paintings from an ecological point of view. Others are outgrowths of his doctoral dissertation topic, "American Attitudes towards the Landscape in New England and the West, 1830–1870" (1954), which discusses our European nature heritage in gardens and art, the perceptions of itinerant travelers along the Oregon Trail, and the development of tourism and the national park system in the United States. The essays also incorporate his extended research in the above-mentioned areas that led to the publication of *Man in the Landscape* (1967). With the exception of the lengthy monograph "An Ecstasy of Admiration," all of the essays presented here have been previously published, some in journals no longer in existence.

These essays are not merely a review of history. The overarching assumption in them is that attitudes toward the landscape determine not only how we view the natural world but also how we treat it. Such attitudes develop through the interaction of contemporary circumstances with past cultural traditions and practices. Comprehending the origin of our perceptions is a necessary first step in studying the antecedents as well as the consequences of the ecological devastation of Planet Earth today.

Paul's ability to identify the underlying attitudes that fueled the alarming exploitation of the natural world helps us understand our nation at the mid–nineteenth century. The stark contrast between wild and domesticated nature was then becoming apparent and sparked the beginning of environmental activism. By questioning our past and present fascination with romanticized landscapes, he helps us understand our need for wild nature as the ground of our being.

In the early 1970s when Paul was named an Avery Professor at Pitzer College, one of the Claremont Schools in California, he chose as a title for that endowed chair Professor of Natural Philosophy and Human Ecology. It was an appropriate name. He was concerned primarily with interrelationships between humans and nature, and his method of study was very similar to the natural philosophy followed by Thoreau.

Paul Shepard's own words best explain the type of research that preceded the writing of these essays: "At the suggestion of my mentors at Yale at mid-century, I examined the work [of the Hudson River painters] as a naturalist, going into the field with copies of the paintings the way a bird-watcher might go, working first to clarify the taxonomy, and then assuming that the culture of nineteenth–century America was part of their natural history. My advisors suggested that I compare the perception of order in the work of the artists to that of the ecologist."

His field and research notes concerning the Hudson River painters (edited slightly by me for brevity) reveal in more detail this serendipitous method:

> Preparation for the [project] involved visiting museums from Washington, D.C. to Boston and scanning the material in reference books and libraries in search of landscape paintings. [He also photographed paintings and photographs when permissible.] There seemed to be a distinct heritage of American landscape painting, particularly from the second third of the nineteenth century. Biographical material on the painters was sought. Out of some three

to four hundred paintings or photographs of paintings I selected about 75 for which there seemed to be some chance of finding the actual site of the painting. Some titles gave specific sites (*Niagara Falls*) while others were very general (*In the Catskills*).

After selecting the pictures, I contacted the owners to obtain official photographs and permission for publication. Thirty-seven museums or individuals were contacted to get pictures of the 75 paintings. Forty-four different artists were represented. [As he collected the paintings and permissions he began working out a plan for visiting the sites. Two separate trips for finding and photographing original sites emerged.] One was up the Hudson Valley, across to the Taconic Mountains on the Massachusetts–New York border, and back down the Housatonic River valley to New Haven. The other went up the Connecticut River valley to the White Mountains, with a swing over into the Green Mountains, then down to the New Hampshire coast, Boston, and south to Newport, Rhode Island and back to New Haven along the Connecticut coast. . . .

As the photographs began to arrive I was at work at the geology, botany, and natural and human history of the regions. The pictures were mounted in transparent holders in a large notebook in the order in which I would visit them. The factual data was typed up and mounted opposite each photograph. Finally all was ready. The Hudson River trip would be the first. After living with these paintings for weeks, I had begun to feel that each painting was an individual with its own character and I attempted to re-create in my imagination the conditions under which it was painted. The twenty to thirty painters who are considered to have belonged to this group were working from 1825 until 1870. I had no prejudice about the time of the painting or the natural philosophy of the painter. That the majority were from the early nineteenth century seemed to indicate the preponderance of landscape painting done at the time – or possibly the failure of museums to accumulate much of the modern landscape work.

Paul goes on to document each of these trips, the first taken with a friend, Gordon Loery, the second with his wife, Melba, and their year-old son, Kenton. Both car trips – which included hiking and camping – are described in his notes with details of back-tracking, talks with residents, dead ends, and amazing discoveries.

This method of going on-site to substantiate his research was repeated in 1958 when, after studying the diaries of itinerant travelers along the Oregon Trail, he retraced their route, taking photographs and notes along the way. Likewise, in preparation for the completion of *Man in the Landscape,* he visited the formal gardens in England, France, and Italy. On a Fulbright Fellowship to New Zealand in 1961, after studying diaries and sites there, Paul wrote the monograph *English Reaction to the New Zealand Landscape before 1850,* replicating there his Oregon Trail research.

Special books and mentors guided Paul in his quest to understand the link between perception and ecology. The idea of "an ecology of vision" began in his undergraduate years at the University of Missouri with a study of *The Vertebrate Eye* by Gordon Walls under the tutelage of his undergraduate mentor, Rudolph Bennett. Later, at Yale, *Scenery and the Sense of Sight* by Vaughan Cornish provided a link into the context of the Hudson River paintings. And also at Yale, in one of that university's first interdisciplinary doctorates, outstanding professors and mentors guided Paul: Paul Sears (ecological conservation), Evelyn Hutchinson (zoology and evolution), William Jordy (art history), Christopher Tunnard (architecture), and Ralph Henry Gabriel (history). It was not until late in his landscape research, upon reading Marshall McLuhan's *Through the Vanishing Point,* that he seriously questioned the validity of landscape perception as a way to ecological understanding. It was at that point that he turned in *Nature and Madness* (1980) to proper nurturance of children in nature as the route to ecological understanding and sanity.

Although a serious student and researcher, Paul Shepard did not spend his life sequestered in a library cubicle. Beginning with his undergraduate work and extending through his graduate work at Yale and his first academic position at Knox College – a period that spanned two decades – he was an environmental activist, a whistle-blower, and an informed conservationist as well as a dedicated teacher. Although he had many knowledgeable mentors along the way, Paul was not one to follow the lead of others. He studied situations carefully and reached his own conclusions, even if they differed from those of the people at the top. For example, as an undergraduate in the summer of 1947, while working at Big Spring State Park in Missouri as an interpreter, he took it upon himself to inform the governor of logging practices that were removing huge old-growth trees that he recognized as having irreplaceable ecological value. His whistle-blowing made the news, and the state policies for management of state parks were completely reviewed and revised as a result.

Following graduation from the University of Missouri in 1949, Paul worked for the Conservation Federation of Missouri for a year, under the direction of Charles Calliston, a foremost conservationist of his time. Along with organizing local conservation organizations, he served as associate editor of *Missouri Wildlife,* where his writing career as well as his active conservation work began.

During Paul's graduate work at Yale University he became aware that the creation of European gardens was an important step in the development of attitudes toward nature and applied to the National Council of State Garden Clubs of America (NCSGCA) for a scholarship to fund this area of study. Following the completion of this work, he was asked to serve as the conservation chairman of the NCSGCA – at the time, one of the largest conservation organizations in the country with a membership of 250,000. As conservation chairman he represented the group on the Natural Resources Council along with officers of other environmental organizations, including Ira Gabrielson, Charles Callison, David Brower, Sigurd Olson, and Howard Zanhiser. With Rachel Carson, he testified before Congress about the dangers of unrestricted use of pesticides. During the period of uncontrolled reclamation and dam building by the government in the 1950s, Paul disagreed with conservationists' decision to approve building Glen Canyon Dam on the Colorado River in Arizona in exchange for the government's agreement to abandon the plan for a dam in Echo Park on the Green River in northern Utah. Consequently, he refused to join other conservation organizations in these negotiations.

As a seasonal park ranger at Olympic National Park in Washington State in 1956, Paul Shepard again became a whistle-blower, this time mustering the membership of the NCSGCA to write letters opposing logging in the park. As a result of this controversy, which created a major crisis in the administration of the park, Paul was permanently banned from further employment in the national parks. Shocked by this action and greatly disappointed, he decided in 1958 to resign his position as conservation chairman of the NCSGCA and withdrew from national conservation issues.

But his conservation work at the local level did not end. He had originally accepted a position at Knox College primarily because it offered him the opportunity to develop a field station for the college. During his ten-year tenure there he directed the development of Green Acres, the college's biological field station, which encompassed reclaimed mining land—including tailings piles and pits—and old cultivated fields. He enlisted students and faculty to help in the restoration. In addition to reintroducing native flora and fauna, they restored certain cultivated fields to tallgrass prairie with seeds gathered along old railroad beds. This tallgrass prairie now thrives; a portion of it bears his name.

As has been my practice in editing Paul's work, I have not extended or altered his ideas in these essays. I made few changes in previously published work beyond softening the unintended sexist language of his time and eliminating repetition. I did not include the extensive notes to the New Zealand monograph. Paul had already edited the original version of "An Ecstasy of Imagination," and I further simplified the language, shortened quoted materials, and reconstituted abstracts at the beginning of each section into a summary statement. I included most of the available photographs Paul had originally selected to accompany his published essays, again avoiding repetition.

Reconstructing Paul's research was a difficult but interesting task. A dedicated and tireless scholar, he left behind published papers and early drafts, vast collections of photographs of landscape paintings as well as his photographs and slides taken of painting sites, extensive field and research notes, and correspondence related to his work. It was a tremendously moving experience to sort through these materials, to follow him intellectually from a young man in his early twenties literally to his deathbed. But most astonishing to me was his unflinching belief from the very beginning in the importance of the natural world to our human evolution and individual development. He never wavered from the belief that human nature depends on the natural world for fulfillment.

After studying his papers and pictures for more than a decade, I am beginning to appreciate what Paul Shepard saw when he looked at the land. Landforms and their representation as landscapes meant something to him. He believed that the discovery of "landscape," "the arrangement of objects in space and time as a synoptic [general] view of human experience," was intimately associated with vision and represented a kind of detachment from the world. Paul surmised that although changes of taste in the appreciation and enjoyment of art and nature occur regularly, humans carry a genetic disposition to certain landforms, an "environmental sensibility" or consciousness that grew out of our evolution in nature. And with proper bonding to caregivers and nature in childhood, we have the capacity to develop sane, ecological, and realistic relationships to people and the natural world.

The essays collected in this volume were written primarily between the 1950s and 1970s. They fulfill two purposes. First, they provide an undergirding for his early books that are now classics in human ecology, the study of humans' complex relationship to their environment. But in their own right they are also an astute critique of our perception of nature as landscape, and as such they help elucidate the origins of our present ecological problems.

In his last years Paul began revisiting his early landscape themes with several essays that appear in the last section of this book. He concluded that landscape, as a visual representation, emerged in the sixteenth century as a secular perspective not only in art and literature but also as a habit of perception that profoundly influenced human relationships to the land. It emerged with print and reading, and was thus a linear way of seeing and a way – he finally realized – that separated us from, rather than brought us closer to, nature.

Sitting beside me in our cabin looking north to the rugged Gros Ventre Mountains one day, Paul explained how the framing of that scene by our window – or, for that matter, a painting of such a scene – acted to distance us from the experience of the mountains. I could understand how "scenery" might replace the real thing in our lives, but, I pointed out, contemporary writers commonly use the word "landscape" to refer to the external world as well as to their internal psychological state. It obviously means something important to them, I insisted. He agreed that it probably did, and added, "It may be the best they can do under the circumstances."

I believe we must do better than that. The implications of Paul Shepard's teachings are evident everywhere in a world that is being relentlessly rent by machines of exploitation operated by unforgiving and mindless masses. We are all a party to this devastation. The imperative before us is to change the course of civilization in support of the health of the earth.

We know there is something deeply flawed about the way we treat our precious earth today. Using Paul's insights as a road map to present-day landscape perception and environmental attitudes, perhaps we can begin to understand where we went wrong. We must make our idealized landscapes congruent with the real world. Only then can we stop the devastating destruction of earth's ecosystems and begin to repair the damage. As landscapes these ecosystems merely reflect our attitudes; as landforms they are our home – the soil and bedrock and precious but limited resources that support the ground of our being.

Landscape

Paintings of the New England Landscape

A Scientist Looks at Their Geomorphology

THE PAINTING OF A LANDSCAPE RAISES A NUMBER OF questions about order in nature and the ways in which it is perceived. Without being condescending, ecologists, who know that landscapes are complex and our knowledge of them limited, may assume that artists know very little about the mysteries with which they deal. Like naturalists, artists have a fragmentary knowledge of what they see. In addition to this they must harmonize their personal apprehension of the landscape with the prerequisites of painting and the organizational problem of a two-dimensional canvas. Art historians and critics perennially discover that a landscape painter's work expresses not only a personality and a measure of understanding, but also a more or less consistent and systematic orientation to the natural world.

Equally diverse forces may be at work in all of us as we examine our corners of the world and attempt to formulate our experience. But the rest of us do not produce a picture. We have, instead, the spectator's pleasure of examining the finished painting, a tangible product of all the historical debris, emotions, factual data, and visual eccentricities that coalesce—often surprisingly well—in a work of art. It is unsafe to generalize about which of these elements is epitomized. But it may be illuminating to narrow the inquiry by comparing some paintings with their landscape sites and asking ourselves, "What part do the landforms and their intrinsic processes play in the painter's attitude toward nature?"

Because of its rich artistic history New England offers a fertile ground for study. Its landforms derive mostly from igneous and metamorphosed crystalline rocks that formerly constituted a northeast–southwest synclinal trough and are now at the surface, exposed by the erosion of a prism of rock several miles in thickness. Because of its north–south alignment the region may be conveniently considered as a series of parallel strips. North and south from Boston are the sedimentaries of a submerged shoreline. West of this is a belt of shale and sandstone lowlands, bordered on their landward side by an upland which is continuous with the granitic White Mountains to the north. Between this upland and another to the west is the Connecticut Valley, which splits New England from north to south, forming the boundary between the White and Green Mountains. The valley contains the Connecticut River and its floodplain, much of which is a glacial lacustrine deposit underlain by sandstone and conglomerates. Fault zones occur along the valley sides, and basaltic trap ridges parallel to the stream rise above the valley floor.

The Berkshires and, to their north, the Green Mountains occupy most of the uplands between the Connecticut River and the Hudson. The area is greatly dissected by streams, and the hills are noted geologically for several accordant summit levels. Along the western edge of the Berkshires are several stream valleys or "intervales" with floors of sedimentary rocks, especially limestone and its altered form, marble. Also between the Berkshires and the Hudson is the narrow Taconic Range, a high, broken ridge of much folded and extremely resistant metamorphics that continue southwestward as the pre-Cambrian Appalachians. The fiordlike Hudson trough is cut out of tilted sedimentaries and is partly filled with alluvium.

The streams throughout New England are well adjusted to surface forms and structures except where recently disturbed by glaciations. The whole region was covered with ice, but its effects were disparate because of varying depth, direction of movement, and duration of the glaciers. West of the Hudson and north of the Highlands is an eastern corner of the Appalachian Plateau, the sedimentary Catskills. Along their margin they are deeply dissected, but their crests extend impressively three thousand feet above the Hudson Valley.

There are many local variations in this general picture, mostly associated with special glacial features, dikes, sills, contact zones, local mineralogy, and differential mass wasting. Other variations, biotically expressed by the transition from mixed deciduous to boreal forest, result from climatic differences between north and south and between seashore and mountaintop.

Contemporary with the young men who would become the first industrial tycoons were their antitheses, a group who represented the culminating bloom of an incandescent faith in the visible face of nature, a faith that had grown out of the early years of the previous century. In its milieu was a quickening of the sense of time, of a natural world of order and continuity, of beauty instead of sin. Emerging from advances in physics and chemistry, the new geology stimulated wide general interest. An educated New Englander in the 1840s found the evolution of landforms excitingly evident and perhaps still an argument for the design of providential intervention. But the forms were nonetheless propelled endlessly by gravity, producing rocky features and plant associations constantly adjusting to the weather by perpetually assuming forms dictated by the structure and solubility of base rock.

The full horror of New York City's slums, annual epidemics, and fires impressed itself upon the sensitive. The artist and naturalist fled, at least periodically, from the city's intrinsic evil. As the new mansions along the Hudson indicated polite approval of the valley's sublime wilderness, new railroads and highways carried the less affluent on vacations far from the city into the mountains of New England. In those mansions and in the glittering new villas in the city itself, for the first time since the founding of New Amsterdam, there was a steady market for paintings of indigenous landscapes.

Scenery-conscious observers could see most of the area because of the extensive clearing of the land. Some counties, now once more covered with forests, were as much as 65 percent deforested.[1] From numerous naked hilltops, the distant mountains loomed. The relationship between the painter and New England's mountains was apparently a compelling one, and yet, in absolute scale, these mountains fell far short of the Alps. This was something of a contradiction and an obstacle at a time when America's bounty was the best oil for chauvinism's wheels. Figures did not lie, of course, but on the other hand, the actual impression of size in the field depended on the observer. Rocks of relatively insignificant proportions had a way of becoming bigger. James Suydam, modifying the scale of men and livestock, saw Paradise Rocks (figures 1 and 2) as an extraordinary form, although some simple calculation shows them to be about 400 percent greater in height in his painting than their actual height of some ten meters. Fifty meters is a modest addition when it comes to mountains, although much depends on how you look at them. It is appar-

Figure 1. *Paradise Rocks, Newport,* 1865. Painting by James Augustus Suydam. Oil on canvas, 25 1/8 x 45 1/8 in. National Academy of Design, New York. Bequest of James A. Suydam, 1865 (1226-P).

Figure 2. Site of *Paradise Rocks, Newport,* 1953. Photograph by Paul Shepard.

ent in *Paradise Rocks* that this addition has determined the whole meaning of the landscape—not only because of the increased height, but because the rocks' clean, angular surfaces are architectural. Sixty meters is an impressive level when it comes to large buildings of the kinds venerated in Europe. It was a rewarding natural substitution in the face of grave historical insufficiencies. Not many hills look like buildings, but those that did helped offset America's paucity of castles and cathedrals, our lack of which Mr. Ruskin so deplored.[2]

There is little doubt about this pseudo-architectural value of some New England hills and rocks. It is perhaps unfair to suppose that such tabernacular rocks as those portrayed in John Kensett's *Cathedral Ledges, North Conway, New Hampshire* (figures 3 and 4) were only salve for the wounds in our national cultural pride. Men of any nation have found them equally architecturally appealing. Nearer specifically to the heart of the early-nineteenth-century Anglo-American was the antiquity and the condition of such timeworn edifices. Present dilapidation compounded former magnificence. The mass wasting of the Cathedral Ledges is most clearly seen from Kensett's position. The acid-stained cliffs, with their newly broken and old exposed surfaces, taluses, the evidence of frost

Figure 3. *Cathedral Ledges, North Conway, New Hampshire*. Painting by John Kensett. Location of painting unknown.

Figure 4. Site of *Cathedral Ledges, North Conway, New Hampshire,* 1953.
Photograph by Paul Shepard.

and water, and the incessant moldering lichens, are the wounds of time. The sharp angles and blocky fracture pattern of this granite, together with the knowledge that granite was a building material, firmly impress the beholder with the delightful illusion of an inexorably decaying pile. Kensett obsessively reproduced the details of the cliff, but he filled in the foreground with a twenty-ton rock and perhaps added a few birches. The number of New England's naked, near-vertical walls of rock is small indeed thanks to glacial thoroughness. Those that do exist—structural faces like those at Cathedral Ledges along with stream- and wave-cut rocks—figure importantly in the art and the tourism of the times.

The contemplation of mountains, as ruins or otherwise, was a pursuit that engrossed the observer for many hours at a time and required sufficient distance from the mountain. New England was remarkably well suited to such landscapes in the manner of Claude Lorraine. The wide Hudson and Connecticut Valleys, the intervales, the shores, and the Monadnockish geography of the mountains ensured ample foreground and the convenience of village lodgings. Vertical enlargement of the distant mountains is almost the rule in these paintings. Changes in slope angle and form are also evident. The concave element of the S-profile is usually shifted nearer the peak, and sometimes the convex crown is completely lost. Geologically, the relative extent of the concave and convex components and the degree of slope that they involve are unique for the conditions of weathering, debris removal, and perhaps uplift in any particular place.

A century ago Americans spoke of the White Mountains as America's Alps. So, the creation of horns and arêtes in New England must be credited to the human imagination and not to the ice ages. Thomas Cole's *View of the White Mountains* (figures 5 and 6) is a view that looks northeast from Bretton Woods toward Mount Washington. It shows crest line modification and lateral compression that modify the profile and add steepness to the gradients. The fore- and middle grounds may have been based on a separate sketch. The painter isolated the mountain with a gesture appropriate to the eclecticism of the times, remaking the top after the geology of glaciations and the bottom after that of the desert.

In these modifications of the quality of New England's smoothness we are reminded that an aesthetic theory still prevailed which separated the *beautiful* from the *picturesque* partly on the nature of surfaces: the beautiful

Figure 5. *View of the White Mountains,* 1827. Painting by Thomas Cole. Oil on canvas, 25.375 x 35.188 in. Wadsworth Atheneum Museum of Art, Hartford, Connecticut. Bequest of Daniel Wadsworth.

Figure 6. Site of *View of the White Mountains,* 1953. Photograph by Paul Shepard.

Figure 7. *Bash-Bish Falls,* 1857. Painting by John Kensett. Oil on canvas, 34 ¼ x 27 ¼ in. Photo courtesy of the Gerald Peters Gallery, Santa Fe, New Mexico.

was smooth-flowing and unbroken while the picturesque was patchy, irregular, and discontinuous. The distant view in New England – provided it did not fall into a third category of vast and awful, the *sublime* – was usually beautiful. Glaciations by an ice sheet and the subsequent slow flow, or "creep," of soil down the slopes were the beautiful's agents. According to the theorists the very models of the beautiful were seventeenth-century paintings by Claude Lorraine.[3] But unlike his contemporary, Salvator Rosa, and unlike the nineteenth-century Americans, Claude never went into the mountains. It was one thing to observe isolated mountains from their foot and imagine that they were buildings, or to survey a distant range beyond a pastoral middle ground; it was something else to scramble up wild ravines.

Once out of the rustic, domestic, alluvial-lacustrine bottoms, the traveler entered the wilderness – with its accumulated connotations from the

Figure 8. Site of *Bash-Bish Falls,* 1953. Photograph by Paul Shepard.

time of Lord Shaftesbury to the then contemporary views of W. F. Cooper
and W. C. Bryant. Often as not, the traveler carried with him, too, an
amateur's enthusiasm for one of the sciences. In a mountain ravine the
landscape was small, the horizons close. But only here were the details
of wild nature undisturbed by farmer and woodcutter. True enough, the
details of the farm dwelling were picturesque, but the mountain chasm
was natural, free, and picturesque too. Seen close at hand, New England's
stony soil is not smooth. The rocky outcrops and the textures of rocks as
well as tree trunks were rough and interesting.

A score of American painters produced hundreds of canvases of New
England's brooks and mountain ravines before the Civil War. John Kensett's *Bash-Bish Falls* (figures 7 and 8) is an example of an extraordinary
preoccupation with the surfaces of crystalline and granite rocks – perhaps
the most extraordinary in the history of painting. His work centers on
these rocks under the impact of relentless mountain streams, the wedg-

ing of time, and sometimes the implacable beat of the sea. He seemed to know every quartz crystal, and to have scrutinized every tenacious lichen and sweeping, water-sculptured curve on the rocks he painted.

In New England, brooks are both abundant and perennial, as they are in Western Europe, and are fairly common in the multitude of short, steep, narrow gullies of the fine-textured and much-dissected landscapes. It was in exactly this geomorphic setting that the actual process of mountain decay was most evident and the agencies of weathering and abrasion most easily determined. Mountains were no longer everlasting. The process instead—the mountain brook—goes on forever, rendering Time, that perpetual presence which William Irvine calls the Victorian equivalent of the medieval Holy Ghost, most strikingly real.[4] It is in this connection that the *sublime* (the vastness of time) and the *picturesque* (the textures of surfaces) are important in American aesthetic and intellectual history in a broader connotation than categories of academic connoisseurship. The picturesque was fundamental to the intellectual preparation of leaders in the arts and sciences who examined with the greatest pleasure rough rocks in their minutest detail and engaged, often with much humility, in speculation about the landscape under their feet. Scores of contemporary travel journals reveal the impact of geology not only on the layman's understanding but also on his pride, taste, and perception. It was not from coaches, steamers, or even horseback, but afoot among the mountain brooks that the encounter with the life of rocks was most insistent.

And yet, urgent as nature seemed in the ravines, it was grandest from the mountain summits. Pilgrims to nature's supreme scenery, as it occurred in New England, left the valleys and the shore and threaded their way above the mountain streams to the peaks. The American mountain summit has never before or since been so relished by so many people as it was in the second third of the nineteenth century. The trails are there still—those that have not been converted into roads—in the crests of the Highlands, the Catskills, and the Taconics and in the trap ridges of the Connecticut Valley and of the White and Green Mountains. Some are still in use for various reasons, but having become hikers' trails, they no longer end at the peaks, and their sojourners, even if fervent about nature, seldom see the sunrise and never gaze for hours at one particular view. Mountain houses monumentalized the most extraordinary summits. Many of these were only log shelters; others were rustic chalets; some were luxurious hotels.

Besides social "sunrising," the summits offered other unique experiences. The subjective tendency to enlarge the distant peak is clearly expressed in the predilection for the summit; more paintings of mountains were made from other mountains than from any other place. This, incidentally, helped toward a solution of the inherent difficulties in dealing with a three-dimensional landscape on a two-dimensional canvas. Not only does the mountain seem to enlarge, but also our field of view tends to tilt downward and to fill with land at the expense of the sky.[5] Only the thinnest line of sky is necessary for reasons of gestalt. Such an effect requires a summit position and the absence of foreground. The most popular summits had this propinquent verticality.

Certain geomorphic situations produce abrupt relief better than others. Large waterfalls are one, the best example of which, Niagara Falls, deserves separate study. The Catskill Escarpment is another. A corner of this cuesta-cemented debris from the vanished Arcadian Mountains extends to within about eight miles of the Hudson River. The escarpment affords a sweeping, two-hundred-degree view from as much as three thousand feet above the valley floor. Much of the Hudson from Albany to the Highlands is visible. To two generations the "Catskills" meant this very small corner of these mountains above the village of Palenville: the lip of a cliff like an incredible limestone pavement, peaks that terminated the westward-dipping rocks, and deep "cloves" cut into the face of the scarp by glacial ice squeezed up and out of the Hudson Valley. The cloves with their present streams grow bigger as they eat farther into the escarpment and capture more and more of the drainage beyond the escarpment crest. From this cliff Cooper's Leatherstocking looked upon "all creation." South of the Catskills is another, equally spectacular form of the abrupt relief which drew the artist and tourist. The Hudson River floodplain is normally several miles in width, but where the river lies across the axis of the Highlands that connect the Taconics on the east with the Appalachians on the west, the floodplain vanishes altogether and the stream is confined between fifteen-hundred-foot-high walls of ancient primary rocks. West Point commands the scene as Fort Putnam, nearby, did before it. Two levels of narrow terraces, on one of which West Point is built, notch the

Figure 9. *West Point from Fort Putnam,* 1867. Painting by David Johnson. Oil on canvas. Fenimore Art Museum, Cooperstown, New York.

Figure 10. Site of *West Point from Fort Putnam,* 1953. Photograph by Paul Shepard.

walls of this intensely scoured chasm. The magnificent view of the river from West Point drew thousands of visitors before the Civil War. David Johnson's *West Point from Fort Putnam* (figures 9 and 10) shows the view upstream. It shows also an intense interest in the erosions of these steep walls, including dissected cliffs that could not have been visible even in winter. This is geological deduction – an observer's assertion of the evanescence of mountains.

The highlands are generically related to Mount Holyoke, a trap ridge in the Connecticut Valley, insofar as they are both sundered by a stream. From Mount Holyoke Thomas Cole painted his *Oxbow* (figures 11 and 12), which exhibits several of the perceptual characteristics mentioned: the profile and gradient of the mountains, the increase in size of distant hills, the downward direction of view. As at the Highlands and Catskills, the observer looked down on the large stream near grade. The rich lacustrine and alluvial soils brought to mind the virtue of the yeoman and

Figure 11. *View from Mount Holyoke, Northhampton, Massachusetts, after a Thunderstorm (The Oxbow)*. Painting by Thomas Cole. Oil on canvas, 51 1/2 x 76 in. The Metropolitan Museum of Art. Gift of Mrs. Russell Sage, 1908 (08.228).

Figure 12. Site of *View from Mount Holyoke, Northhampton, Massachusetts, after a Thunderstorm (The Oxbow)*, with Melba and Kenton Shepard, 1953. Photograph by Paul Shepard.

the advance of culture. But these streams have breached the long axis of the mountain wall at Holyoke and at West Point. Geology had not yet answered the question of how they had done so. A dark, cataclysmic past was still feasible, and a kind of judgment day atmosphere seemed to hang about the water gaps.

Even to the casual observer these views of "all creation" from high points were charged with unique problems and opportunities. The texture of the topography was neither too large nor too small, and the relationships of all kinds – of highlands to lowlands, drainage to landforms, land use to stream patterns, valley floors and terraces to stream levels, removal to deposition – encouraged recognition of patterns. A patient visual habit and a degree of curiosity were not unusual among observers. These factors played an intimate role in the aesthetic discovery of the region, a discovery that began with the contemporaries of Timothy Dwight and reached its acme before the Civil War. Landscape painters phrased this development in pictures. Their work was panoramic and detailed, not necessarily because they had set out to document the beauty of New England, or because of vague naturalistic philosophies slavishly separated from the discovery of nature as it constitutes the visible landscape. No science prospered more than geology in the period we have considered. Though it was not formally related to painting, the enthusiasm that it engendered enlivened the discovery of the indigenous landscape.

Artists found various scenes: some classically beautiful, some resembling the great architectural ornaments of civilization, and some providing a spatial situation in which a heightened, even ecstatic, experience was possible. Painters' demands were, then as now, rigorous; and although they might have been the last to classify their preferences geologically, it is evident that they had them. The polarity of macrocosm and microcosm had not yet lost its meaning. A rock in its finest detail was fully as paintable as a glorious panorama; the streams were ceaselessly at work on each.

The Cross Valley Syndrome

CROSS VALLEYS ARE STREAMS OR RIVERS THAT CROSS ridges or mountains. They result from at least four situations: from the overflow of a basin, from being gently lowered across a buried ridge as the stream removes materials by erosion, from a stream's capacity to maintain its position as the ridge rises by uplift at right angles to it, and from erosion into the hillside until the crest of the hill is notched. There are refinements and combinations, of course, but in a given set of conditions a geologist can predict where streams are likely to breach mountains or where this occurred in the past.

In terms of human geography, these water gaps provide passageways. They tend to become historical and economic landmarks. In the settlement of America, for instance, water gaps were especially important because the westward movement of settlers was at right angles to the general north–south lineaments of the continental ranges. Cities and roads developed a definite spatial relationship to these passages. The water gap might be cited as the classic example of the topographic passageway.

Another characteristic of the water gap is that it is usually admired as scenery. It is frequently described as a sublime spectacle of great forces at work. The valley is narrow and the current speeded. The rough walls and rocky debris seem evidence of upheaval and destruction, or scars of former gigantic earth movements. The slopes are too sharply inclined to cultivate and may be covered with forest, except where there are cliffs. Forest and cliff are conventional signs of natural catastrophe and wildness; they have evoked some of the most rapturous descriptions in travel literature. From a distance the cross valley has an emotional impact since, unlike most mountain-valley landscapes, it may be observed looming above a horizontal foreground.

The water gap was intimately associated with the discovery of American scenery in the first half of the nineteenth century. Although travelers had described New England from the time of settlement, a genuine enthusiasm for its landscapes matured only in the intellectual and artistic renaissance that began in the 1820s. The water gaps of New England are particularly associated with the rise of landscape painting, travel literature, nature poetry, and the sentiment for the outdoors that was to lead in one of its branches to the conservation movement.

Evidence for this linkage between water gaps and an intensified American attitude toward nature may be found in the history of some of the principal examples. About one hundred miles north of New York, the Hudson Valley, here about ten miles wide, lies in the afternoon shadow of the spectacular escarpment of the Allegheny Plateau. This rocky outcrop, rising three thousand feet above the valley floor, is the extreme eastern point of an upland, the Catskill Mountains. This escarpment is deeply dissected at intervals along its face of sedimentary rocks. Washington Irving set many of his tales drawn from Dutch folklore in these glens, which drain toward the Hudson. Sleepy Hollow is part of a mountain stream valley, a clove (or "kill") working headward into the face of the escarpment. James Fenimore Cooper used this immediate area as a setting for some of Leatherstocking's adventures. The steep ravines on the face of the escarpment next attracted poets and painters. Asher Durand, Thomas Doughty, and Thomas Cole came up the river on the heels of William Cullen Bryant, and were pursued in turn by admirers, aspiring artists, people of taste, and tourists. The aesthetic enjoyment of this area precipitated new popular interest in the scenery of the Hudson River and

Figure 13. *White Mountain Scenery, Franconia Notch,* 1857. Painting by Asher B. Durand. Oil on canvas, 48 ½ x 72 ½ in. Accession number s-105, negative number 27105. Collection of The New-York Historical Society.

focused it in the Catskills. This burst of awareness of the native landscape may be considered, ecologically, to mark a revolution in the American sensitivity to the habitat.

Access to New England scenery proper was up the Connecticut River valley. In southern Massachusetts the river crosses the axis of an igneous trap ridge; the peaks on either side of the breach are Mount Tom and Mount Holyoke. Immediately above the passage is a wide lacustrine fill upon which the river has formed an oxbow, a landmark on the river. The panorama of the valley and oxbow from Mount Holyoke evoked the construction of one of the first and most popular of the New England mountain houses. The mountain house tradition was, in fact, an integral part of the nineteenth-century effort to absorb the benefits of grand scenery. From shacks to luxurious hotels, they marked the most prized viewpoints in the region.

In the Mount Washington area of the White Mountains are the Franconia and Crawford Notches. These incipient gaps were, from the time

Figure 14. Site of *White Mountain Scenery, Franconia Notch,* 1953. Photograph by
Paul Shepard.

of Timothy Dwight, highly prized for their scenery. Here, as in the glens
of the Catskills, glaciated notches and their associated drainages are developing cross-axial patterns (figures 13 and 14).

It is one thing to claim that these cross valleys, including the Delaware
Water Gap, the gaps on the Susquehanna, and other rivers, catalyzed
American ideas of scenic beauty, and quite another to uncover the nature
of their peculiar attraction. We can detect something of the motivation in
the paintings of these water gaps made during a period of aesthetic discovery by comparing them with the sites themselves, by using the same
basic approach used in distorted mirror studies in psychology.

Another way of gaining insight into this motivation is to consider the
response of travelers to the first sight of such gaps in another environment, the semiarid West. About halfway along the Oregon Trail between
Independence, Missouri, and Astoria, Oregon, is a remote water gap that
was seen and recorded in diaries by hundreds of westbound Americans
before 1850. As Bernard DeVoto has pointed out, these people had few

visual expectations of the West, for at that time almost no pictures of it had been published. If the cross valley has unique evocative qualities, gaps like the Devil's Gate on the old Oregon Trail would be unusually interesting: they are removed from the tame context of familiar surroundings because the temperate forest openings with the town-and-country patterns of Western civilization are stripped away.

Devil's Gate is a spur of the Granite Range transected by the Sweetwater River of south-central Wyoming (figure 15). The walls are less than four hundred feet in height above the stream, and the passage is only about one hundred yards in length. At this point the Oregon traveler was a thousand miles from civilization and had been weeks in what seemed a desert. The way had been first along the Platte and was now beside the Sweetwater River. There was an easy detour around the gap, so wagons were not forced to go through it. But many of the travelers who kept journals found it awe-inspiring and lingered to climb, sketch, measure, explore, and engage in geological speculation. The conventional figure of a harassed, plains-weary, fearful emigrant is scarcely consistent with the name-carving, rock-collecting, scenery-hunting tourist that he occasionally became.

This vaguely familiar landform was unaccountably fascinating in its novel surroundings; but why should it have been called Devil's Gate? Father Jean De Smet, who stopped to sketch the gate in 1841, believed that it should have been named "Heaven's Avenue." Referring to the distant mountains, he wrote, "If it resembles hell on account of the frightful disorder which frowns around it, it is still a mere passage, and it should rather be compared to the way of heaven on account of the scene to which it leads." He noted its perpendicular walls, the tree trunks caught in the rocks, the overhead masses of shadow and gloom where dark pines and cedar grew. "Lofty galleries" could be seen among the rocks. "In the midst of this chaos of obstacles, the roaring waves force a passage," the water coming first furiously, then with majesty, and finally gently. The gate itself was horrid, but it led to paradise. Thus the gap is characterized by contradictions and by the contrasts of barrier and penetration. De Smet's account of the Devil's Gate was probably in some measure influenced by the eighteenth-century aesthetics of the Sublime; but the aesthetic was itself merely a means of formalizing and sorting out spontaneous responses to

Figure 15. *Devil's Gate,* 1837. Painting by Alfred J. Miller. The Walters Art Museum, Baltimore, Maryland.

the landscape. De Smet refers to a geomorphic feature, but there is – for want of a better term – fantasy in his description of it. His encounter with the Devil's Gate is what might be called an ecological event.

Certain aspects of this cross valley syndrome are unusually distinct in this strange habitat. We may examine them further by turning to a wholly fantastic description in a story by Edgar Allan Poe. Poe's "Domain of Arnheim" is a first-person narration of a mysterious journey. The narrator is en route to visit the estate of a wealthy friend. The way is by water. In a beautiful and elaborate skiff he glides along a heavenly avenue. "The channel grew more narrow; the banks more and more precipitous . . . clothed in richer, more profuse, and more sombre foliage." Past the walls of foliage the voyageur enters a gorge in which "intertwining shrubberies overhead gave the whole chasm an air of funereal gloom." Suddenly the boat enters a large basin of great "softness" and "voluptuousness" with slopes whose flowers look like precious gems. Transferring to another fairy canoe propelled by an unknown force, he floats through a gigantic gate of burnished gold, "elaborately carved and fretted, and reflecting the direct rays of the now fast-sinking sun with an effulgence that seems to wreathe the whole surrounding forest in flames." Then "the whole paradise of Arnheim bursts upon the view" with its melody, sweet odors, and amphitheater begirt with purple mountains and a gleaming river, flocks of golden birds, meadows full of blooms, lakes, tall slender trees, and "a mass of semi-Gothic, semi-Saracenic architecture, sustaining itself as if by miracle in mid-air, glittering in the red sunlight with a hundred oriels, minarets, and pinnacles; and weaving the phantom handiwork, conjointly, of the Sylphs, of the Fairies, of the Genii and of the Gnomes." This paradisiacal garden with its ornate hanging structures, preternatural light, fragrance, flowers, birds, and parks belongs to a class of landscape images that frequently recurs in eschatological and epic lore. It is worth noting that these images are almost identical with those of hallucinatory and visionary landscapes. Studies of induced hallucinations strongly suggest that spontaneous visions of this sort are not uncommon, especially under conditions of physiological stress. Even the perception of the normal individual who seldom or never has traumatic visions can be affected by hallucinatory sense experiences. Aldous Huxley has pointed out in "Heaven and Hell" that, given sufficient doses of certain chemical agents, the normal observer perceives objects in his daily life in terms of a truly visionary landscape reminiscent of something not consciously remembered. Among the geographical forms that play a compelling part in these visions is the cross valley—the defile or precipitous pass or ravine.

How are we to explain this recurrent vision, and the elation of travelers, tourists, and artists when confronted with this type of scenery? One answer, I believe, is to be found in our deep-seated, unconscious tendency to liken earth forms to human forms, to think of the earth itself as a body. The prevalence of the primordial image of the earth mother is a familiar instance. There are primitive societies that reject work in the fields because the body of the earth mother is not to be injured. There, stones are likened to the bones of the earth, soil to her flesh, plants to her hair. Anthropologists have long recognized the special significance of the passages of the body in primitive cultures. "If the earth is thought of as a living and fecund mother," Mircea Eliade observes,

> all that she produces is both organic and animated, not only men and plants, but also stones and minerals. . . . Such concepts are extremely ancient. Mines, like the mouths of rivers, have been likened to the matrix of the earth mother. The word bi in Egyptian is translated as vagina or shaft of a mine . . . and the same symbolism can be applied a fortiori to grottoes and eaves; it is recognized that caves have played a religious role from Paleolithic times. To penetrate a labyrinth of a cave was the equivalent of a mystic return to the Mother—the object of rites of initiation as well as funeral rites.

If this correspondence is no longer part of our conscious perception of the landscape, it is nevertheless still part of the vision of artists; such persons retain the power to apprehend and symbolize what others only vaguely sense. To this first group belong prophets, storytellers, and legend-makers as well as painters.

The river issuing from the cloven stone or from a mountain in paradise is in fact part of an ancient core of myth. The Grail legends and the Tannhauser epic contain such earthly paradises: the deep gorge with its gloomy forest and torrent, obstacles such as bridges and gates. Ornate castles and parks beyond the defile are consistent themes. Tannhauser's goal was the Venusberg, and many persons in the Middle Ages actually searched for the Venusberg in Germany, Italy, and elsewhere. Nor did the Arthurian or Tannhauser quests end with the Middle Ages; both remain with us in a modified, scarcely recognizable form. In an age of easy transportation and egalitarian culture every man may set out on such an errand. It survives to this day in the search for wild and remote places, passes through forbidding mountains, hidden landscapes beyond barriers.

It is in this light that much of our American agitation for wilderness preservation can be interpreted. The rationale for the preservation of Yosemite Valley in 1864 was based less on scientific than on aesthetic grounds. The articles and diaries of early travelers to Yosemite contain many pseudo-psychological expressions; observers attributed their feelings to spiritual transcendence, to formal aesthetic responses, or to the unexplained virtues of a natural Wonder. Yet, however rationalized in the extensive travel literature that has developed since the discovery of the Yosemite in 1851, it is permissible to believe that the attributes of the valley owe at least part of their allure to a profound and unarticulated recognition that their morphology reflects an inner image of a fundamental kind.

Yosemite was the first wilderness in history to be preserved for its scenery by an official act of the government. Public interest in the Dinosaur National Monument is another example of the same geopsychic experience. Within this area along the Colorado-Utah boundary is a junction of the Green and Yampa Rivers. As part of the Colorado River system it was included in a valley development program that came before Congress early in the 1950s. The ensuing controversy over the construction of a dam in the monument drew to a close after a six-year dispute in Congress, in magazines and newspapers, and among a group of private organizations and individuals. Opponents of the dam won, and Echo Park Dam was omitted from the legislation passed by Congress in 1956.

The public debate serves in its way to illustrate the prevalence of the cross valley (or in this case, canyon) syndrome. Although Dinosaur National Monument had been little visited, much money and energy were expended in opposing the dam. It was claimed by the dam proponents that this particular piece of desert was not greatly unlike much of the rest of the Great Basin country. But in this section of the monument is a cross valley, a place where the Green River transects a spur of the Uinta

Mountains. The exciting passage through the turbulent canyon waters was publicized by pictures showing whole families – children, elderly men and women, and ordinary people – as they emerged from rubber boats onto the green, gardenlike fringe at the mouth of the canyon. Their triumph through the perilous mountain valley had been possible because of strong young men who, like Tannhauser, had forsaken the humdrum world.

If the application of this hypothesis to the Dinosaur controversy appears highly speculative, it should be recalled that an unconscious identification between bodily image and geological form is a widely held theory however it may be explained. The early history of geographical exploration includes many extraordinary examples of the delicate interplay between a complex psychic image and its geomorphic correspondent. It was an experience particularly common in the early Renaissance, when Christianity had lost some of its ascetic character and had adopted (or was invaded by) pagan, magic, and mystic elements. In the present century we are not accustomed to allegorical art forms; we do not consciously see the natural world as symbol. Positivism and materialism have all but overwhelmed the art and myth that in the past seemed at times even more real than objective experience. Perception of the landscape as anatomy now seems primitive and irrelevant; in our culture, where technology rather than affirmation connects man to nature, it is merely a romantic anthropomorphism – it would be difficult to say much in its praise that would be accepted happily.

Yet the Dinosaur episode suggests that these attitudes continue to operate in the formation of personal and collective ideas of the landscape, in the evaluation of scenery, and in the motivation of much tourism.

One might venture further and suggest that the study of the relationship between psychological processes and their geomorphic or ecological components is a potentially fruitful approach to the broader areas of man's relationship to nature. This brief examination of a cross valley syndrome – a persistent theme of a mountain barrier and sundering stream in vision, romance, art, and in travel and exploration – is a provisional effort in this direction. Even the underlying concept, that of the earth mother, merits in this connection a far closer study. "The obscure memory of a pre-existence in the womb of the earth" (to quote once more from Eliade) "has had considerable consequences. It produced in man a sentiment of cosmic relationship to his environment. One might say that at a remote period man was less aware of belonging to the human species than of a cosmobiological participation in the life of his surroundings. . . . This sort of experience established a mystic solidarity with the place, the intensity of which extends to our day in popular traditions and in folklore. . . . We have not yet begun to explore the benefits of such 'illusions.'" The ecological interconnections of the living members of a landscape have an organic fragility needing protection. We must even appreciate the tenuous projection of the human form into the environment if that is part of the process by which we acknowledge the world as living and perishable.

Ugly Is Better

"WHAT'S WRONG WITH PLASTIC TREES? MY GUESS IS THAT there is very little wrong with them. Much more can be done with plastic trees and the like to give most people the feeling that they are experiencing nature."[1]

We may have to make do more and more with "proxy" and "simulated" environments, says the author of the above statement in *Science*. What is natural and rare is only relative, he adds, and if it is rare, it isn't necessarily worth preserving. After all, who is more important, man or nature?

No doubt he intended to shock the reader, especially those naturalists who sentimentally suppose the natural to be better than the artificial. His is the culminating statement of the recognition of intangible values, the high point to which two centuries of nature aesthetics have led us. He has taken the aesthetes and hoisted them on the point of their own logic. Given natural beauty, as we now understand it, the ersatz is as essential and good as the real. The real solution to the Los Angeles smog problem is to put perfume in gasoline.

The "antilitter" and "Keep America Beautiful" campaigns were prob-ably, in all, a worse disaster for the American environment than the Santa Barbara oil spill. The Spanish, and the Spanish parts of the New World, were never infected with puritanical tidiness until recently. Like much of the non-Western world, they accepted the smells of the body and the real-ity of excreta as necessary aspects of life. Antilitter campaigns and freeway plantings are Airwick and deodorant soap – sensory crutches protecting our own perceptions from unwelcome data. In rural Mexico and Spain, wrappings and bones and junk are still just thrown out – measures of the use of the world, reminders not just of our consumption of things, but of our gorging on the ecosystem. Every bread wrapper is a score in our war with nature that should be seen a thousand times. In fact, it is a double score, first because it wasn't necessary to begin with, and some tree was cut to make bread wrappers, and second, it simply marks success in our caloric demand. Pie wrappers and all other luxury containers signal to us a third score: superfluous consumption.

It is not only that litter is judged ugly in its lack of asepsis. More impor-tant, it is not beautiful. It has to do with the category of aesthetic values. Aesthetics is that invention by which sensory qualities can be disassoci-ated from things and classified abstractly. The term "landscape" came into use in the sixteenth century to represent the pictorial abstractions of ecosystems. Such pictures were at first imaginary scenes composed from literary images and were soon formulated by aesthetic theory. Places were in time classified as sublime, beautiful, picturesque – or without aesthetic significance. It all became dialectic and esoteric, a proper subject for the leisured, educated connoisseur. Its eventual breakout into the realm of public concern took place in the nineteenth century as part of the spoils system: not as opposed to the spoils system, but as part of it.

American attitudes in the nineteenth century seem ambiguous; there was the common "root, hog, or die," and the great spoiler barons in land, timber, and oil; but there were also Central Park, pastoral graveyards, Yosemite, save the buffalo, Burroughs, Muir, the Audubon Society, and an enormous popular addiction to picture books and sentimental nature poetry in every newspaper. It looks at first like counterculture, and it may have been for some. Mostly it was the system taking over the old landscape aesthetic, one with which it could live, making illusory options – like the modern soap company that really owns its own competition.

Look what the industrial society could do with landscape aesthetics. It could shunt it into pictures and other symbolic tokens; it could be geared to style, taste, and fashion, in that order – the clear-cut slope and strip-mine spoils really are beautiful, they just don't happen to be à la mode. The beautiful places could be identified and isolated from the rest of the biosphere, and the qualities could be detotalized and translated into technique: A patina of pastoral planting was laid on virtually every college campus built after 1850.

And the concern for scenery was profitable. Somebody said to me during a trip to the desert, "This is great. I can't wait to get home and look at my slides." To appreciate what it has meant to the travel industry, you must travel in a place where there are no accommodations for tourists. But more important, scenery unfettered the spoilers; nature is really resources – except where we have made parks – because man does not live by bread alone. Aldous Huxley once observed that Wordsworth was inapplicable to a tropical jungle. But he needn't have gone that far. Wordsworth doesn't apply to much of Texas, Georgia, Alberta, Baja, or New Jersey.

Conservation is the rubric under which landscape aesthetics was incorporated into enlightened exploitation. Officially, it had to do with spiritual values, but for the hard core it could always be translated into money values by feeding its raw data of participation through a translating machine called Recreation. "Scenic Resources" fit well with "human resources." Then, for the corporate agencies, 1970 was the traumatic year of confrontation. The mountain heaved and gave birth to two peas, two changes in terminology. They struck out "conservation" and "nature," inserting in their places, "ecology" and "environment." A great rhetorical year.

The difficulty is that it is practically impossible to discuss our experience of the nonhuman without recourse to a jargon that is the property of an outmoded and destructive enterprise. Worse yet, in the field of action it is the same. Recycling is the ecological slave in the front office. We seem determined to engage in the most frenetic charades and games to avoid reducing consumption and human numbers. The strategy of the system and the options provided by the barons has always been to quietly provide harmless alternatives.

To hell with conservation and nature aesthetics. The confrontation with the nonhuman occurs every second. Every breath is an encounter with nature and every bite of food is part of a language. We have been conditioned to reserve feeling and thoughtfulness and attention to the nonhuman for our visits to those scenic enclaves or their pictorial representations. For whooping cranes and rhinoceroses we may indeed have to provide protected terrain, but that is the last desperate measure, not the best one. The protected lands on which threatened species live should not be open to the public at all: The species should be regarded as in a retreat from which they may once again emerge in a functional relationship with people. To reduce creatures to spectacle is part of the game, making them merely beautiful. The famous remark, "Seen one redwood, seen 'em all" is true. It refers to retinal forms, curiosities, architectural and pillared spaces through which one moves; they are objects from another world, repetitive surfaces filling the visual screen. The observation has candor and courage; it puts the aesthetics of the beautiful where it belongs.

The nongame alternative is that the redwoods are beings. Since they are more remote from us than other human cultures and races, more circumspection, not less, is necessary. We cannot so easily "know" them. If there are means of doing so they are long neglected by our culture. If there are no means of doing so, then the mystery itself is manifest. Perhaps both are true. In any case, we cannot formulate a new relationship out of air. Religiosity is the trap that idealism and ideology set for the antinomian. We cannot achieve a fundamentally different worldview by an act of will alone—some individuals can, perhaps, but not societies.

For the present it is just as well. We have only begun to recognize the extent to which the Faustian hubris has usurped aesthetic and ethical categories. We have just recently started to appreciate the modes of consciousness possible and to apprehend the incredible richness and otherness of nonhuman being and the impossibility of surviving a man-made world. A century of ethology has hardly touched the ways of being open to other species and the ecological wisdom that has been realized in some places and some times.

This is not a cop-out. It is not the curiosity of the inventor and capability of the engineer that have been at fault, but rather the zeal to employ every technological innovation for change and newness as ends in themselves. Changing culture is open to the same mistake. It is not simply that understanding must precede action; it is that at present further understanding is the most important action.

If you must have some symbolic actions, I recommend the following: throw your wrappers, papers, butts anywhere, beer cans in the streets, bottles on the berms and terraces; uproot and cut down all ornamental trees and replace them with native fruit-bearing trees and bushes; sabotage all watering systems on all lawns everywhere; pile leaves, manure, and garbage among growing things; return used oil, tires, mattresses, bedsprings, machines, appliances, boxes, foil, plastic containers, rubber goods, and all other debris to their origins – seller or manufacturer, whichever is easier – and dump them there; unwrap packages in the place of purchase and leave the wrappings.

When this has gone on long enough, some tokens of the glut of over-consumption will at least be evident. Equally important, there will be less refuge from the countryside with its regimented monocultures, scalped slopes, poisoned rivers, and degraded rangelands. Our society goes for letting it all hang out, so let's do it. Are encounter groups in? Let's raise the encounter a whole octave and confront the real human ecosystem that we live in. Some great Avon lady keeps rouge on the cheeks of the middle-class neighborhood, the industrial park, and the college campus; the same tinsel earth mother in whose name the slaughterhouse is hidden, the zoo's dead are unobtrusively replaced, and the human dead are pseudo-fossilized.

We may, as the Sierra Club maintains, need wilderness as a spiritual tonic. But if so, it has nothing to do with glorious picture books or even with landscapes. For John Muir, the club's founder, the landscape was the canvas painted by God. Henry Thoreau, by contrast, knew better. He edited no picture books, did no landscaping. Looking for kindred spirits, he once read William Gilpin, the English vicar who also wandered over the hills. Gilpin observed that a horse was aesthetic because of the effects of light and color in its coat. Thoreau said, "And this is the reason why a pampered stud can be painted! Mark that there is not the slightest reference to the fact that the surface with its lights and shades, belongs to a horse and not to a bag of wind." The observations of terrain in Thoreau are prospects, the descriptive opposite of the landscape scene.

The prospect was the unfettered view of the ambient from a high place. You can see it in the paintings by the elder Brueghel. The prospect is not a pastoral dream or an interesting texture. In one of the few paintings of a man cultivating the soil (*The Fall of Icarus*) Brueghel has included the unscenic details, and Icarus splashes in the distance while the horse goes on farting down the furrows.

Despite the old masters' perspicacity, pictures themselves are part of our present problem. Theirs was an iconic reality and Brueghel could not have foreseen our dilemma. He was not concerned with the picturesque ("the scenery's capabilities of being formed into pictures," as Christopher Hussey describes it in *The Picturesque*) or the terrain's "capabilities" for being reshaped into garden landscapes in imitation of old paintings by eighteenth-century landscape architects like Capability Brown. The substitution of pictures for places was the step toward making places that match pictures. Now we are taking pictures of places whose patterns happen to suggest those gardens built in imitation of paintings, which were originally done as visual expressions of literary evocations of "classical" scenes.

"Scenery" is from a Greek word meaning stage prop.

Five Green Thoughts

THE SHEEP AS CUSTODIAN

The idea of an ovine sentry came to me as I stood on a large ring of earth in southern England, trying to imagine the medieval castle keep of which it was the ruined foundation. Sheep grazed quietly in the center, and it was *their* turf that protected the relicts buried beneath from the erosion of the centuries. Their droppings fertilized the green shroud. Like a company of mild wardens they occupied the space, giving it an air of permanence, of keeping.

But that air, like the static feel of a museum, is an illusion, for such places are the sites of old havoc, piles of the dismembered and disjointed. The unspoiled-looking site had long since been sliced through and the old mounds built up again.

Why must one dig up the past? How and by what agency do all those fragments get buried in the first place? In the Western world in particular our sense of history is intimately related to exhumation. Of course, graves are a part of the explanation, and the walls of villages and cities from England to Teheran were built on top of the ruins of predecessors. Fallen ceilings became new floors in a hundred cities across the Mediterranean world. Our roots are down there and we – represented by archaeologists – are like moles, otherwise blind to our origins, tunneling and nibbling at them.

Any archaeologist will tell you that relatively little of the remains of seven thousand years of town and city life actually got buried. Most of the products and belongings of vanished peoples simply disappeared – not buried, just kicked around, worked on by weather and time, carried away, broken up, dissolved, disintegrated. Yet the fragments of old pottery, hardware, and masonry were not randomly buried. Much depended on the local drainage: the city's place in the watershed.

The mortality of those ancient cities was itself related to the impact of people and their animals on the terrain. Throughout the "cradle lands" of civilization, the agriculture upon which the city depended developed a tangled network of canals, reservoirs, gates, and channels presided over by engineers, slaves, and bureaucrats.

The elaboration of the state was dependent on making land usable, and it in turn supported greater populations. As irrigable land ran out, the tensions between neighboring tribes and chieftains escalated, and as human numbers overflowed the centers, the surplus went higher up the watershed. There they cut timber and grazed their animals and sent down wood, skins, wool, meat – and the soil.

Upstream denudation, valley floor saturation, and conflict: The debacle came when some war, famine, or epidemic combined with the weather disrupted the hydraulic works.

The pretty sheep in grassy places represent the whole tribe of "hoofed locusts" who have toppled so much of the highlands down upon doomed societies. They (the sheep, goats, asses, horses, cows, mules, yaks, camels) administered the interment of eleven successive Mesopotamian empires. They were the barbers or scalpers of the Judean highlands, the Peloponnesian and the Syrian upper slopes, where their dexterous tooth work and footwork buried cities. King Solomon paved the way three thousand years ago when he sent eighty thousand ax men and seventy thousand haulers to take cedar and cypress from Phoenicia. Two thousand square miles of forest was thereafter reduced to four tiny groves today, the largest of which has about four hundred trees. The livestock followed on the loggers' heels and sent forest humus into the sea – or into the valleys where it simply buried the pillaged and burned remains of whatever army happened to have swept through.

Many generations were involved in a series of such debacles. The magnificent forests of the Mediterranean rim and islands were progressively demolished and their seedlings and root-shoots chewed and trampled by livestock. The relics of that vegetation – the maquis (myrtle, box, oak, olive, and oleander shrubbery) and the even more degraded garique (heath, juniper, pistachio, viburnum) – cling to raw earth between the rocks, giving an appearance of timeless austerity. The blanket of soil, once the sponge for a million springs, vanished so long ago that even the educated traveler, who finds the region so picturesque, considers the rough, raw land as "natural."

Still, the classicist writes of the "puzzle" of the demise of Minoan civilization. The historian calculates the political and military factors that destroyed Jerash, now a village of 3,000 that was once a city of 250,000. The cities of Mesopotamia faded before bloody invaders and "natural" catastrophes.

It is possible that in some places this cycle of buildup and collapse was run through relatively quickly, while in others there were periods of stability when the downstream main works and the upstream plundering were not so intense and a stable ecological relationship prevailed. Such places were, so to speak, in the process of not being buried. Having left us less to dig up, they are less well known and, being unknown, are omitted from our official history.

So we come to the inverse relation of land use and history: The worse the land practices, the more surely the "culture" was buried. No wonder Western consciousness is an overheated drama of God's vengeance and catastrophe, preoccupation with sacrifice, portents and omens of punishment by a heavy-handed Jehovah. Like the dinosaurs, which are known mainly for their vanishing, the ancestors we know best, and from whom we take our style, are those who seem to have lived mainly to call down calamity upon themselves.

The whole thing seen from the standpoint of the goat or sheep might seem utterly reasonable. First the centuries of teeth and hooves, slowly cutting loose the sides of the mountains, and finally their own silent presence in the lowlands, like woolly old museum docents, inane munchers, watchful angels over all that stuff filed away in the basement.

WHY THE GREEKS HAD NO LANDSCAPES

The lack of landscape painting—lack of description, of setting or scenery, in literature, poetry, and painting—does not mean that the ancient Greeks lived suspended in the sky with Apollo or spent all their time at sea with Poseidon. They, like us, had their feet on the ground most of the time. The Romans, in contrast, had whole walls covered with the mosaic views and a tradition of pastoral poetry with images of the country retreat.

This seeming lack of attention to the terrain, or accounts of plants and animals as part of narrative or myth, led early scholars at one time to conclude that the Greeks were either not interested in nature or had no talent for exploring it. "The literary genius of Greece," writes Walter Greg, "showed little aptitude for landscape, and seldom treated inanimate nature except as a background for human action and emotion." Together with the ancient relics of the sculpted human figure, pottery painting that depicted figures but not place, and "classic" architecture, this absence of surroundings was seen as part of Greek narcissism and as reflecting the Greeks' interest in the relations between humans and God or human and human.

In Homeric epics there is no "scene," no purely external description, no nature at all in our mode of portraits of place, picturesque settings, or charming atmosphere. The nonhuman context is not an aesthetic container of the action. Homer does not depict events against a background, as in the barren sets of a play by Samuel Beckett, or conjured scenery, as in Virgilian poetry. For Ulysses, objects are never only things. Hence things are not simply acted upon; they participate, standing out brightly for the sake of the relations among them that are messages from mind to mind.

For the old Greeks, nature was not "treated" by the artist, but was for all consciousness part of the animation. Creatures, plants, rocks did not surrender their otherness to scenery. They abided in their own right and moved in relation to the psyche, converging without simile, a true kindred reality, never merely symbolic. All terrain was an extension of what men experienced mentally and metaphysically, occupying places of existence but not different parts of a dual reality.

Paolo Vivante, in *The Homeric Imagination*, says that we must imagine a consciousness in which there are no literary associations, but in which all events, human and otherwise, derive from common vital principles. The human feelings are expressions or extensions of more profound commotions. Greek verbs combine human and natural action, which have both a psychic and physical meaning. The word for "melt" refers to both a state of snow and human tears. Things are not "like" other things but share their process.

Although there is little reference to the features of particular places in Homer, each place is profoundly unique. The sanctity of the earth is locally signified by the *memos:* a place often defined by cleft horizon lines in which a goddess is immanent. Divinity resides, characterizes it; mind and feeling have worked upon it. Shrines are possessed by deities, not built for or dedicated to them. Because of the universality of events, human action is never separate from its other forms. Thus intense human action, says Vivante, may stop while the actors attend to the glitter of bronze or the resounding sea, which are part of their action. In this the significance of one thing is heightened by the mutually responsive qualities in another.

Our modern perspective of space and time in which human action is located and described may also have some of its roots in later Greek thought—particularly in Plato, in Euclid, and in certain aspects of Greek theater with its scenes and its parabasis, in which the chorus removes its disguises to comment on the action. It is this detached observer for whom the pictorial view becomes possible.

Socrates scorned the old oral traditions. By the time of Periclean Athens the Greeks may have been philosophically capable of conceiving landscapes. The Roman frescoes of the first century are Greek thought in pictures; painted portraits involve a distancing and eventually a setting. In Flemish painting of the fourteenth century there appear beyond the faces of saints, fragments of landscape, the harbingers of a new subject matter. The revolution in visual thought, keyed to mathematics, was first incorporated in panels painted by an architect, Filippo Brunelleschi. This perspective of distance was discussed theoretically by Alberti Leon Batista in 1435 and came to be called Euclidean, distance-point representation in which space was "mathematically homogeneous" and ruled by the "laws" of convergence. From this, various other abstract rules developed for describing the "unity" of pictures – hence of nature. Marshall McLuhan has been at pains to point out how the application of mathematics to space organized the visual world into perspective, isolating the seer from the seen and creating secular space and human alienation from nature. "Civilization," he writes, "is founded upon the isolation and dominion of society by the visual sense." This visual sense is associated with a fragmented human identity. Outside the picture, viewers become onlookers, spectators. They become connected to the picture itself, not to what is shown, a part of a work of art. Life as a work of art is born. Its relationship to nature is a *stasis:* a presentation of selected fragments of visual experience. Like literature, and through literature, the "scenes from a life" are connected by a story.

Panofsky has said that the painting – unlike its medieval predecessors – became a kind of window. The modern reader may find this idea confusing, as we now think of windows as *connecting* us to nature. What they connect us to, however, is landscape: the window makes real the wall as a separation, its fenestration a calculated visual portrayal of certain external "symbolic" objects. An interior with no windows is a whole canvas. The unity that is achieved is of physical space, while what is fractured is the continuity in time without which there is no life. The optic culture tries to repair this by an association of the scene with a literary idea or story, but the repair is purely intellectual. It is not lived. The multisensuousness, especially the auditory quality, of the Homeric world did continue in medieval Europe as *participation,* in which speech and the word continued to be a shared principle in the whole of nature.

For most of Western history, two different approaches to experience existed. One, evident in Homeric and primitive thought, the other, apparent in art in Athens as early as the fifth century and inseparable from Euclidean space, increased with phonetic literacy and was essential to the idea of nature as distinct from humans. A contrived picture of the world is a landscape, which in our time we have come to think of as synonymous with "nature."

VIRGIL IN WESTCHESTER COUNTY

The appeal of suburban (or exurban) life is that it provides a bucolic setting without the concomitant monotony and trash of agriculture. Its popularity implies that we share a pervasive, almost compulsive ideal – not an ideal hammered out of personal reflection or social dialogue, but one that the culture imparts. It is an adjustable ideal. Basically, it is composed of a large yard (from *jardin*, or garden) separating the house from the street, and extensive, unbroken but undulating meadows with scattered trees that set the house off and yet blend it gracefully with the surrounding countryside. Subordinate buildings, pools, stream, rockwork, paths are incidental to it. Its original theme was the association of hoofed animals and dogs in a tight symbiosis with people. What it does not include in its most perfect expression is naked wire or steel fences, cultivated ground, standing crops, farm machinery, fuel tanks, storage bins, loading docks, junk or garbage piles, woodpiles, manure heaps, old vehicles, wheelbarrows, wagons, a cordon of old barns, electric wires, washtubs and clotheslines, pigs, or any other paraphernalia of the working farm.

Yet the suburban concept is not derived from a tidied-up farm. It is not a sort of Puritan or Dutch housewife or modern sanitized version. It has wholly other sources that come not directly from agriculture but via an urban dream and its aesthetic consequences interposed between distant rural antecedents and middle-class taste. Without being aware of it, even the educated inhabitant knows little or nothing of the convoluted history of The Pastoral.

Modern writers sometimes use "pastoral" to mean anything outside the city, from farmland to the wilderness. Actually they know better, for the pastoral is a literary genre. Those whose theme is the contrast between the city and the country utter this slipshod use of the term deliberately to minimize the variety of nonurban landscapes. The genre has a long history. Its lineage includes Theocritus, certain Romans, and a number of poets and dramatists – Boethius, Jean de Meung, Boccaccio, Sannazaro, Spenser, Sidney, and Milton. Its best-known exponent is probably Virgil, whose name, for anyone with a smattering of literature, conjures just such idyllic scenes of shepherds and their animals that the layout of the modern country house is intended to imitate.

What is one to say today of a two-thousand-year-old body of poetry that alone created the images of the idyllic and bucolic that still fill our heads? How are we to deal with the magisterial pronouncement of Johan Huizinga that "however artificial it might be, pastoral fancy still tended to bring the loving soul into touch with nature and its beauties. The pastoral genre was a school where a keener perception and a stronger affection towards nature were learned." But what "loving souls" does he mean – shepherds themselves, urban people, naturalists, or just lovers? And what "nature" does he refer to – the denuded slopes of a half-million square miles of Mediterranean watersheds?

Theocritus knew the real harshness of the Greek terrain so well that he placed his poems in Sicily. The Roman, Virgil, no less aware of the gap between the campagna and "nature," set his version in Arcady. Only if you put it far enough away could the illusion of goats scrounging sprouts among the rocks be accepted as "nature." Huizinga must mean educated loving souls whose "keener perception" of classical lands was that enhancement of landscape through Virgil's spectacles and those of the great "naturalists": Petrarch, Boccaccio, and the rest who used the pastoral for tales of social intrigue, satires of prominent politicians of the day, nostalgia, allegory, escape, a model of the Christian paradise, or other metaphysical imagery.

The main connection between that ancestral body of defunct literature and modern expression is by way of certain landscape painting and, in turn, landscape architecture. This series of emulations, each removing the modern reality further from its model in ancient Sicily (Theocritus's boyhood home), has been written upon at length. It can be quickly reviewed in Elizabeth Mainwaring's work and its American extensions understood in the influence of nineteenth-century architects such as Andrew Jackson Downing and Frederick Law Olmstead. The point is that ancient reverie about pastures made its way through the arts steadily and perniciously, emerging finally as the stereotype for suburban dwellings and rural beauty.

It is ironic that the term has come to symbolize the whole of nonurban environment, for its antecedent has no equal for ecological destitution. Looking at the epitome of its type – the country house with its graceful horses and purebred dogs – it is difficult to believe that this pattern and style of the occupation of habitat is the product of a great ecological lie.

As for the social metaphor made from the relationship of humans and sheep, Aldous Huxley makes the rueful observation: "We go on talking sentimentally about the shepherd of his people, about pastors and their folks, about stray lambs and a Good Shepherd. We never pause to reflect that a shepherd is not in business for his health, still less for the health of his sheep. If he takes good care of his animals it is in order that he may rob them of their wool and milk, castrate their male offspring, and finally cut their throats and convert them into mutton." How is it that an economic activity that, as much as any single factor, is one of the most destructive forces in the world could be so beautiful? Anyone who wishes to look at the evidence will understand that grazing and browsing animals have been agents of the collapse of Mediterranean empires, nations, and city-states and the principal means of the impoverishment of equatorial lands more decisively than all of the wars men have fought. On any slope at all the goat is simply the nemesis of the land that he sends rapidly off to fill deltas, estuaries, and lower river valleys around the sea.

The lie is that the goat and its fellow grazers and browsers and the denuded and eroded lands are an enchantment. It might be imagined that the ancient Greeks and Romans, the Renaissance Spanish, or the modern Moroccans and Syrians, and the American westerners, are blind to it, but the record does not show it. On the contrary, there is written evidence in every age that some people have been totally blind to the effects of overgrazing, but there has always been some evidence, too, that some people could see what was happening. It was not a question of ignorance.

Rather, I think, the pastoral fraud is based on a selective vision. Whatever the motivations for perpetuating the geological calamity of grazing, that economy over the centuries evoked artistic expressions. The most deceptive feature of such land systems is their stability. Economies create their own justifying demons. Indeed, pastoral art has often been criticized as "static": Things go on for centuries without apparent change. Large ecosystems do not vanish, but they do change, often imperceptibly. Their productivity and composition diminish to a low equilibrium. So there is built into this complex of flocks, fields, and herdsmen an image of endurance: the abiding earth. The city has often been sacked and burned, redesigned and rebuilt, and destroyed again. Even the farm was altered – or disappeared as its fertility was exhausted. Against these riptides of political turmoil and upheaval, the merchant and bureaucrat found unfailing consolation in the peace of meadow and sylvan glen, flocks and murmuring brooks, piping shepherds, sunshine and birds.

That the shepherd was usually brutal, hostile, stinking, and stupid, that the order of magnitude of destruction was more like that of glaciers and climatic change than of battles and plagues, that the potential of the land for human well-being was degraded under asses, sheep, cattle, horses, and goats – these were not what the harassed bureaucrat, military chief, or tradesman wanted to see. What they did see was physical evidence of Elysium: a land of leisure where drudgery was unnecessary and bribery and conniving unknown or innocent by comparison. They needed respite from the stench of cities without sewers, from rats, epidemics, assassins, noise, and the treadmills of survival. Compared to all that, the dung of cattle was sweet and the vacancy behind the shepherd's eyes a relief. Things could have been seen this way especially when the magic of art could make it so.

Theocritus, roasting in Alexandria, was dreaming of his boyhood. Virgil is not known ever to have held a hoe in his hand; he was a gentleman farmer. Spencer and Sannazaro were allegorists and Pope a dandy. Bellini and Claude Lorraine, the landscape painters, were not doing portraits of place but imagined scenes from Greek Arcady or the biblical. The landscape architects like William Kent, Capability Brown, and Humphrey Repton, using plants instead of paint, mimicked scenes already twice removed from the physical world, first by the poets, then by the "classical" landscape painters.

Theocritus had been interested in the play of joy and sorrow in life, while Virgil is said to have "discovered the evening," that is, to have associated melancholy with certain terrain effects and with dusk or time-gone-by. Thus the past instead of the distance was associated with the elegiac sentiment: The twilight reminds us solemnly of the idyllic world of long ago.

The emphasis on images and vision tells us that what was sought was a picture of that eternal prospect in the mind's eye: a world made simple and endlessly comfortable. Since the world, naturally and socially, is not in fact simple, what can one do to realize it? The goat, under our guidance, has solved it for us. It amounts to a kind of lobotomy on the land, done not with scalpel but with teeth and hooves. There is the victim, placidly like an ex-patient in a threadbare green robe, no longer full of primeval thunder and night creatures, all sunny and sweet, or at least mild, and, as they say, "spacious."

LAWN OF THE GIANTS

Enlarging on Huxley's observation that Wordsworth could not have felt the same about nature had he spent some time in the tropics – its density and fecundity would have swamped his sensibility – it follows that any culture tends to form standards of judgment about the environments from its own habitat. When individuals encounter radically unfamiliar vegetation and terrain forms they often feel uncomfortable. One reaction is swiftly and unconsciously to ransack the clues from their heritage: sizes, forms, images, utility, working assumptions about how their ideal standard types would have to be altered to make something like what they see.

Among the habitats for which Anglo-Saxons were unprepared, besides the jungle, there was the steppe. Nowhere in temperate-climate northwestern Europe is there sufficient natural grassland to provide an adequate cultural perspective. Not since the Hun horsemen overran much of the continent in the fifth century had such memories been fresh. Moors there were, but their vegetation was typically a heath association, mostly of shrubs and herbaceous plants. Grasslands would, by that scanning computer in the European mind, be assumed to be the result of human action and to have replaced the natural forest. Whether that was felt to be a loss or a gain depended much on individual perspective, as we shall see.

The historical test case was the grasslands of North America, particularly the tallgrass prairies of the midwestern states. As emigrants expanded into this new frontier west of Ohio in the early part of the nineteenth century they found, first on the uplands, openings in the forest, then intermixtures of scattered trees and grasses, and finally great stretches of prairie, sometimes miles in extent, with scattered groves of trees and shrubs along the streams. What could one say about such a place? How to explain it? Would it be a good place to live? How did it strike the itinerant's sense of beauty and utility? What did God have in mind here, and what could humans do here?

Much of the earliest Caucasian experience in the prairies was by the French Jesuits, who gave them their name. But the Jesuits in the eighteenth century were merely traversing a foreign, heathen land. Although they wrote of the soil, forests, grasses, and fires, their main concern was with souls, and the comments are brief: "beautiful," "verdant," "boundless," "frightening," even "pleasure grounds." But in general the Jesuits were not looking for a home or trying to make sense of a place. It was the later settlers and eastern visitors who puzzled out appropriate descriptions.

The pleasure-garden theme was certainly one of them. With any education at all, the traveler saw "a magnificence of park-scenery, complete from the hand of Nature, and unrivaled by the same sort of scenery by European art." Even "[e]nchanted ground," of all things, grasslands "gemmed with wildflowers of every hue, the stately forest and valleys interspersed with shady groves – the wild and bounding deer in great numbers" where the eye "wanders from grove to grove, charmed and refreshed by an endless variety of scenic beauty." And in the rocky bluffs "along the banks of the Upper Mississippi there stretch for hundreds of miles the ruined facades of stately castles and magnificent temples, built by Nature's hand."

One was, I suppose, at once Adam and God's Protestant elite. "I have no morbid sensibility," said William R. Smith, "on the subject of taking possession of a land which was worthless in the hands, and under the dominion of roving savages . . . a country so recently rescued by the enterprise and valor of our hardy pioneers from the wandering Indian, whose only occupation was to hunt deer and spear fish, although dwelling in a Western Eden."

Then came the cultivation of Eden. The moldboard plow, which could handle the tough prairie grasses, was invented. Some were not so sure of the fertility of a soil that did not support trees. "Oak barrens" they called the savannas between prairie and forest. It was clear to others, however, that the annual prairie fires caused the lack of trees. Along the prairie borders the first farmers planted themselves close to the woods, somewhat off the fire's path and the forest edge that hovered, to their mind, like a protective mother. "As I rode leisurely along upon the prairie edge," wrote an itinerant, "I passed many noble farms, with their log-cabins crouched in a corner beneath the forest."

For those with an eye for the sublime spectacle, the great prairie fires were indeed exciting. So were the storms and the wind that made the grass look like sea waves. William Cullen Bryant put it all in his poem "The Prairies," and more—beyond its sheer sensory impact there was the mystery of its presence. Taking his cue from the signs of a shaping intelligence, the past he created was that of pastoral civilization gone to ruin, its builders vanished, its livestock degenerated into buffalo and "prairie chickens." The land was now to be rescued from its barbarity.

In spite of the extraordinary effect of the prairie "on the mind," it was doomed. The ideal of the garden granary of the world would sweep away any persisting notions of pleasure gardens as fast as hedgerows could be planted or fences built. Robert Ridgway wrote, of a return to the Fox Prairie near Olney, Illinois, twelve years after an earlier trip, "the change which had taken place was almost beyond belief. Instead of an absolutely open prairie some six miles broad by ten in extreme length, covered with its original characteristic vegetation, there remained only 160 acres not under fence . . . the entire area was covered by thriving farm. . . . We searched in vain for the characteristic prairie birds." And he noted that the same was true throughout the state. "The buffalo has entirely left us," observed a writer in the *Illinois Monthly Magazine* in 1830. So had the elk. The beaver, otter, and bear were scarce. The badger, like the smaller birds, would survive in fencerows.

So the hypothesis with which we began must be modified. What do invaders in an alien habitat do about its strangeness? They concoct explanations for it, and may make it an imaginative and aesthetic experience—but only if they have no practical interest in it. If they have a practical interest in it, they change it into something familiar. The tallgrass prairie of Illinois, in which a man, it was said, had to stand on his saddle to find his cattle, was exterminated as a natural community within a lifetime of the beginning of settlement. Its extensions in Indiana, Wisconsin, Iowa, and Missouri met a similar fate.

Colleges and universities have re-created some tiny bits of prairie from its scattered species. But the opportunity to smell, hear, and see it through the seasons, especially to walk alone in a prairie that extends to the horizon, is gone. The soil the prairie made is too valuable to leave it to nature.

PLASTIC TREES AND PLASTIC MINDS

Seen too close in time, it is hard to know when an era ends. It was indeed becoming clear by 1980 that a remarkable period had passed. When *Science,* the weekly journal, carried a full-scale piece called "What's Wrong with Plastic Trees?" it was clear that the economic cowboys, harshly criticized by environmentalists during the previous fifteen years, were back in the saddle again.

The plastic tree article was about as sensational as that publication gets. But despite its trendy intellectual chic the viewpoint presented was not one that simply blew in on the winds of change. The argument that the artificial and man-made are as good as or even preferable to the natural touched a theme that could easily be traced to the ancient Greeks or beyond, and that has surfaced strongly in Western thought ever since Francis Bacon made it clear that the purpose of nature is to serve humans. But the splash with which it hit the fans of public dialogue signified not only some shift in rhythm but also a pressure that had been building since about 1965. The barons of technology, the main targets of that crescendo of environmental voices, had been caught off guard. Intellectually and academically they were ill prepared. It took a little time for them to build a better rationale than "growth is good." By the late 1970s their festering had matured and they had their own stable of scholars and adjusted P.R. The era of ecological conscience as a popular movement was to have on its tombstone an avalanche of advertising full of logical, humane, aesthetic, reasonable, economic, and philosophical tirades. If advertising is nothing more than the spindrift by which one judges the temper of the sea, beneath it were all sorts of theses, doctrines, programs, and all the dialectics pertinent thereto. A great overkill of justification and vindication of The System had begun that seems to go on forever—at least to the graying warriors of the "ecology movement."

One sensed the plastic trees argument was a bit tongue in cheek, but the assertion is interesting at the heart—or the root—of the claim that human works must be consonant with ecosystems and must build themselves into systems that are millions of years old. Much of technomania defends itself on the grounds that it loves nature more than anybody, but the old Faustian thought is that the whole kit and caboodle of nature is out of date and will eventually have to go. With so many garden-clubbers, backpackers, and fishermen about, that assertion cannot be said too brazenly, for the engineers of the new world know that otherwise they would soon find themselves knee-deep in restrictive legislation. The plastic tree is one small step toward making humankind the only living thing in the new world order.

It is a clever wedge. Fourteenth-century Arabs were extremely fond of mechanical birds – delicately made gadgets that sang and moved. No one can imagine Islamic science half a millennium ago as forging ahead in the area of metal avianoids as whimsy; it was more likely a response to some felt need. My guess is that three or four thousand years of land abuse combined with a harsh, dry climate had so decimated most natural habitats that the birds had vanished. There is abundant evidence of the love of luxurious gardens and parks stocked with animals of all kinds by those who could afford them. Where that was not possible, a finely done likeness was perhaps the logical alternative. There is certainly no reason to suppose that Islamic taste would find the idea any more objectionable than that of Christians. Perhaps it makes the lack of things natural easier to take.

If I were an all-powerful king, convinced that the pests eating my well-regimented crops or parasitizing my highly bred animals were transmitted by wild plants and animals, that my concrete pavements and asphalt surfaces were cracking from the barbaric forces of living roots, that random photosynthesis was intolerably inefficient and that other creatures were still getting half of the energy produced, that the weather was too accidental for human good and needed to be regulated, that the prodigal wafting of seeds and wanderings of animals was inimical to a well-planned society – if I were a benign tyrant I would put a stop to it all. But not in such a way that would alarm my subjects (with their primate bodies and Pleistocene minds).

I would begin by declaring that the world is beautiful – indeed, that its beauty is its most valuable attribute. I would lament that it is difficult and costly to keep things growing in the many perimeter and decorative plantings and little parks that accompany enlightened progress. Direct impact by trucks, careless tromping by many feet, buildings below ground and roofs above, and cables and pipelines, the lack of pollinating insects for flowers, the disappearance of symbiotic fungi and other necessary partners, the very air itself—all seem to "do in" those things we all love—nay, those necessary aesthetic elements in a highly developed world. However important we find film substitutes and science backdrops, garden wallpaper and organic motifs in finishes and surfaces of all kinds, we must keep some truly beautiful, real landscapes. This I would insist on.

"Landscape" is the pivotal word. It is not a synonym for habitat or place, certainly not for natural community or ecosystem. A landscape is a representation of a certain kind of visual experience. The word was first used to mean a painting. The earliest of these "landskip" paintings (in the West) were imaginary scenes inspired by biblical and classical themes—that is, literary images. "Scenery," as mentioned previously, was originally a Greek term for stage props. Thus landscape is a way of tangibly representing a dramatic moment by using terrain and sky and plants as stage props, eventually as actors. Gardens made to be seen, or which are designed around viewpoints, are another tangible expression of the idea.

H. V. S. Ogden and his wife, Margaret Ogden, have documented the historical sequence by which a body of criticism and language of connoisseurship developed first around imaginary or ideal scenes and was then applied to actual places by Dutch itinerant limners doing portraits of country houses for English aristocrats in the seventeenth century. A place that looked good as a picture was regarded as "picturesque," and Christopher Hussey has shown us how such pictures trained the eye or became a veritable language for an aesthetic of nature. Others have unraveled the profound interconnection between paintings of idealized scenes and the rise of a style of gardening in eighteenth-century England more completely visual than anything previously done in Europe. That pictures were the standard by which raw nature was to be judged and its aesthetic value established is a trap escaped by only a few (of which Henry Thoreau was one). Bernard Smith has traced the steps by which a whole section of the planet—the South Pacific—was perceived by Europeans in terms of pictures.

My program as a kindly monarch would be to dwell on the idea of landscape, to use the terminology of analysis and description that it shares with the arts, to talk about aesthetic and spiritual values as identical, and to refer to art, artists, inspiration, and creativity as the supreme human qualities, the great achievements of civilization. When the natural came up, I would assume that it referred to that idyllic relationship between humans and nature exemplified by pastoral poetry. Even ferocious beasts, as seen in the paintings by Delacroix and Henri Rousseau, have a "place" in nature, that is, in parks created for their "preservation." Everything depends on the manner in which nature is "treated," to use the language of art criticism. We all want harmonious, dynamic, balanced, integrated, relationships to nature. (Isn't that what ecology says, too?)

For a few years – and it may have had some permanent effects – a wave of doubt swept across the modern mind that nature and art had the same purpose. There was a sort of rebellion by some scruffy types who agreed with Thoreau that they did not find the play of light and shade on a dead horse in a meat stall to be as satisfying as sunshine on a live horse in a field. Those "romantics" were barred from the technocratic centers of power as Thoreau's century ended. Today we can imagine the hee-haws with which Thoreau would have greeted the substitution of Astroturf for meadow. And yet it makes perfect sense as long as we regard the purpose of the world as a setting for the human romance – or tragedy – and order to be a matter of form.

The reverse romanticism of plastic trees is not one of birds and flowers as moral lessons and kindred beings, but a vicious fantasy that justifies the extirpation of nonhuman life. No one doubts that we will have our plastic trees and that they will do even better than seeming like the real thing, for they will be horribly real.

Place

Place in American Culture

PLACE IN AMERICAN LIFE BEGINS WITH ONE OF THE MOST distinctive bodies of art in the United States. The Hudson River School painters produced several thousand canvases of New England landscapes in only about three decades before the Civil War. Almost everyone is familiar in a general way with these pictures, some of which are in the larger American galleries. Their real abundance is not often appreciated, for they are stored by the hundreds in gallery cellars and are owned privately in great numbers.

The question of why they were painted has been seldom asked and poorly answered. Usually the subject is confined to the notion of frontiers, a sense of scale, conquering the wilderness, or it emerges within the history of art, a consideration of the styles, training, and influences of the painters in a cultural era called romanticism. In that idiom the paintings are provincial expressions of painterly traditions of England and northwestern Europe, with its centuries of "Italianate" influences and Dutch predecessors.

Figure 16. *Kindred Spirits,* 1849. Painting by Asher B. Durand. Oil on canvas. Collections of the New York Public Library. Astor, Lenox and Tilden Foundations.

But why they are set in such a restricted geography, compressed in time, homogeneous in subject and naturalism cannot be explained simply as American manifestations of a larger tradition. The American paintings are unique in several ways, mainly in that they are portraits of places, especially wild places.

Their homogeneity disappears when they are examined through the eyes of the naturalist. What to the ordinary viewer appear to be repetitive scenes of forest and mountain are actually meticulous explorations of the diversity within a unity, the variations of themes of a certain biome and geography. Seldom, perhaps never, in modern Western art has there been such focused scrutiny of the appearance of a region, especially of the geological and botanical details.

Asher B. Durand, who immortalized William Cullen Bryant and his friend, the artist Thomas Cole, in *Kindred Spirits,* one of the most widely known paintings of the period, chose such a landscape for its setting. *Kindred Spirits* (figure 16) shows Bryant and Cole conversing at the foot of Kaaterskill Creek near Old Palenville. This painting shows the stream deeply incised in sandstone, its abraded chasm walls, potholes, and typical ovate limestone fragments from upstream. Successive layers of sedimentary rocks offer differing resistance to the down-cutting stream, developing stair steps and waterfalls. Washington Irving, who started it all, identified Sleepy Hollow nearby. Like many of the painters, Durand painted a composite: the cliffs at the right are from farther upstream, and so is the falls. In figure 17, Paul Shepard stands on the same rock, now undercut and fallen into the streambed.

If you drive through these landscapes today, you see a phenomenon that is happening almost everywhere—changes whose origins and materials, designs and purposes do not originate locally: roads, buildings, transmission lines, vehicles—the whole paraphernalia of technophilia—brought from elsewhere, from common centers of planning and production. The countrysides produced by such means are themselves duplications of one another. Among an educated and somewhat supercilious class this produces a familiar lament: the loss of native crafts and local industry to the enveloping tentacles of centralized political and industrial forces in a society whose mastery of nature is based on the replication of machines and the modification of terrain to make them work.

Figure 17. Paul Shepard at the site of
Kindred Spirits, 1953. Photograph by
Melba Shepard.

But why do we mourn the loss of the native ambience? Critics say it
is only self-indulgent nostalgia, sentimental attachment for a past when
life was simpler or cleaner—largely a self-deluded view. The opinion is
echoed by the minions of change: our attachment to obsolete, old-fashioned economies, skills, or styles is but a romantic dream. Those afraid
of progress are said to cling to the past and impede growth and affluence.
Indicted by this accusation of weakness and immaturity we yield to its
logic, and the worldwide blenderizing goes on, with the blessings of the
industrial state, converting the globe piece by piece into a business network of uniform parts and identical places.

The angry reaction to romanticism—past or present—has just about run
its course. Whatever the foibles of romanticism, its concern for the organic,
for the wholeness of things, for feeling as well as reason, has outlived the
spurts of bad taste and emotional affectation that it generated. Even so,
the romantic in each of us remains a whipping boy, an excuse for our
own lack of conviction. The yearning for scenery, nostalgia for the family
farm, for respite from the urban roar, and sensitivity to wildlife: these are
regarded still as the indulgences of those who can afford them, symbols
of wealth and privilege. Enthusiasm for the local and unique, the customs
and environments that differentiate one region from another, handicrafts

and skills, things homemade, exotic places, "primitive" peoples – all are associated with the idle amusement of the few.

And, in a sense, they should be scorned. They have been the playthings of fossil-fuel man, a part of his connoisseurship of cute objects and color-ful places. Parochial values are debauched by layers of exploitation and misunderstanding. Picturesqueness reduces everything it touches to mere surfaces. In the eighteenth century the gentility went about Italy speaking of the *genius loci* as though it were a landscape painting. They pimped for tourism's whoring of place. The admirers of landscape were not the op-ponents but the agents of the Faustian spirit, the founders of the aesthetic passion of nature, who would facilitate the destruction of peoples and places for the arts by perceiving them as "local color" and subordinating them through commercial travel to the movers and changers at the heart of Progress.

To the old Romans, whose poetry created the pastoral, the *genius loci* had not meant picturesqueness at all but referred to a tutelary divinity, a guardian spirit. It had been the same among the Greeks, whose temples were expressions of the character of particular goddesses in whose laps the temples were placed. The subtlety with which they were accommo-dated to the terrain extended even to the configuration of the horizon; the temple passages were designed to guide ritual processions whose central themes were a dialogue between the people and the earth.[1]

However much they admired the old arts, educated persons more than a millennium later could feel little of the old pagan interior sense in which these sacred places were experienced as part of themselves. The Jews and Christians had methodically sought out the old shrines and turned them into churches whose essential purpose was to direct the religious inspira-tion away from that place.[2] To the bishops who consecrated them and the liturgy they followed, they referred to a Holy Land elsewhere, a heaven and hell that were nowhere and everywhere.

In his widely read book *The Sacred and the Profane,* Mircea Eliade has instructed a whole generation on the history of sacred places: the rites and ceremonies that "cosmosize" a hearth or an altar.[3] But there is for him no real chthonic, no real spirits, only human beliefs. Eliade is a Christian historian. Although at pains to insist on the religious man's loyalty to the heterogeneity of space, he sees it only as something made by men. The intrinsic qualities of the spring or cave or mountain are for him little more than markers. There is not the slightest hint that the spiritual entities that the Romans, Greeks, and scores of so-called primitives conceived as indwelling and indigenous were anything but cultural assertions. One always called in the forces from a centralized heaven the way one dials a long-distance operator.

Of course, the Christians did not invent this making of place by will and designation. The ancient civilizations of the Near East are speckled with temples built where they would be convenient to the bureaucracy, the keepers of the grain, and the army barracks. The shift of attention away from the uniqueness of habitat began long before the Church fathers declared that all places on this earth are pretty much the same. Eliade's view is ultimately no different from that of municipal street-namers: the world behind the human facade is homogeneous. One *founds* rather than *discovers* place. It doesn't matter whether a priest blesses an altar or the mayor cuts a ribbon. The autochthonous forces by which the earth speaks are not part of nature but only elements in myths through which the peasants rationalize their designations of sacredness. This view assumes that we know what is given and what is made.

But the polarity of the given and the made will not go away. It is the duality of the heart of knowledge, the central enigma of our private and collective identities. Arthur Modell has observed that the painting and sculpturing of the Paleolithic caves of southern Europe often use the erosional forms of the rock as a part or whole of the animal figure.[4] This "transitional" synthesis of what is there and what is created externalizes the linked polarity between the culture, the artist, and the stone, between our selves and our bodies. The artist formalizes that tension which is the core of the maturing self-consciousness.

Art, says Modell, is always a love affair with the world. Henry Moore, the sculptor, liberates his massive reclining figures from within the stone; they do not escape so much as articulate their own particular mineral substance. Like the cave art, his work is a search for self that was not solely defined by the acts of transcendence and domination that energized romantic tragedy, feelings for which the self-styled "neoclassicist" and modern highway-pipeline–parking lot for builders cannot conceal their antipathy. Romantic tears seem to them like infantile weakness. The temples and caves were part of an irretrievable past, they say.

And infantile they were, for the stresses of deprivation have regressive effects. Miss a developmental episode that belongs in your sixth year, and in some respect you never get older. Even when the connections are made you are drawn back sometimes to your roots for renewal. Between the natural and the human, the given and the made, the other and the self, what the romantics sought was "a place in which to discover a self." This apt phrase of Edith Cobb's is a way of describing a childhood process by which the terrain and its natural things become a model of cognitive structure for the plastic, order-seeking juvenile.[5]

The child, she says, seeks to make a world the way the world is made. Her studies of the biographies of geniuses led her to the conclusion that the terrain itself provided the durable gestalt upon which the intellect germinated. Home range for the eight-year-old is prime, patterned, concrete reality in life, upon which the wavering and nubile powers of memory and logic cling and develop, like seals climbing out onto the rocks to give birth.

In his book *The Mind of a Mnemonist,* A. R. Luria describes a man whom he observed and studied for many years, a man whose phenomenal power of memory enabled him to remember everything and anything – all the words in all the paragraphs in all the pages he ever read – a man who could repeat the names of a hundred spices or a hundred flowers in order, regardless of how much time had elapsed since he saw the list.[6] To Luria's question "How do you do it?" the man replied that he could visually recall the book pages and that when he was given a list he took an imaginary walk in a landscape, placing each object in view along the path. To recall them he had only to picture that place again and his walk through it, to see objects. The man was abnormal. Most of us have the blessing of remembering trivia only in the unconscious, if at all. But his anomaly was a clue to a strange and necessary relationship between place and mind.

Cobb's study of genius was a search for the genesis of thought and creativity by studying the lives of the gifted. That genius is both the "spirit of place" in its classical sense and a personal divine spark among the most powerful minds is not coincidental. That early formation of the self in children who are yet untouched by ideology is a growing awareness of one's own anatomy, the discreteness of body parts: both organs within and complexity of surface, sensory location, and feelings and moods as well. Experience for a small infant is a formless sea of feelings that engulf the individual. Their subjective separation requires a spatial detachment. They are intuited from external models and introjected. The constituents of self need externality and distance to be comprehended. Considering how admirable the human individual is, as Shakespeare tirelessly reminded us, the burden on the environment is great indeed. Diversity, richness, all those terms of multiplicity that describe a heterogeneous world, have been demonstrated repeatedly by biologists as essential to the development of intelligence. From nutritional and environmental studies of laboratory maze-running rats to the observation of babies with and without playpens, institutionalized children, and the psychology of the playground, the evidence is strong that heterogeneity is like an essential nutrient.[7]

But how does it work? You cannot, after all, just put a baby in a bag with a thousand objects and shake well before using. Claude Lévi-Strauss believes that the species system of plants and animals is a durable, dependable, concrete model for the development of the powers of categorizing, or basic cognition. Edith Cobb holds that the fixation on terrain is an organizing process by which the precept of relatedness is interiorized. White and his associates at Harvard find that the intelligence of children emerges relative to a spatial movement among objects, coupled with naming. All of these imply real changes in the nervous system. We can visualize the possibilities at the individual level among people by an analogy to differences that occur in the nervous systems of different species of animals that live in different habitats.

A series of paintings done in about 1901 and published by the Royal Society represents a kind of extension of the terrain into the inner eye.[8] These were the first color representations of the ocular fundus, the retinas of living animals. The patterns have a likeness to environments that is inescapable among those animals living in horizontally structured habitats – sheep, horses, lions, dogs, humans – while the fundus of others, who live in the trees or underwater, lacks the landscape-like patterns. There is nothing mystical about this. The structure and content of the visual cells correspond to differences in the frequencies of light in sections of the visual field. In open terrestrial habitats the field is roughly divided into bands of light from the sky, the ground, and the horizon. It suggests in a way perhaps more symbolic than evidential the capacity for structuring the nervous system on an external model. To me these retinas look like impressionist landscapes. In an evolutionary sense, the habitat has impressed its form upon the neural tissue, and the individual organism seeks out those places in which its sensory and nervous systems work, orienting its head and eyes to light patterns matching its visual anatomy.

The individual's intrinsic needs all have spatial settings that are not inventions but a mammalian heritage. In a seminal paper on what he calls "archetypal place," Mayer Spivak has enumerated thirteen subdivisions of the habitat.[9] One can live without special places for resting, feeding, conviviality, grooming, courting, and so on, but without them we become, like deprived, captive mammals, increasingly stressed and pathological.[10] Such places are not arbitrarily labeled in this ancient tradition of mammals but are the psychological and physical prerequisites of the different behaviors. All of them have perceptual and psychological dimensions.

The development of this continuity of internal and external, the reciprocity of place and person, takes place at every level of experience. James V. Neel, studying the most remote Indians of Central and South America, was struck by the lack of parental concern for the groveling play of crawling infants.[11] They frolicked happily in the debris of village and camp, dusty or mud-smeared, thrusting everything in their mouths, tasting their way, so to speak, into the environment. Neel knew that infants everywhere do the same if given the chance. But what to our sanitary-minded society looks like infantile perversity has the wisdom of enabling the child to begin building a repertoire of antibodies against the local antigens while still in part protected by the immunoglobulins of its mother's milk. To do so they had to "meet" the local antigens, and the result was that the children he examined had extremely high levels of antibodies against infection. In a somewhat different perspective the child was building into its physiology an immunological counterpart of the antigenic landscape, a sensual mapping of home territory done by children the world over.

The foregoing suggests that the habitat is not merely a container but a structured surround in which the developing individual makes tenacious affiliations, that something extremely important to the individual is going on between the complex structure of those particular places and the emerging, maturing self, a process of macro-micro correlation, mostly unconscious, essential to the growth of personal identity.

Figure 18. *View of the Round-Top in the Catskill Mountains,* 1827. Painting by Thomas Cole. Oil on panel, 18⅝ x 25⅜ in. Gift of Martha C. Karolik for the M. and M. Karolik Collection of American Paintings, 1815–1865, 47.1200. Courtesy, Museum of Fine Arts, Boston. Reproduced with permission. ©2002 Museum of Fine Arts, Boston. All rights reserved.

With this in mind, we can turn again to those large, excruciatingly detailed paintings made along the rivers and among the mountains of the Northeast during the second third of the nineteenth century. Up to the Revolution, the American knew himself in three contexts: as Christian, English colonial, and village community member. As this scaffolding was cut away by independence, secularization, and industrial urbanization, he suffered an acute attack of inchoateness from which he still has not recovered. The landscapes of those institutions had been the stable, rural countryside tightly and hierarchically ordered around the church and town, making zones upon the land and interpenetrations with the wild that changed little between 1520 and 1820.[12] In an era of rapid change we may forget how constant was American life for three centuries, and we may overlook how traumatic the collapse of the old order was.

Figure 19. Site of *View of the Round-Top in the Catskill Mountains,* 1953.
Photograph by Paul Shepard.

The main body of the Hudson River School was preceded by a literature of travel and description, but more significantly by an indigenous
prose and poetry (even though imitative of European themes and styles).
Preeminent are the works of Washington Irving, James Fenimore Cooper,
and William Cullen Bryant. From time immemorial the myths of creation
have been presented as epic tales, and perhaps could be comprehended
only that way. The "legends" of Sleepy Hollow and the adventures of
Natty Bumppo and Leatherstocking among the Indians are geographi-
cally explicit.

From the "actual" sites of such places, which much of the early painting
scrutinized with an almost frenetic intensity, the painters moved out in
search of correspondingly dramatic sites appropriate to the imagination of
episodes of pioneering life, or even storms or mountain geology. Thomas
Cole was its most fervent spokesman. He painted and wrote long essays.
To be lost in the wilderness, he said, was the supreme experience. The

view painted in *View of the Round-Top in the Catskill Mountains* was a two-hour hike from the Mountain House on the Catskill Escarpment, where the Hudson River is not easily seen. It was a sunrise view requiring over-nighting on the mountaintop – a way of seeking one's roots, a primitive regression (figures 18 and 19).

Neither the eroticism nor the adolescent emotionality of Cole's work has gone unnoticed. This sentiment, for which later critics had only contempt, had its purposes, for it turned Americans back to maternal themes, to the land itself, in a search for their beginnings, without which they would re-main lost. Cynics after the Civil War saw the romantics as merely weak and undisciplined, as the Victorian considered women to be. To rhapso-dize about trees and waterfalls seemed to them to have been sentimental and silly. The artists' own personalities were indeed rife with immaturity. But they were, in a sense, childish for us all.

Until then, the Europeans who settled America were on alien ground. With few exceptions their concrete connection to locality remained in Europe. The painters in America tried, in a few decades, to overhaul that whole troubled subjectivity, to imprint on our nervous systems a wild mountain spectacle as home, to do in the New World what had taken centuries to accomplish in Europe. Of course they could not possibly succeed, but in some ways no concept of place and landscape in America since then has been without something of their mark.

We are reminded with painful regularity of our continuing sense of dislocation, the neuroses of personal identity problems and the terror of loneliness in the crowd, of isolation both from society and from the rest of nature. These anxieties are linked to doubts about the purpose of life, even of order in the creation. Traditional psychology, scientific humanism, and even our religious preoccupation with the self have tried to explain these dilemmas of unconnectedness as arising within society and its works – in the family, the home, the job, or the church. But the failure of these explanations to either elucidate or remedy our chronic fragmentation raises doubts that our loneliness stems from inadequate social planning or ideology, or that we make or unmake ourselves apart from a nonhuman gestalt.

It is easy to blame rootlessness, mobility, and the fluidity of American life for our anguish, but all the hunting and gathering cultures that have ever been studied moved serenely through hundreds of miles without such troubles. Although they traveled through vast spaces, there is an organismic scale about their lives; W. H. Auden once observed that for us today the megaworld of the galaxy and the miniworld of the atom are real mainly in frightening ways. In "Ode to Terminus" he speaks of the earth:

> where all visibles do have a definite
> outline they stick to and are undoubtedly
>   at rest or in motion, where lovers
>   recognize each other by their surface,
> where to all species except the talkative
> have been allotted the niche and diet that
>   becomes them. This, whatever micro-
>   biology may think, is the world we
> really live in and that saves our sanity.[13]

"Saving our sanity," in this mesocosm, might well require that we forget the heaven of the other world religions along with the Adlerian psychology of simply willing our own world, as we have forgotten other tall stories.

Eliade wants us to believe that places differ according to the amount of universal holy oil we pour on them. He is in company with the cartographers, whose surveys of latitude, longitude, township, and range we have also accepted as the terms of location, of "defining space." But the world is not a billiard table until we finally turn it into one. It is unique everywhere in combining differently features that, in some unknown way, both reflect and create an inner geography by which we locate the self.

However exact the mathematical, political, or ecclesiastical subdivision of space may be, if it is imposed from a distant culture, it cannot refer to place in the sense that is meant here, any more than maturity is achieved through ceremonies by which those institutions confer power on the individual, however much symbolic scenery they frame it in. British drama critic Tyrone Guthrie once wrote of Thornton Wilder's keen sense of place in his play *Our Town* "that such a close attachment to, and interpretation of a particular part of the earth is an absolute essential to any work of art which can ever be of deep or lasting significance. . . . It is one of the paradoxes of art that a work can only be universal if it is rooted in a part

Figure 20. *Catskill Mountain House,* 1855. Painting by Jasper Cropsey. Oil on canvas, 29 x 44 in. The Minneapolis Institute of Arts. The William Hood Dunwoody Fund.

of its creator which is most privately and particularly himself. Such roots must sprout not only from the people but also the places, which have meant most to him in his most impressionable years."[14]

Wilder creates not only place but an instrument of its recognition and affirmation. His own experience is one of discovery. He is like Carlos Castaneda, who tells us how difficult it is for one coming from a culture of the human domination of nature to discover, even in a room twelve by eight feet, the spot on which he could sit without fatigue. His frustrating search under the tutelage of Don Juan took all night.[15] Again one thinks of the nineteenth-century painters, who roved on foot back and forth across the White and Green Mountains, the Berkshires, the Taconics, the Hudson Highlands, and the Catskills, endlessly searching. They along with tourists visited Kaaterskill House, which faces east overlooking the Hudson Valley twenty-five hundred feet below. Perhaps no other place taught Americans to enjoy scenery like this one. The neoclassic remains

Figure 21. Site of *Catskill Mountain House,* 1953. Photograph by Paul Shepard.

were still standing when the photograph was made in 1953 but have since vanished (figures 20 and 21). The heterogeneity of the land is not made by humans – only discovered and enhanced or ignored and diminished by them.

An example of this reciprocity in which the given and the made play complementary roles is described in Jacquetta Hawkes's beautiful book *A Land,* an exercise in the gestalt-making powers where local rock is used for architecture, as it has been in many regions of England. The mind resonates between the stone as geology or terrain and its arrangement in man-made structures, between a unique regional architecture of the earth and the constraints and opportunities it offers in style and design. She is especially sensitive to the evolution of mind and consciousness, whose records occur as fossils in the same rocks that are used to build libraries, laboratories, and churches in which to contemplate the past.

Europe, as May Watts observed, had its cultural history written in the regional materials. Her guidebooks to the landscapes of Europe and

America are achievements of a high order because she recognized that the value of place differences is not a matter of scenery but of the interaction of people and their natural environment, a claim to which they cling despite the leveling bulldozer and premolded structures.[16] In America this is clearly less so than in Europe. True, there are the stone fences of Frost's New England and the grave slabs of Yankee marble, the limestone storefronts and banks of the Midwest, the sandstone campus at Boulder, and the adobes of New Mexico. Types of wood may also be identified with the local architecture, though modern lumberyards have virtually lost their local connections. Wood does not last long enough to signify the earlier dependence on local trees in the way rock does. One is reminded of John Ruskin's refusal to come to America, saying that he could never visit a country that had no old castles. If you had no old castles you had no history, and if you had no history, there was no place in which the events that made you sanctified the ground.

But Ruskin was inordinately attached to the picturesque, to the necessity of ruins and the moral qualities of painting. Some dimensions of place do not depend on the interpenetration of geology and architecture. In her introduction to the poetry of Carl Sandburg, Rebecca West describes the loquaciousness of Americans in public, their readiness to discuss their lives with total strangers, and the leisure they take in self-explanation:

It occurs to one, as such experiences accumulate, that one has encountered in art, though not in life, people who talk and behave like this: in Russian novels. There one gets precisely the same universal addiction to self-analysis. And then it occurs to one also that this place is in certain respects very like Russia. Chicago, like Leningrad, like Moscow, is a high spot, to use its own idiom, on the monotony of great plains, a catchment area of vitality that rejoices extravagantly in its preservation because elsewhere in this region it might have trickled away from its source and been swallowed up in the vastness of the earth. All round Chicago lays the Middle Western plain. . . . The physical resemblance between Russia and the Middle West is certainly close enough. And it may be that life which finds itself lost in the heart of a vast continent, whether that be Old or New, has a tendency to take the same forms. Life in another case, which flows in a number of channels and is divided into small nations, has an audience, who will give it a verdict on its performance, which is none the less useful if its inevitable function is to be disbelieved, and it has a basis for optimism about the universe since it sees the neighboring nations surviving and flourishing in spite of what it is bound to consider their inferiorities. But a nation that is isolated in its vastness has no audience but itself, and it has no guarantee that continued existence is possible or worth while, save its own findings. Therefore, Russia and Middle West alike, it is committed to introspection, to a constant stocktaking of its own life and a constant search for the meaning of it.

In the Middle West more than anywhere else the introspective inhabitants have developed an idiom suited for describing the events of the inner life and entirely inadequate in dealing with the events of the outer life.[17]

In celebrating Chicago and the prairies Carl Sandburg threw the raw land right back in John Ruskin's face, for the prairie and Chicago were the least aesthetic places by the canons of painterly aesthetics, the concept of scenery.[18] The beauty of Missouri and Illinois will never come from matching them against the abstract standards of the picturesque, but from the affirmation by people in those places and by an integrity that is violated neither by alien aesthetics nor by alien machinery. The commerce that tends to homogenize the world is not just physical, while its opponents are aesthetic. Modern tourism is not a defender of the world's difference against the utilitarian onslaught. Recreation, leisure, and art are the ministers of abstract scenery just as the centralized religions are of the abstract holy. Because of abstract theory, a park might be established where nature happens to fit the standard. But the making of parks has been a license to surrender the rest.

Tourism and the park mentality, like that which pushed American Indians onto reservations, makes enclaves—not on the theory that quality is everywhere different, but on the theory that the alternative to dispersed points of sanctity is a continuous, weary uniformity. Sandburg was not signing parks and petrified village monuments like Lincoln's New Salem today. He belonged. Belonging, says Erik Erikson, is the pivot of life, the point at which selfhood becomes possible—not just belonging in general, but in particular. One belongs to a universe of order and purpose that must initially be realized as a particular society in a natural community of certain species in a terrain of unique geology. What Rebecca West sees as the empty plains of Illinois and Russia betrays her own bias, for they are empty only – as noted – of close neighbors.

My theme can now be drawn together. It can be signified by the wandering of certain Australian Aborigines. In going on the pilgrimage called walkabout, the Aborigine travels to a succession of named places, each familiar from childhood and each the place of some episode in the story of creation. Symbolic art forms and religious relics heighten the sacred qualities of each. The journey is into the interior in every sense, as myth is the dramatic externalization of the events of an inner history. To the pilgrims these places are profoundly moving. The landscape is a kind of archive where the individual moves simultaneously through his personal and tribal past, renewing contact with crucial points, a journey into time and space refreshing the meaning of his own being.[19]

Terrain structure is the model for the patterns of cognition. As children we internalize its order as we practice "going" from thought to thought, and learn to recognize perceptions and ideas as details in the sweep of larger generalizations. We intuit these textures into a personal uniqueness. Mind has the pattern of place predicated upon it, and we describe its excursions, like this essay, as a ramble between "points," the exploration of "fields," following "paths," and finding "boundaries," "wastelands," or "jungles," of the difficulty of seeing forests for the trees, of making mountains of molehills, of dark and light sides, of going downhill or uphill.

Cognition, personality, creativity, maturity – all are in some way tied to particular gestalts of space, to locality partly given and partly found.

What does this say to us as Americans? From the standpoint of society as a whole, our disadvantages seem obvious and enormous. We have little cultural continuity with the land; history has few tangible relics. The vestiges of precolonial art and earthworks remain, but their meanings we do not know or feel. At the time of its settlement by Europeans the continent had vast diversity, as indicated by the different Indian tribes, numbering in the hundreds. Almost everything we have done to it in the past two centuries has worked toward the destruction of these differences. We idealized this uniformity in the image of the melting pot and standard of living. The industrial complex levels mountains, drains swamps, opens forests, plants trees in grasslands, and domesticates and exterminates the wild. We have long been aware of this and of the rejoinder that it is a small price to pay for convenience, security, and comfort – that entertainment, travel, instant news, electrified homes, and an unlimited array of goods are made available in this way. Diversity, in fact, is suspect because it is divisive, or at best it is said to be just one more source of pleasure in a complex equation whose theme is "trade-offs." We are doubtful and ambivalent about diversity. Phyllis McGinley put it this way:

Since the ingenious earth began
    To shape itself from fire and rubble,
Since God invented man, and man
    At once fell to, inventing trouble,
One virtue, one subversive grace
Has chiefly vexed the human race.

One whimsical beatitude,
    Concocted for his gain and glory,
Has man most stoutly misconstrued
    Of all the primal category –
Counting no blessing, but a flaw
That difference is the mortal law.[20]

But the trouble is not that as a nation we lose the multifold character of a continent or lack architecture that affirms its diversity. We do not actually experience anything as a nation, but as individuals. To the corporation or bureaucracy the quality of place is merely an amenity, because our mythology of collective power confirms the transcendence of the individual.

The crucial point is that the child must have a residential opportunity to soak in a place, and that the adolescent and adult must be able to return to that place to ponder the visible substrate of his or her own personality. Place in human genesis has this episodic quality. Knowing who you are is a quest across the first forty years of life. Knowing who you are is impossible without knowing where you are. But it cannot be learned in a single stroke. This is what makes the commercial ravagement of the American countryside so tragic – not that it is changed and modernized, but that the tempo of alteration so outstrips the rhythms of individual human life.

In the 1830s it was said that hardly a Dutch house remained in Manhattan. Ax, fire, and merino sheep had deforested much of New England. Half-a-hundred painters went out in a furious attempt to find what might persist, attaching themselves to the most rugged terrain in their adolescent dismay and desire. In a hopeless frenzy of sheer will and stamina, they tried to establish grounds for self-discovery that would perhaps be stable, the way the European countryside was, across at least a generation of time.

Everywhere in America we continue to be engaged in that unspoken drama, to know the frustrations of being unable to grow up. Samuel Beckett, in his plays, has rightly set out our quandary in an empty landscape, where we wait at crossroads marked only by signposts for something to happen, surrounded by a terrain that is both featureless and meaningless.[21] Signposts do not make a *whereness* or beliefs a *whoness*.

If we were all as alike as eggs—and as eggs in our personal genesis we are unaware of our identities and potential relationships—it would not matter. But we hatch into a world where everything we do can help make or unmake the possibilities for our further growth. Intellectuals or eggheads like to think that we live in a world of ideas that we invent, as we create the domestic plants and animals. But in some part of our skulls there is wilderness. We call it the unconscious because we cannot cultivate it the way you would a field of grain or a field of thought. In it forces as enduring as climate and bedrock maintain our uniqueness in spite of the works of progress. It is the source of our private diversity. Together, our collective unconscious seems almost to exist apart from ourselves, like a great wild region where we can get in touch with the sources of life. It is a retreat where we wait out the movers and builders, who scramble continually to revamp our surroundings in search of a solution to a problem that is a result of their own activity.

Place and Human Development

THE HUMAN REQUISITE OF THE NATURAL ENVIRONMENT has nothing to do with recreation in the sense of exercise, challenge, aesthetics, scenery, or release from work. It has little to do with "the outdoors" as a hobby or inspirational spectacle. It does have to do with ontogenesis, the development of a human from infant to maturity, and is the respondent in events as essential to the health of children as proper nurturance. The exact nature of the connection of human development to place is still unclear, but some of the lineaments are distinct in kind and timing and plug into the life cycle in specific ways. They are the outcome of phylogeny as it occurred in the latter phases of human evolution during the middle and upper Pleistocene. What follows is an attempt to identify these episodes during the first twenty years of life. Each is arranged in age sequence and, where possible, associated with certain environments in regard to urban life.

ANTIBODY PRODUCTION

The importance of the natural environment for the crawling infant has to do with pathogen/antibody development. Infants are programmed to taste repeatedly the surroundings within reach, particularly the soil. Over time, enough dirt and objects are stuffed in their mouths to build an antibiotic repertoire appropriate to the precise pathogen taxonomy of the area. Place, for crawlers, is a special collection of indigenous germs ingested that stimulate their antibody-producing system while they still have the protection of immunity provided by their mother's milk.[1]

Tasting the environment is a normal and ongoing experience for people who harvest their own food. It relates them to the earth in chains of connection that may be the foundation of all ecological relationships. The lack of these relationships in our culture may have physiological and psychological consequences. What Mircea Eliade has called "the homogenization of space" refers not only to visual and mythological but also to biochemical aspects in a society committed to specialized regional agribusiness, massive transport, and eclectic consumption patterns.[2]

COGNITIVE DEVELOPMENT

A certain natural environment is "expected" by the human genome for cognitive development to proceed. Diversity of natural species is essential, as they become both the object and code of thought. The first operations of cognition are related to taxonomic strategies: discriminating, comparing, sorting, grouping, categorizing, and naming.[3] The language-acquisition schedule of young children is consonant with taxonomic identification. So the language of a child at the idyllic and practical age of ten is naïve taxonomy – not yet having metaphorical significance. That the strategy of mental operations coincides with both the linguistic and the categorical enterprise in a world rich in fascinating different species is probably no coincidence.[4]

ANIMAL MIMICRY

James Fernandez has called a certain kind of fantasy play in children "animal predication."[5] The mimicry of animals by children and juveniles is included in extemporaneous individual and group play. Such mimicry involves the subjective internalizing of commonly recognized traits, through turn taking at performances and interactions by which certain qualities are assimilated into the inchoate self and others are rejected. Running across as much as five years of such play is a resolution of self and the Other—represented primarily by animals—a direct and prosaic acknowledgment of qualities of which the self is a synthesis. These early cognitive activities pave the way for later abstraction and analytical operations by which we understand characterization and personality.

At first glance, animal predication seems to be largely independent of place, an impression that seems to be verified by the imaginative play of children at "Fox and Geese" or "Run, Sheepie, Run" on bare playgrounds. But the questions that an ecologist might raise about the context of this play do involve the environment: To what extent do these animal referents evoke appropriate habitat or actual behavior of the prototypes? Does it make any difference whether these animals are wild or barnyard forms? What range of experiences do modern urban children need to adequately predicate human consciousness, and how does this differ from indigenous children? What happens to this internalizing process when machines are substituted for animals? Is this behavior itself a part of the broad dysfunctional syndrome that arose with the altered horizons of sedentary agriculture and is undertaken in hunting/gathering societies in wholly different ways?

TERRESTRIAL ANLAGE

A terrestrial anlage, or foundation for human development, is evident but is highly diverse. Children of hunters in the Aleutians learn anatomy at the same time they learn place-names, which implies a linguistic connection.[6] Psychologists separate children into "field dependent" and "field independent" groups, the latter articulating both internal anatomical and terrestrial detail more completely, which implies to me a reciprocal and interdependent resolution.[7] Edith Cobb, surveying the biographies of geniuses, finds repeated return in memory to childhood places to renew order-giving intuition that was initially formed by the textures and pattern of juvenile play space.[8] Space is structured differently in juvenile life than in later ages: in early childhood, it is much more critically defined. It is intensely concerned with paths and boundaries, with hiding places and other special places associated with particular things. This whole home range (its radius measured by the range of the care-giver's voice) is, in effect, imprinted on the child. Such a construct works imperceptibly on the memory and consciousness and is especially important in creative adults who are introspective about the generation of their own ideas and who tend to be fascinated by their autobiographical terrain. At just that age where their movement follows the patterns of the environment, some future ineffable claim is made. The searching mind of genius recontacts the child's world and an ancient game: the stalking and tracking of the predator and the refuge – the retreat, solitude, and disengagement – of the prey.

Nostalgic returns to places always contain the surprise of how small they are. The garden, the symbolic source and first home of all life, is translated by architecture in a language and style of its time but is universally unspoiled cosmos made small. In Newton's time it was mathematically precise and geometrically pruned; in Wordsworth's, it was grassy and pastoral. Gardens are but one example of place as a kind of diminutive externalization of a mental set. The mental apparatus may be perceived, in turn, as a place, and the landscape as a metaphor of it.[9]

Margaret Mead once proposed that all children spend some time on an island.[10] Perhaps she meant only that the social forms convey a sense of finiteness, but I took her to mean that the physical and sensory experience as a whole does not simply frame but constitutes the limited nature of human habitat, a prototype of reality. Within the confines of the island a universe operates; it is a natural miniature. The implications of this anlage are many, one of them being its contained livingness: the organic unfolding, growing, and dying. Even the desert oasis has this biotic insistence. What intellectual schemata does the no-longer-walled city with its paved and paneled surfaces offer? What are the consequences of its gestalt-making power? The nostalgic return of the adult to juvenile home ranges may have crucial bearing on transitional phases of later ontogeny. What do these demands require of the nature of such places?

For the juvenile, the peripatetic round of Pleistocene life involved a succession of hearth-centered ranges with constitutional similarity – having spatial order and taxonomic diversity and familiarity. The moves of

nomadic peoples built across the years of latency a series of tightly con-
stricted spaces, each related to the others in a spatial and temporal order
that eventually formed a mosaic of band or tribal range. In slightly different compositions, the juvenile rehearsed the creation of textured space
again and again. All these places were probably ecologically mature biotic
communities. Habitat stability persisted in spite of constant movement of
the tribe and in spite of the passage of the years, a stability that formed
a perennial continuity of surround for individuals whose social relations
were constantly changing. Returning adults in such societies do not come
back to juvenile yards and fixed abodes but to a world created by successive understandings of small spaces, which they now see as a whole.

Amos Rapoport has touchingly described the visits of middle-aged
Australian Aborigines from church or government camps to their tribal
lands, where every year is remembered from childhood and the terrain
"is an archive of the ancestral past."[11] For the middle-aged everywhere,
past experience is a journey. How much must be lost to the quality of life
among those who have no easily accessible natural landscapes. One sus-
pects that its possession is related to the maturity and strength that marks
the endurance of American Indian cultures that have retained a home
land base.[12]

PREPUBERTAL EXODUS

In our society, Scout camps provide a prepubertal exodus as children
follow nonparental leaders into "wild" terrain. In America this began as
a woodcraft movement, which Ernest Thompson Seton designed after an
English model; but Seton's real theme was the preinitiatory experience of
American Indians. The camping phenomenon for eleven-year-olds sets the
tone of the departure from childhood and the preamble to an adolescent
ordeal in solitude. Skills and mastery are central to this experience just as
they are to a young Eskimo learning to use a kayak. Group membership,
symbolized by hypnotic orientation to a campfire and by group singing,
is no arbitrary device of middle-class life; it is an autogenic attempt by
people in affluent societies to read out the genes.

The camp exodus may seem to be a penumbral phase in the lee of latency and windward of adolescence. But we need to have much more care

than in the past in writing off age classes as "transitional." The eleven- to twelve-year-old group may be special in certain ontogenetic respects rather than merely in-between. These are heroic years in which the hero has not yet been exalted beyond mortality: cliques are bound by unexamined spontaneity rather than by ideology; joys of escape from surveillance are unsullied by doubt; and the reality of nature is exquisitely explicit and tangible. In terms of place, they are indeed developmental, with excursions out of juvenile home range, if only for a little while. But the admiration of older adolescents or young adult leaders and attunement to limited exploration are not necessarily mere foreshadowing, but instead form a unique whole for that period of life with its own essential purposes.

Adolescence has its own karma and its particular ecological requirements. "Adolescence" is a misleading term, for the period of life is not unitary; the thirteenth is very different from the fourteenth year, and a diverse series of events is involved. But there are three identifiable stages with their own special relationship to the environment.

Adolescent Regression

Adolescent behavior is widely recognized as regressive, but infantile behaviors are symptomatic of deep renewal, the excavation of what Joseph Campbell calls "infantile imprints of experience," the homological basis of mythical structures.[13] The regression carries strong implications for the figure of the mother. The grand shower of poetic perception in adolescence allows the maternal affiliation to be reexperienced in cosmic terms – an insight into reproduction and generation that carries with it the love of one's own mother in infancy. "Back to nature" and "the love of nature" are the hackneyed expressions of this movement of adolescent feeling toward the "mother of the hunt," the "mother of herds," or the "mother of us all." For the initiated, the earth is a body. An organic metaphor as the basis of geohuman relationships is a functional one. The nonliving is thereby understood never to be without life. Presumably this grows from continuous movement of the infant with respect to its mother's body.

For the most part our culture fails to provide the rituals and myths this powerful insight compels. Self-generated substitutes created by adolescents are a virtual catalog of delinquency and neurosis. Another aspect of the renewal of the mother motif as a catalyst toward the nonhuman world is that the individual has the opportunity to surmount deficient parenting when it was an infant, to straighten a crooked path by walking it again. It hardly needs saying that the implications of this rebirth and its potential for shaping the attitudes of modern society toward nature are scarcely explored.

Ecological Knowledge

An extension of taxonomic knowledge learned by children serves an ultimate achievement in adolescence as ecological knowledge. The species system and its ecological interconnections — especially food chains — if perceived through the lens of a mythical drama, related, and acted, provide guidance and a model for human social relations. In a degenerate form domestic animals are involved in social hierarchies with humans. In urban thought, in storytelling, and in experience, transformational forms, such as frogs, manifest or symbolize complex relationships that in tribal cultures take the form of taboos.[14]

Initiation

The test of solitude is particularly environmentally related in initiation. Testing the spirit of the initiate surrounded by the majestic and terrifying natural world is a widespread practice. There are no equivalents in the city or in a sensory deprivation tank, despite their isolating effects. Indeed, sensory deprivation is more likely to alienate than connect the individual to the concrete world. The autogenous and myth-depleted contemporary expression involves thousands of young people hiking in the wilderness making bold but secular and therefore emasculated simulations. What many individuals feel about the wilderness is that they have personally *approached* a spiritual experience. Without a liturgy it is largely wasted, though there may be psychological benefits.

We all know that one effect of national and multinational corporations and bureaucracies is to distribute identical structures and forms and to modify the terrain into duplicated units. Because of its repeatability, the abstract world of duplicated spaces is a nonplace, a landscape without historical depth or definable named places. It is my contention that the initiatory process empowers adolescents to make place by cosmosizing the world known to them.[15] "To make" in the modern world means, in fact, to transform. The physical making follows the ideational. Fully mature humans – the product of adolescent spiritual initiation – will not make a world of repeatable segments.

The test of the end of childhood is the ability to confront and to wear the Other, to enter it like a garment. The perceptual otherness of the visible cosmos, its explicit nonhuman concreteness, lies in true wilderness. If the individual's spiritual cosmology is adequate to his test of isolation, it can be adequate also to the whole arc of life. Having faced the Other in its diversity, adolescents may then face themselves, an expression of which may be the otherness of the city. Like infants who must see love in action before they can discover it in themselves, adolescents cannot discover their maturity in the city. We are surrounded by their ludicrous and pathetic efforts to create a universe in which to measure their own achievements.

As Erik Erikson and Harold Searles have demonstrated, the adolescent critical periods are in the service of identity resolutions through the establishment of a vast network of relations with the nonhuman as well as the human environment. If the landscape is fixated by juvenile perception as an extension of mental operations – as suggested earlier – then the wilderness may be the epigraph of the unconscious.[16] If the earth's wildernesses are finally domesticated as part of the mythology of Fossilfuelman's "control of nature," the immediate loss to wild species and ecosystems may be incalculable. But earth's wilderness is like some cosmic embassy where the adolescent pilgrimage ends in the birth of maturity – the final test and shaping of sanity is confrontation with the Other. In this its loss to us may be incalculable; we already see the signs of this deprivation.

Above I have suggested ontogenetic critical-period episodes in which human development in the first twenty years of life may be related to the natural world in the context of place. I have suggested that this ontogeny and its environmental complement are the outcome of human phylogeny in the Pleistocene and in Paleolithic hunting/gathering life.[17] Our present distance from that setting seems enormous, and the hunting/gathering past is easily seen as a ludicrous model for ourselves. That distance, however, may only be projected by the myth of historical humankind, augmented by recent commitments to progress and humanism. To the contrary, through the study of primitive cultures one sees the convergence of urban and hunting/gathering life. Throughout this essay I have alluded to the opportunity of urban peoples to recover elements of human ecology warped by millennia of immersion in domesticated landscapes. Paramount among these is the opportunity to be free of domestic animals both as social partners and as models of the nonhuman. The enormous human desire for animal figures is seen by their ubiquity in popular culture. "Pet therapy" notwithstanding, the psychology of this is poorly known. There is evidence for us in the impoverishment of peasant thought: a perception of nature as an extension or enemy of animals – degraded monsters – of the barnyard.

That city life suffers from the lack of green in daily experience may be an exaggeration – an irrelevant, sentimental fragment from an aesthetic that aligns its vision on an urban-rural axis. Far more important are components of nature that have deep psychological but not necessarily scenic import. Chief among these is the system of food chains. Wherever our attention falls on the schemata of alimentation it becomes the very model of relatedness. The nearly universal reciprocity of food and marriage regulations in tribal cultures signifies the two preoccupations of kinship – one connecting social ties, the other ecological ones. It is widely lamented that urban children think that groceries come from the store and milk from a carton, but the problem is usually seen in terms of mere information; the motor and participatory bases of learning in children and the way that kind of learning becomes a scaffold for seemingly unrelated data later in life are disregarded. Picture-book explanations are no help; nor is help from grownups who repudiate the very thesis of trophic centrality, whose denial of the life-giving nature of death is a prison for their own children. That we do not and cannot find it in ourselves to affirm as good and beautiful a world where creature eats creature – where butchering is a ritual act and decay an affirmation of wholeness – is a measure of the impoverishment of the urban mind. To treat this emptiness with better classroom materials or more open spaces is not only insufficient but misses the issue. Parks and pets are not the crucial points of contact with "nature" but only therapeutic exercises in the treatment of symptoms of deprivation.

The ontogenetic, critical-period approach to this subject is extremely hopeful and positive. It asks the prescriptive counsel from the social and psychological sciences for making childhood environments measure its plans against Pleistocene models, against the hunting/gathering life, against the demands of ontogeny and its critical-period phenomena. It implies that cities are as livable as the people in them are sane and mature – and that the journey into ecological maturity does not require continuous immersion in a garden. It is centered on focal experiences and episodes, which do need special spaces, resources, and – most urgently – mentors who mediate fantasy in childhood as apprehension of the biotic world instead of a trick for avoiding it. It is a general and probably valid intuition that the destruction of the natural world somehow impairs our humanity. The amount of wild nature necessary may be surprisingly modest if we can recover a sense of timing and purpose that makes us human.

Perceptions of the
Landscape by Pioneers

An Ecstasy of Admiration

The Romance of the High Plains and Oregon Trail in the Eyes of Travelers before 1850

INTRODUCTION

The westward movement of settlers over the Oregon Trail in the mid–nineteenth century marks a heroic era of American history. Their tales of the hardship, adventure, and danger of pioneering illumine the national memory. A kind of mythology belongs to that wagon train syndrome that owes its rigid imagery of the harried frontiersman to mass education and entertainment in the twentieth century. The trials of the hostile wilderness — usually in the form of rampaging Indians, bandits, and marauding animals — are typical of the convention, exploited beyond reason and reality in the commercialization of the history of the frontier. The bold risk of emigration into the unknown, the feats of daring and grim determination, the deprivation and struggle

Figure 22. *Hiawatha*, 1869. Painting by Thomas Moran. Oil on canvas. Museum purchase. The Philbrook Museum of Art, Tulsa, Oklahoma. 1944.9.

all have a real and true history, but they are only one aspect of pioneer life.

I do not mean only that instead of constant excitement there was monotony, weariness, and dull drudgery; nor only that there was gaiety, music, and fellowship. Even further from the stereotype of pioneering there was, among westering hearts, a powerful, positive, emotional rapport with the wilderness. Such a burst of sentiment and admiration for the environment may come as a surprise to many who think of the pioneers—as I did before I read their diaries—as dim and stolid figures perpetually struggling and dying. Perhaps it is true that many American pioneers on the trail or at their rustic homesteads *were* too busy with life's physical essentials to enjoy their surroundings aesthetically or to cultivate a deeper sense of kinship based on reflection and taste. But there was a golden moment—nearly a decade—in the first years of the Oregon Trail on its eastern portion, which rises to the continental divide, an exceptional time when bright pleasures of the imagination alternated with rather mild hardship and monotony. I speak not of the blunt strain of mountaineering, the regimented mindlessness of soldiery, or the later era of the Plains Indians' death struggles. I refer to the people in passage during the ten years prior to 1850 along the trace that crosses the plains from Independence, Missouri, to South Pass, Wyoming. It was a time when treaties still held, before railroads and buffalo slaughters, before the wave of prospectors and speculators. The Oregon Trace was still clean and verdant, its waters yet little polluted; its grass, wildflowers, and wildlife intact; its landscapes largely unsullied by the debris of civilization or the denudation that would soon mark the swath of the west-flowing river of humanity.

There were hard times and bad moments. People sickened and died. The fainthearted turned back. But the minds and hearts of the travelers were not entirely on these difficulties.

Perhaps at no other place or time in the American experience were pioneers so enveloped in an atmosphere of visual and kinesthetic discovery. In the course of the 1840s thousands of pairs of new eyes looked upon a new creation. They had come a long way from the "Howling Wilderness" of New England and its gothic antecedents in Europe. Their delight in nature and sense of awe and wonder placed them far in spirit from the Puritans, the earlier world of Daniel Boone, or the later one of Kit Carson.

They came in the great tradition of travelers: as observers of the milieu, collectors of information, amateurs of natural history, lookers at scenery, tourists hoping for a glimpse of American Indians and bison, and, perhaps most singularly, witnesses. They were poised between two geographies of plunder—the East and the Far West—between the "root, hog, or die" of the past and the furious land rush to come. They testify to a profound sense of historical moment and nature encounter, when pioneering could be truly lyrical. It was the halcyon decade of the Oregon Trail. Without the promptings of pictures or guidebooks or the voices of experience to prejudice them, their confrontation with the land was nearly free of the conventions that were later framed in the American mind as its idea of the plains of the great West.

VIRGIN LAND

Although the fur trade, the dominant motive for westering, was in decline by 1840, missionaries from the East had established settlements in Oregon. Full-scale emigration began with the thousands who crossed the prairie in the summer of 1843. By 1850 the wagon wheels had already worn deep ruts in solid rock.

The only settlements along the way were at Shawnee Mission, just inside Kansas at the beginning of the south fork of the trail, and at Council Bluffs, on the north fork. The two routes joined to form the main trail short of the Platte River in Nebraska. A third settlement was just inside what is now the Wyoming boundary at St. Joseph and Council Bluffs. The trail in Kansas followed close to the extreme ice line of the earliest "Nebraskan" glaciation of the Pleistocene ice ages, then crossed the Kansas River and traced the southern boundary of the "Kansas" glaciation. Along the Little Blue River in eastern Kansas it left the glacial landscape and struck out across a broad divide to the Platte River in Nebraska.

The rocks of the Great Plains are shales and other sedimentaries of an uplifted Cretaceous and Tertiary sea bottom. The Laramide, or Rocky

Figure 23. *The Oregon Trail*, 1956. Photograph by Paul Shepard.

Mountain Orogeny, tilted the plains up to the west. Resistant strata of this gentle synclinal trough form cuestas, or cliffs, at the eastern and western boundaries of the plains. Sheetlike series of alluvial deposits from the mass wasting of the mountains are scattered over the whole of the plains, and on them have been deposited finer, wind-transported materials. Early Pleistocene uplifting changed the stream regimen of the Platte from deposition to cutting, first in the West and then eastward, so that at present all the major streams are still down-cutting over the plains.

At the latitude of Independence, Missouri, the eastern boundary of the prairie vegetation is approximately in conjunction with the Missouri state line. A long arm of the prairie grassland community extends eastward across northern Missouri, Iowa, and the southern part of the lake states as far east as Ohio. In the Midwest the prairie is dominated by head-high grasses, which tend to be overgrown by forest where the invading trees are not burned back. Farther along, short or desert grasses and desert shrub communities are common. Deciduous forests in the form of a few characteristic trees, such as cottonwood, ash, elder, and willow, occupy the stream banks and wet places as far west as there is sufficient year-round moisture. Between the oak-hickory forest of Missouri and the high plains of central Nebraska is a transition zone, or ecotone, in which open groves of trees occupy lowlands and north slopes as savannas and woodlands contain "openings."

In spite of the extension of the hardwoods along the western streams, the visual experience of the plains is abrupt. A delicate moisture balance determines whether the vegetation is trees or grass. At the plains' western limits, the transition from the glaciated topography to the poorly consolidated fluvial materials is distinct. "At few places on this continent and, in fact, at very few places in the world," noted Wallace Atwood, "is there so great a change in topography within such a short distance as at the western margin of the Great Plains."[1] The plains' boundaries are obvious.

Before 1850, almost all of the emigrants who crossed the Great Plains were headed for the west coast. In some sixty diaries written in the 1840s there is scarcely a serious consideration to homestead anywhere along the route. Most of these travelers were not farmers and hence were not concerned with the agricultural qualifications of the prairie; their spirit of adventure and optimism was great. Furthermore, the plains were the property of the American Indians by government treaty. In short, crossing the plains was a kind of tour.

Comments on the potential utility of the landscape are not uncommon in the journals, but they have a peculiar detachment. They exist alongside thoroughly aesthetic observations. A prairie spring, for example, reminded Edwin Bryant of the "the fabled deities of heathen mythology." He proceeded then to note that the stream would "afford fine water power for mills" and to name the useful trees growing out of the "carpet" of the vegetation.[2]

As for navigability, the Platte was "nine hundred miles in length, but utterly worthless for navigation."[3] The Platte's unavailability even found its way into descriptive poetry:

> Its banks are all plat,
> and its islands are flat
> Its waters are tranquil, and turbid at that
> Protrusion of sand bars are seen all along,
> To hinder the boatman – here's nought of his song.[4]

Readers of Benjamin Silliman's *Journal of Science and Arts* pictured the river as part of the general barrenness: "Soon after leaving the State of Missouri, the country becomes comparatively barren, with little timber except along the streams, and the grass not of sufficient growth to carry fire over the undulating prairies. . . . The river is very broad and shallow, unfit for any kind of navigation, and sweeps along its due proportion of sand and mud to the main Missouri."[5]

The terrace along the Platte that resulted from spasmodic uplift of the floodplain made good roads in dry weather. Although the country around Fort Laramie was a "barren waste," G. S. Isham also found there "the best road that I ever saw." That was in 1849 in a climate where trails do not vanish quickly. Considering the gold fever of the time, surprisingly few emigrants saw signs of gold in every streambed. But John Evans Brown had no sooner left Independence than he reported of the Little Blue River, "The land has the appearance of gold formation."[6]

Richard G. Lillard said in *The Great Forest* that Europeans and their American descendants were prone to judge the fertility of soil before clearing and settling it by the species of trees it bore. He gave excellent examples of the application of these indicators in the settlement of Georgia, where soil belts are distinct in both fertility and forest types. The comments of the Great Plains travelers make it clear that many of them knew fertile soil when they saw it as well, trees or not.[7]

The absence of trees on the Kansas and Nebraska prairies fooled only those observers who had followed Long's and Pike's judgments that it all was a desert, and whose literary gullibility inhibited their perception of the ground beneath their feet. Even some gold seekers could see that the Kansas soil "is deep and of first-rate quality; and at no distant day this must become one of the richest and most productive agricultural regions of the country."[8] "The soil of these prairies is of the most inexhaustibly fertile composition, being a black loam, usually several feet in depth," said another.[9] And again, "On the 14th we entered and passed over a broad district of prairie land, equal for farming purposes to any soil in the world; but it was all solitary wild prairie, and scarcely relieved by the slightest rise or fall."[10] Flat, fertile valleys were traditionally the finest of agricultural lands, but in the East they were always "relieved" by the hills beyond.

Others found the grassy prairie monotonous in spite of its vegetative cover and fertile-looking soil, and to them the sandier areas farther west were no better or worse. At the junction of the north and south forks of the Platte in western Nebraska the country seemed to change, wrote John Townsend, the naturalist, but it was not an improvement. "Instead of the extensive and apparently interminable green plains, the monotony of the which had become so wearisome to the eye, here was great sandy waste, without a single green thing to vary and enliven the dreary scene."[11]

Cyrus Shepard had also recognized the fertility of the Kansas prairies, even where there were no trees. In western Nebraska a few pines appeared on the slopes of the "Black Hills." "Their sterile tops are thinly scattered over with stunted cedars which by their diminutive size seem to tell the traveler that they lack good soil."[12] The form of the vegetation seemed quite as indicative as its species. Shepard was happy to sit in their "agreeable shade" and was "agreeably delighted with the appearance of several luxuriant thistles, simply because they remind me of my native land and the scenes of pleasant home."[13] The presence of thistles in his native land suggests that it was no longer fertile. West of the Black Hills in the Laramie Range in the Wyoming Basin, where semiaridity changes the vegetation from short grasses to sagebrush, there was no doubt of the limited soil productivity, except right along the rivers.

The Oregon Trail left the Platte to follow up the Sweetwater near Independence Rock in south-central Wyoming. Here, "the country . . . is very barren, destitute of timber, with very little grass or other vegetation, except wild sage. Much of the water is alkali, poisonous to cattle and horses and is entirely unfit for use."[14]

Mountains were not necessarily signs of sterility, although mountains without vegetation might be unattractive. "On either side of us extends a range of mountains which imparts an aspect of dreariness and barrenness to this desolate tract of country," wrote Lorenzo Aldrich. But a few days later his opinion changed. "Today's travel has afforded more magnificent scenery than any we have yet seen. Extending far away to the left is a mountain range terminating in lofty table land, its base garnished with healthful looking shrubbery and its sides adorned by majestic cedar. The mountains from their appearance would favor the belief that they are occasionally the theatre of volcanic eruptions."[15] Apparently, when he approached near enough to see the vegetation on them, his attitude toward the mountains changed.

Consideration of soil fertility led to discussions of agriculture in general, and upon it the travelers disagreed. While most thought Kansas a most fruitful-looking place, there were still some unwilling to admit exceptions to the general defects of the Great Plains. That the country between the Missouri River and the Arkansas River could support civilized man except at scattered springs was "an idea too preposterous to be entertained for a single moment," pontificated Rufous B. Sage.[16] The scarcity of trees in Kansas was conclusive: "With the exception of distant and detached trees and groves, no timber of any kind was to be seen, and the features of the country assumed a desert character."[17] But the majority held the opinion that "this would make a great farming country if it only had timber enough to make fires and fences." The Indians' fires, said B. F. Dowell, prevented the timber from growing.[18]

J. Quinn Thornton saw Kansas as "a landscape of unsurpassed loveliness. Springs of pure cold water gushed from the banks of small streams, or bubbled up in ravines. A few small groves adorned the scene. The soil was very fertile, and covered with a heavy coat of green grass. The country was high and undulating, and had the appearance of being very healthy. But the lack of timber disallows that it will ever become a great 'producing country.'"[19] Even as far west as Fort Kearney along the Platte in south-central Nebraska, men were uneasy about the lack of wood: "Fort Kearney, that once was, is beautifully situated on a fine slope of prairie, as beautiful as ever laid out of doors. . . . Country beautiful rolling prairie, fine for agriculture, but no timber to support it."[20]

Riley Root described the whole of eastern Nebraska, from St. Joseph to the Platte, as a country of "soil and fertility." The wild, uncultivated "natural meadow" from which the timber had been burned and replaced by grass was "an inferior but oftentimes resplendent robe. . . . On arriving at the Platte River, a beautifully flat country presents itself, where nature, it would seem, had but an easy task to burden the ground with excessive vegetation, but behold a country of extensive bottom lands, of feeble soil much of the way, and still more feeble at the distance, among the bluffs and rolling country."[21]

From central Nebraska west, few could see agricultural possibilities in the land; but they were not altogether blind to its grazing potential. The Reverend H. H. Spaulding wrote in 1836, "On leaving Laramie the whole face of the country is changed in appearance – East of that meridian the principal objects that strike the eye of the traveler are the absence of timber, the immense expanse of prairie covered with a rich verdure of grass, wonderfully adapted for pasturage." He noted the great herds of buffalo in support of his observation.[22]

Yet, others said of exactly the same landscape, "The eye can rest on nothing all round but a dreary waste, an uncultivated country." Just beyond the juncture of the Platte forks, travelers touched the south border of the Nebraska sand hills, dunes covered by sparse vegetation and subject to blowing. Near this point the trail crossed the south fork and continued northwest along the north fork. Here was "a high, open, and rolling, or rather, hilly prairie, presenting a very desolate and forbidding aspect. Much of the way was sandy and in some places we saw immense numbers of lizards. . . . Many persons in camp were quite unwell, and so many of them had been so during the previous ten days, that it was suspected we had been traveling over an unhealthy region."[23]

It should be noted that, between the time of Rev. Spaulding's trip in 1836 and the forty-niners, a tremendous number of livestock came along the trail, not only draft animals—horses, oxen, and mules—but herds of milk cows as well. By 1845 the forage along the main trail was gone, and the journalists reported "taking the stock three miles to find grass." The greenery of May and June was gone by midsummer, although the buffalo and antelope were heavily hunted within a ten-mile corridor along the trail, and the "normal" grazing by those animals must have been reduced.

Fertile soil was a beautiful thing, but alone it was not enough. Sixty miles downstream from the junction of the Platte forks where the river bottom was still broad enough to farm, Mormon Howard Egan found "the first place I have seen since we left winter quarters where I should like to live. . . . The land is good and plenty of timber and the warbling of the birds makes it very pleasant."[24] Near the mouth of the Sweetwater the sublime and the fruitful mingled. The stream valley marked a "sudden change of scenery" from the plain above, which was "odious and hateful" because of its sterility, having the unpleasant "appearance of a brown heath." In the valley below there were rich meadows and a serpentine stream with flowers, diversity, and a rich verdure, from which "granite masses rise abruptly in sterile grandeur" to the naked rocks, and "forbidding looking mountains on the south" were visible across the sandy plain.[25]

Kansas was almost perfect: "Nothing was wanting to render the scene enchanting, but a supply of water." But this enchantment must not prevent Americans from exploiting the land. The soil is "very deep, covered at this season of the year with a beautiful coat of deep green, varigated with delicious flowers. Whatever emotions of the beautiful, the grand, the sublime, different persons may have on first viewing and traveling over those plains so properly denominated the 'Eden of the West,' one impression must press itself on every reflecting mind, viz: their vast agricultural resources; let them be but fully developed, and North America is second to no other country on the earth."[26]

The suggestion of Kansas as an Eden evoked the Christian conviction that God provided the world and all its fruits for man's use. "It is impossible to travel through this country with the utilitarian eye and appreciation natural to all Americans, without a sensation of regret, that an agricultural resource of such immense capacity as is here supplied by a bountiful Providence, is so utterly neglected and waste."[27]

The journalists seem to have viewed these "uncultivated" tracts with remorse, if not guilt. Immorality seemed to sprout with the native plants in the unplowed field and uncut wood. Rev. Spaulding wrote:

> On rising the bluff at the Fort [at Shawnee Mission], my eye rested for the first time on the "Great West." To one reared in a timbered country, and accustomed to wait a generation for timber, stumps, and the roots to pass away, the scene, the view was grand and impressive beyond the power of words—I felt as never before the force of those words of God at the close of His work: "and behold, it was very good!" A vast expanse of green meadow reaching beyond the distant blue, cleared and seeded down by providence to the hand of the husbandman; but farmer, nor tree, nor fence, nor town were there. Great silence resting on the bosom of the sublime, both personified. The ocean has its beauty and heavens their charms, but the great prairie reflects the lovely smiles of our Father in Heaven. Awe-struck at the living panorama . . . I forgot to present our passport from the War Department to the officers of the garrison. . . . Aware of our mission, the officers threw open the gates, and we stepped from the civilized world into this then "great and terrible wilderness," where thick moral darkness had reigned for ages unknown.[28]

Man established contact with God by working in the fields, and therefore the only real value of the fields lay in their exploitation, not for money, but for the benefit of the soul. Near Council Bluffs Spaulding's colleague, Rev. Samuel Parker, took a last look at the corn and stock that "diversify the scene" and plunged into the kingdom of moral darkness. Approaching the Platte he observed, "No country could be more inviting to the farmer, with only one exception, the want of woodland. . . . The earth was created for the habitation of man, and for a theatre, on which God will manifest his perfections." This amazing extent of fertile land would not continue to be an Indian "wandering ground," he asserted, with little cultivation and wasted forage. "Shall solitude reign here till the end of time? No: here shall be heard the din of business and the church-going bell."[29] This was his favorite theme, and he repeated it often: "The soil of this part of the country is rich, and the grass for our horses excellent; but there are none here to till the ground, nor to gather in the ten thousand tons of hay, which might be made from the spontaneous growth. This part of the country does not yet answer the end for which it was created. The time will come when a dense population will cover this country, who will render the sacrifice of prayer and praise to our God."[30]

And what was the good Christian going to leave the Indian? Nothing, it seemed. A third missionary, Cyrus Shepard, going west with Wyeth in 1834, censured the party's wanton killing of buffalo. It pained his heart because these animals had been provided by our heavenly Father for "*support* to the poor Indians."[31]

SCIENCE AND SYMBOLS: EXPLAINING THE CURIOSITY

From the righteous utilitarianism that rendered the prairie immoral for its lack of cultivation it is only a step to the landscape of symbols, if not of ordained utility then of benignity, omniscience, or the power of God. "This heathen, inhospitable land" contained only animals that had no status in heaven; American Indians, who were pagans and therefore damned; and out-of-work trappers who acted as guides and hunters for most of the wagon trains until about 1847.[32] The parties were always torn between resting on the Sabbath and pushing on. Usually they pushed on, to the detriment of livestock and the general level of their housekeeping. Many keepers of journals lamented the fact but went along.

The trappers were wild-looking men whose behavior was mostly incomprehensible to the emigrants, but they were beautifully adjusted to the requirements of the environment and a product of natural selection. Tom Fitzpatrick was one of the most famous. He led the party of 1841 of which Joseph Williams of Cincinnati was a member. But it was not Fitzpatrick whom Williams meant when he wrote: "O my soul – praise him who takes care of us in the desert!" He considered Fitzpatrick "a wicked and worldly man, . . . much opposed to missionaries going among Indian. On Sabbath we have nothing but swearing, fishing and c–. . . . At night I tried to preach to the deists and swearers. Some of them seemed angry."[33]

As elsewhere, certain geomorphic features acquired the name of devil's this or that, suggesting a loose association of sin and the landscape. It

Figure 24. *Devil's Gate,* 1956. Photograph by Paul Shepard.

would have been illogical for the beautiful things in the landscape to be the spadework of the devil, however, and their names were generally associated with the divinity. Joseph Williams's comment that there were deists as well as atheists in his party is illuminating.

To the orthodox, the landscape was sometimes allegorical. Mrs. Thornton told her husband that as the Sweetwater River flowed to refresh the dry parched valley, "so may his grace flow in on my thirsty spirit, which longs for my savior as does the panting hart for the cooling stream."[34] An almost ineffable relationship between the landscape, the observer, and God was only slightly less vague but an equally real sign of beneficence. Journeying through a part of the prairie full of rich and beautiful "drapery," it seemed to Cyrus Shepard that "[t]here's not a plant or flower below, but makes God's glory known!"[35] But even the flowers paled next to the glory of the mountains. Alexander Love climbed to the top of a bluff after fording the Platte in Wyoming and decided that "[h]ere might with propriety be said is one of the Mighty Structures of the Hand of God."[36] All things showed their own part in the great design.

The mode of joining science and religion was popular: "The imagination of the traveler can detect in the very deformities of nature many elements of beauty; and in the wild disorder of hill and forest, and the sandy plain the established order of nature's great Architect; the Lord Jehovah himself."[37]

Aesthetically, the Protestant missionaries were still medieval in outlook, with their landscapes of symbols and Puritanical gloom. In contrast, Father Jean De Smet's letters sparkle with pleasure in the landscape and an appreciation of eighteenth-century aesthetic theory. He was enthralled, for example, by the Rocky Mountains:

> It is because on yon proud height,
> The standard floats of life and light;
> It is, that there the omnipotent
> Hath pitched his everlasting tent.[38]

God was much closer to the landscape – if not in it – than most western travelers believed. He was right there on the mountaintops.

Insofar as science helped to prove scriptural revelation, one might expect to discover new revelation in a new landscape. De Smet found the "petrified hills" near Independence Rock "incontestable proofs of the deluge."[39] If he did not mean the monoliths themselves, he may have referred to the conglomerates or indurated alluvial debris from the mountains. Edwin Bryant camped in what he called an extinct volcanic crater along the upper Platte and dreamed of violence and convulsion "breaking the granite crust of the globe and afrightening the huge monster animals which then existed. . . . Such are the beneficent changes ordered by that Power."[40]

Mr. and Mrs. J. Quinn Thornton, an elderly couple going to Oregon for their health in 1848, were full of the spirit of science as it was interpreted and extended by amateurs. Along the Oregon Trail, they scurried about enjoying the scenery and naturalizing on whatever they could find. "Mrs. Thornton and myself were said to be 'always either writing, or prowling around after weeds, and grass, and stones and such truck' or going off on an 'exploring expedition,'" Mr. Thornton noted proudly.[41] He occasionally quoted Torrey on the plants and expressed the opinion that the barrenness of the country was caused by dryness of climate, not geology.

Their inability to estimate distances and sizes across the broad panorama was a source of considerable surprise and interest to many. By the time the emigrants approached Fort Laramie the texture (or pattern of erosion) of the landscape and the increasing predominance of mechanical over chemical weathering had upset the usual clues to spatial distance and scale. With increased altitude and drier air, the atmosphere was clearer and one could see much farther. Everybody was fooled; some rode hours to examine a rock that seemed only minutes away. The exhilaration of the visual experience of great spaces is apparent in the journals written along the north fork of the Platte where it cuts bluffs from the shale and sandstone bedrock and its tributaries isolate huge remnants that looked like houses in the distance. The deceptive distance to Chimney Rock reminded Mr. Thornton of optical phenomena such as a mirage or the specter of the "Brocken." He quoted Dr. Vince from an 1834 penny magazine: "Whenever the ray of light strikes a medium less refracting than that in which it was previously moving, it is turned back into the original medium."[42] It did not explain the situation, but somehow it seemed appropriate.

Geology had put ready answers on many lips for a landscape where processes were no longer obscured by vegetation. Nearly everyone knew something about minerals and was quick to name and save specimens, and later to abandon them when wagonloads had to be lightened. Fewer, perhaps, knew the rocks, but most could pick out bluffs "striped with strata of lime and sandstone." Igneous rocks and the obvious signs of volcanism in Wyoming indicated that "[t]he whole country seems to have been thrown into a mass of confusion by volcanic eruptions," and volcanism was used to explain almost any topographic feature otherwise enigmatic.[43] Just past Laramie the La Bonte, a Platte tributary, was surrounded by granite "upheaved by subterranean convulsions of nature," and there was a lovely grassy bottom with "rock thrown up in careless heaps."[44] This was an echo of Cuvier's view of the world.

There was considerable appreciation of the dynamic quality of the topography. Shepard noted some "profound ravines, one of which must have been at least sixty feet deep worn out by the action of water for ages past in its descent from the surrounding hills to the river below." The weathering of rock was more or less obvious and could be examined in detail. Shepard observed: "The hills in the distance presented the remarkable appearance of having had their tops reduced by art to a common horizontal line; each system of hills . . . has its own peculiar line which, although broken by valleys coming down to the plain, lay stretched in fragments, showing that no hills of that chain rose above it."[45] This recognition of accordant summits of an eroded surface is the most scientific observation in Shepard's journal. It is an example of the objectivity that a totally new environment lends to ordinary vision.

Although the land along the Platte was rich and green, Rufous Sage noted that "[b]ack from the valley ranges broken sand-hills mark the transition to the high arid prairies in the rear, where vegetation becomes more dwarfed and stinted in its growth, and intermingled with frequent cacti." The distinction between the plant communities was thus recognized and associated with the topography. The soil, he continued, is a "thin vegetable mould upon a substratum of indurated sand gravel."[46] Most observers saw the plant life as a tapestry of blooms rather than as communities, enumerating the species that "ornament the velvety carpet of flowers."[47]

As for the minute plant life – the molds, fungi, and bacteria – some noted that food did not spoil as quickly in the high plains as it did at home. Father De Smet quoted mountain man Jim Bridger's reply when asked if his wounds from arrows soon began to suppurate, to the effect that "among the mountains nothing corrupts."[48] One can readily imagine De Smet's pleasure in the statement's double entendre.

Popular science graded indistiguishably into pseudoscience. Although considerable strides had been made in science in the early nineteenth century, it was still true, as Sir Archibald Geikie would later note, that "the growth of a belief in the natural origin of all the features of the earth [had] grown faster than the capacity of science to guide it. Nowhere may the lasting influence of scenery on the imagination be more strikingly recognized than in the vague tentative efforts of the popular mind to apply what it supposes to be the scientific method."[49]

Preconceived ideas about what science was and did sometimes put limits on what was seen. There was nothing in eastern Nebraska to interest the geologist, reported Rev. Samuel Parker. "The meadows spread out almost without bounds," and he saw hardly any stones all day. Later in the journey, finally finding something geologically noteworthy, he observed that the Wind River Mountains "are found by measurement to be eighteen thousand feet above the level of the sea" (he was about four thousand feet off).[50]

By the mid-1840s cholera was not uncommon along the route, and various other ailments attacked the emigrants as well, usually with similar symptoms of intestinal disorder, nausea, fever, and chills. Swampy ground had an "unhealthy" look, and there were evidently some uncertainties about what the altitude might do. At least one man had fever, pains, and shortness of breath "as if produced by the want of proper atmosphere pressure."[51]

With the exception of the prairie dog towns, few of the overland travelers bothered to mention the small mammals they encountered. Although the species of ground squirrel changed as often as the vegetation type between Independence and the Rockies, apparently only naturalists were aware of it. One ground squirrel in Wyoming might be a "prairie dog or it may be a connection link between the prairie dog and the ground squirrel," A. Delano noted—a rather unusual statement considering popular understanding of evolutionary theory in 1849.[52]

There was something deeply mysterious about the plains: Where were the trees? The absence of trees did not cause as much speculation among the pioneers as one might suppose. Some were reminded of the steppes of Asia and the pampas of Argentina. Europeans and New Englanders tended to conclude that the trees had been cleared. Rufous Sage and probably many of his contemporaries thought that the forest had been destroyed by fire and sufficient time had not yet elapsed for its return.

In the western half of Nebraska the tall grasses disappeared as well. Head-high in eastern Kansas, they were only a few inches tall here. This aroused only slight interest. It was explained as evidence of drought; or perhaps the growing season in the higher country was later.[53] No one really seemed to care.

More acceptable curiosities were certain residual phenomena from normal dry or semiarid mass wasting such as the spindles of rock left when an isolated block was cut away by streams; even stranger were the resistant granite ridges that the river had inextricably breached and now drained cross-axially. Chimney Rock, which rises from a conelike base of rock and debris, was one of those spindles. The new geology left little doubt in anyone's mind how it had been formed. It and nearby Castle Rock had been "worn, in the lapse of ages, to their present fantastic forms. Every year, probably, wears them more and it is not improbable, that at some former period, even Courthouse and Chimney Rocks were portions of hills which have decayed."[54]

Those who thought about it usually came to the same conclusion. "I am very sure," said G. S. Isham, that "it cannot stand many years before large flakes will slide to the ground, if it all does not come down in a general crash."[55] Indeed, once they had grasped the process, the amateurs were way ahead of science, and the climate seemed to be melting Chimney Rock before their very eyes. It was "a pirimidiale pile of marly earth of 200 feet in height which tradition says was 500 feet high when first discovered by the voyager across the plains. It is fast wearing away under the action of the weather, and will soon be a mound of earth," predicted Simon Doyle.[56] Everyone agreed that it was "an extraordinary natural curiosity," and scores of people from every party rode the six miles across the Platte bottoms to examine it.[57]

Also of interest as a "curious natural production" were four places along the north fork of the Platte where the river is cross-axial to a ridge of granite hills. The Devil's Gate on the Sweetwater was one of them. Such places were particularly noticeable because they forced the wagon train to detour from the flat bottoms over the ridge, often at some distance from the stream and with some hardship. The Devil's Gate, however, was worth the trouble, probably because it was more spectacular than the others. The road approached within easy view of it. "A very curious object, truly," said Bennett C. Clark; others were inclined to agree.[58] Only one of the other sites, near the Red Buttes along the Platte in central Wyoming, is mentioned often in the journals. From the campground there, one was "in sight of this strange looking place, which has the appearance of the river having forced its way through the mountains and leaving there buttes standing high in the air, a monument of what existed in the past."[59]

Some were satisfied merely to describe the Devil's Gate. C. Truesdael, for example, noted: "The Devil's Gate, 10 miles above Independence Rock is quite a curiosity; it is where the river passes through and cuts off a point from the main body of Granite mountains. The mountain is about 300 feet high where the river passes through, the passage is 30 yards in width, and perpendicular on either side."[60] The idea that it was a symbol of God's puissance did not seem to fit its name – and yet, something mighty had happened here. "It looked like the passage way of some higher power anyway it is one of those wonders of nature that man likes to admire," wrote David Staples.[61]

Some gave serious consideration to the origin of the Devil's Gate. The eastern part of Wyoming is intermittently covered with volcanic pumice and lava, and almost anything could be explained by the convulsive upheavals that were supposed to have produced all those igneous and crystalline rocks. And most knew who was behind *that* sort of activity. The gate's name was considered appropriate because "his Satanic majesty had been cutting some queer antics in this wild region."[62]

Others thought the gate might have developed by degrees: "Through this romantic pass the river brawls and frets over broken masses of rock that obstructs its passage, affording one of the most lovely, cool and refreshing retreats from the dry and scorching sunshine in the valley."[63] The Devil's Gate might have developed, A. J. McCall continued, along a weak vein of sedimentary rock – with the aid of an earthquake. "This river appears to have run around the mountain point formerly," wrote Samuel Dundass, "and found its way here through a large crevice, which has gradually crumbled down and washed away until the cut is clear to the top of the mountain."[64] Dundass approached the rationale behind one of the four processes by which streams become cross-axial, namely headward erosion along a structural weakness, but his guess was not correct here. The Platte crosses the granite mountains of the Black Hills because it was superposed across those mountains as it removed its own bed and the ancient granite ridges were uncovered. That Dundass should have come so close with his carefully reasoned explanation of the Devil's Gate is interesting in light of his earlier assertion that "the wild disorder of hill and forest" is really the established order of "the Lord Jehovah himself."

The science of these amateurs was clearly not mechanistic or dualistic. That nature is both orderly and within God's plan – and therefore good – was the primary assumption. To see this belief in full perspective it might be contrasted to the orthodox Christian viewpoint that nature is evil

Figure 25. *Along the Platte,* 1956. Photograph by Paul Shepard.

or at best features isolated symbols of divinity; or, at the other extreme, to the modern scientific specialist's detachment and refined technique, which disallows a priori assumptions. It was distinctly one world and one universe to Mr. Dundass, though he misinterpreted the processes he saw. He occupied the crest of a wave of intuitive perception. Probably no generation before or after his was so personally involved with the remote place where a river cut through a mountain.

THE LAND OF DREAMS

The Sublime and Picturesque

Thomas J. Farnham, who crossed the prairie in 1839, was captivated by it. "A sense of vastness—beautiful vastness was the single and sole conception of the mind!"[65] The idea of an infinitely great God could fill the soul to overflowing. Seventeenth-century astronomy had added a new dimension to the mind as well as to the sky, and infinite space and infinite God were so nearly similar that "sublime" would describe either. The earth itself forms an arc, if one has but space and height enough to see it. The height of the eyes on the plains does not place human sight high enough to see the sweep of the great circle, especially near a forest edge. The immensity of the sky in the prairie is the surprising result of the addition of a very small ring of sky around the horizon where there would otherwise be hills; this small addition is psychically enlarged to create an almost endless vista.[66]

To the pioneers camped at night, the field of stars seemed to be infinitely greater and to acquire an "imposing sublimity," which contributed to the generally awesome nature of the sky.[67] "After ascending a long . . . hill we came in sight of the mighty prairie . . . so extensive as to make it seem as though the earth and sky were moulded together."[68] Almost everyone, however untutored in the finer points of aesthetic history, could say, "I gazed around with wonder at the distant plains."[69]

"As we approached what is called the Blue Prairie," Edwin Bryant reported,

> the road became much drier and less difficult. The vast prairie it-self opened before us in all its grandeur and beauty. I had never before beheld extensive scenery of this kind. The many descriptions of the prairies of the west had forestalled in some measure the first impressions produced by the magnificent landscape that lay spread out before me as far as the eye could reach, bounded alone by the blue wall of the sky. The view of the illimitable succession of green undulations and flowery slopes of every gentle and graceful configuration, stretching away and away, until they fade from the sight in the dim distance, creates a wild and scarcely controllable ecstasy of admiration.[70]

Edmund Burke, whose aesthetic theory of 1757 distinguished the sublime from the beautiful, never saw the Great Plains. Bryant's description of the prairie quoted above does not quite fit into any of the categories of aesthetic theories because the concept of vastness had always been associated with mountaintop or ocean. Green slopes and flowery meadows had to do with the friendly nature of the beautiful countryside. Yet here, rather than hills "crowned with forests of primeval vastness and magnificence," were little groves like "clusters of islets that dot a waveless sea" that were undoubtedly beautiful.[71] Here too one might exclaim in rapture, "Oh! I felt then, 'There is pleasure in the pathless woods / There was society where none intrudes!'"[72] In eastern Kansas the woods were pathless enough if one overlooked animal trails, but they were eminently passable. The combination of the primeval forest and vast space with the meadow rather than the rocky foreground confounded aesthetic theory. But those who saw it were deeply impressed by it. Most overland travelers commented in their diaries on the vastness and beauty of the prairie.

Progressing west up the Platte River, the traveler ascended in elevation to the high plains, which were uplifted along with the Rocky Mountains. The rivers there have been cutting faster and longer than those in the eastern plains, and have carved deeper gorges. As the Black Hills of the Laramie Range came into view near the Wyoming boundary, and, beyond, the Wind River Range of the Rockies, the landscape became more variegated, the prairie more lawnlike, the flowers more ephemeral and striking, the valleys deeper and more abrupt, the dry places sandier – more alkaline and desertlike – and the distant peaks higher by emphasis with the plains.

On the prairie there were dangers and thrilling events that stimulated that awareness of power, fear, and pleasurable honor that defines the sublime. The prairie storms were more intense than any the easterners had experienced. The rains of May and June were cold and the winds harsh. There was little comfort or cover; the greenhorns always got wet and had no place to change into dry clothes, or no dry clothes to change into. "None but those who have fallen in with one of these storms can have an idea what they are," wrote Rev. Spaulding. "The earth shook with continued peals; the black night trembled and blazed with the forked lightening; the cattle bellowed; the picket lines snapped, and the horses snorted and plunged away; the wagons upset, the tent was twisted into a dish cloth; the pouring torrents of rain were driven against man and beast as if by steam engines."[73]

Rev. Samuel Parker likewise experienced a very bad storm that "was alarming, and yet grand and truly sublime."[74] Bryant said, "The scene during the violence of the storm was inexpressively grand. . . . A more sublime and awful meteoric display I never witnessed or could conceive."[75] To Thomas Farnham the troubled clouds "appeared rent in fragments by an explosion of electricity, that all my previous conceptions of grandeur and sublimity could never have allowed me to believe might exist."[76] The

Thorntons were enchanted: "I exulted in the view of nature in her most terrible majesty"; and "The scene was so sublime, and I could not but rejoice that I was here to witness it."[77] It reminded Mr. Thornton of the Deity. Others thought of God and sublimity too. Farnham was fortunate enough to observe a herd of buffalo in the midst of a prairie storm. It was, he said, "a funeral scene of nature a reeling world tottering under the great arm of its Maker."[78] A tornado, which plainsmen today watch in fear for their buildings and belongings, was "sublime" to Father De Smet.[79]

Prairie fires also presented "a grand and most pleasing effect."[80] At night and as "noonday splendor . . . a sublime spectacle . . . terrible in its beauty. How awful and how grand."[81]

The Black Hills, named for the dark pines growing on them, loomed ominously above westward travelers. "We were compelled to go on all day, with naked Black Hills peering down upon us, like goblins, laughing at our way-worn wretchedness," wrote A. Delano, who quoted Macbeth: "Double double, toil and trouble."[82] Why did he think of goblins? The goblin is originally a woodland creature, and it seems probable that it was not the nakedness of the hills that really impressed the writer but the darkness of the scattered trees.

The "sublime prairie wilderness" changed form as one approached the hills. It became a "scene of desolation scarcely equaled on the continent . . . when viewed in the dearth of mid-summer from the bases of the hills. Above you rise in sublime confusion, mass upon mass, of shattered cliffs through which are struggling the dark foliage of the stinted shrub-cedars; while below you spreads far and wide the burnt and arid desert, whose solemn silence is seldom broken."[83] The sublime and the beautiful could be confused on the eastern part of the plains. The vastness was beautiful because of its verdant appearance, but sublime, perhaps, because it was a genuine wilderness.

To those with a proper sense of terror, the Black Hills were not only solemn and forbidding but also threatening. "The general aspect here, was dreary," noted John Townsend; "the soil was intersected by deep and craggy fissures; rock jutted over rock, and precipice frowned over precipice in frightful, and apparently endless succession."[84] But real horror came, as it did for Englishmen in the Alps, with the high mountains: "They struck us with terror their lofty peaks seemed a resting place for the clouds."[85]

Father De Smet, a disciple of mountain scenery, "was ecstatic" at the sight of the Rocky Mountains:

> I had before seen landscapes of awful grandeur, but this one certainly surpassed all others in horror. My courage failed at the first sight; it was impossible to remain on horseback. My mule, Lizette, was sufficiently docile and kind to allow me to grasp her tail, to which I held on firmly, crying at one moment aloud, and at other times making use of the whip to excite her courage, until the good beast conducted me safely to the very top of the mountain – There I breathed freely for a while, and contemplated the magnificent prospect that presented itself to my sight.[86]

To some extent the sublime was separated from other types of scenery as the emigrants reached landscapes in which it was readily distinguishable. Some places could then be beautiful in the word's more restricted sense, and other scenes merely picturesque. The general merging of aesthetic categories persisted, however. J. Q. Thornton said of the Devil's Gate, "Of the varied scenery for which the surrounding country is so much celebrated, I regard this particular locality as presenting views so exceedingly picturesque that it is felt at once to be more grand, and at the same time more beautiful, than any other collection of objects within the whole compass of vision."[87] Bryant agreed: "The view . . . is strikingly picturesque, although the extensive landscape presents a wild, desolate, and inhospitable aspect."[88]

The scene contained the roughness and irregularity that made it a suitable subject for a picture. De Smet may have been thinking that when he sat down and took out his sketchpad. He preferred the lower side of the gate, which is rockier, the debris having been moved down by the current. It should have been called "Heaven's Avenue," he said. "If it resembles hell on account of the frightful disorder which frowns around it, it is still a mere passage, and it should rather be compared to the way of heaven on account of the scene to which it leads." Through the "chaos of obstacles" surrounding the gate, "the roaring waves force a passage: with fury, majesty, and finally gentleness. Overhead are masses of shadow, the gloom of pine and cedar, and lofty galleries.[89] The generalization that most perfectly encompasses these aesthetic ideas is "romantic." Many rode out from camp in the evening to see the Devil's Gate because of its "romantic appearance" with the rocky ridges on both sides and the mountains in the distance.[90]

Romantic, too, was the braided channel of the Platte where the trail first touched it near Grand Island: "[T]he River is covered with small islands presenting a most romantic and picturesque appearance," wrote Jacob Snider. "The hills here approach nearer the river than at any point that we have yet reached."[91]

Completing the triad of picturesque and romantic objects was Independence Rock. "There is many high hills or ridges and masses of granite rock in this neighborhood all destitute of vegetation and present a very wild and desolate as well as romantic appearance," wrote Howard Egan.[92]

Even the bluffs along the Platte, without cross-axial drainage, stimulated the imagination: "We soon came to the bluffs, which generally are several miles from the river but in this place rise abruptly from its banks. We now had to pass over these rough places from the space of several miles presenting the most beautiful, wild and romantic scenery in nature."[93]

Through literature, the travelers had learned to associate "gloom" and "melancholy" with certain scenery. In the sand hills along the Platte, for example, Simon Doyle reported: "A rather gloomy but romantic scene was presented to view. Range after range of these peaks appeared piled one upon the top of the other as far as the eye could see. Between many of these peaks are beautiful dry valleys from 2 to 25 yds wide which abound with a luxuriant growth of the most nutritious grass and shrubs and near the head is always found a cluster of ash timber with some fir, cottonwood, and cedar."[94]

Why was it gloomy? "Beautiful as the country is, the silence and desolation reigning over it excite irrepressible emotions of sadness and melancholy."[95] The bluffs were eroded into many fanciful shapes, and while none were said to resemble the bust of Pallas, the spell was clearly on Mr. McCall when he drifted off among the sand hills to shoot a raven but desisted as an angel stopped him, whispering, "Never More!"[96]

The stream through the Devil's Gate was romantic in literary terms too. It went "leaping" and "shouting" with fury through its passage among the "fancifully appearing" and grotesque fragments and the craggy, broken masses overhanging the "dark recesses."[97]

Along the Platte the travelers climbed the hills to see the view: up the bluffs along the river, up Courthouse Rock, to the top of the Devil's Gate, and onto Independence Rock. The Thorntons, in spite of their age, seem to have been unusually enthusiastic climbers. Mrs. Thornton, "who was . . . still suffering from ill health, with the aid of some of her female companions, ascended one of the very high bluffs from the top of which she had a fine view of the country."[98]

The cosmic view that spread out below the hilltop was perceived as a great picture. Even the sublime prairie storm with its "troubled clouds which appeared rent in fragments by an explosion of electricity, that all my previous conceptions of grandeur and sublimity could never have allowed me to believe exist" was a scene fit for a Raphael, said Thomas Farnham. It would enable him to sketch "the bursting foundations of the world" as the "ark of scripture loosed its cable on the bellows of the flood."[99] In spite of four days of "diarea," David Staples looked over the Kansas River and found it a worthy subject. "Our camp tonight is on a beautiful rise with a creek on our right and the Kansas on the left, a grand scene for a painter."[100] From a swell, Edwin Bryant noted that "the configuration of the vast diameter of the plain which can be observed from this, presents all the graceful and gentle curves, and the delicate shading and coloring that would charm the enthusiastic landscape artist in his dreaming sketches."[101] There was "a beautiful prospect on the opposite side of the [Platte] river – the dark Black Hills, with bright spots of sunshine on them, and the rest partially enshrouded in mist and clouds, while around us it was murky and drizzling."[102]

"From the top of the hill we had the pleasantest view of the surrounding country," Mr. Egan noted. "The scenery was truly romantic. The country is very broken, with a forest of pine covering the surface. From this hill we have a fair view of Laravamia [Laramie] Peak. There appears to be snow on top of it."[103]

Rev. Spaulding was equally impressed by the vista. "When we arrived at the top of the Hill a most magnificent prospect – on our left and seemingly very near us was Laramie Peak the summit of which ascended to the clouds and was covered with snow. The eye from this point might rest in any direction on a variegated landscape from 50 to 100 miles in extent."[104]

Sometimes the writer's education colored the description of a landscape. Few displayed Father De Smet's erudition, but the generalized
landscapes of the Yankee emigrants are full of broad pictorial interest
and variety. "From a high stand-point two miles to the South of this
[Independence] Rock, the beholder is presented with a wild and grand
scenery," noted Rev. Parker. In the distance were the Red Buttes, and at
his feet sat Independence Rock, looking as though it were traveling west
and "contemplating one of two passages before him – either the Devil's
Gate, six miles above and only 40 feet wide . . . through which his own
Sweetwater forces its way with difficulty to enliven the little patches
of grass and shrubbery and beautiful flowers at his feet[,] or the 'Hot
Spring Gate' some 25 miles to the southwest, 70 yards wide, with walls
of white sand rock rising 350 feet high through which the Platte escapes
the mountains."[105]

In sum, the prairies had a vastness new and almost overwhelming to
these travelers, who perceived beauty, the sublime, and an ominous melancholy in the prairie's uncertain desolation – that pleasurable melancholy
of eighteenth-century poetry. As examined below, their reactions to this
vast and open space form a revealing profile of American attitudes at the
time the Oregon emigrants moved into unfamiliar landscapes.

The Prairie Sea

The only visual comparison to the space of the Great Plains seems to have
been the sea. Their reverence for the ocean is not directly associated with
the overland travelers' sailing experience. It is instead fraught with the
excitement of men living a simile – the allegory of life as a voyage. They
reacted to the prairie, that is, with the same emotions inspired by the sea.
It had been a century and a half since aesthetic theorists in England had
first listed the sea as one of the sources of the sublime, and they were only
labeling something that people had probably felt since the first savages
ventured out onto it.

Land, to Rev. Samuel Parker from Ithaca, New York, meant a place
characterized by familiar vegetation. To his utilitarian mind, the sea and
the prairie were similar in having the same deficiencies. "When out of
sight of land, that is, when nothing but green grass could be seen, we eat
our bacon without cooking."[106]

Along the Santa Fe Trail in central Kansas the country became less un-dulating, but it still had sealike qualities. "The heaving ridge which had made our trail thus far, appears to pass over an immense sea, the billows of which had been changed to waving meadows . . . gave place to wide and gentle swells," wrote Mr. Farnham.[107] When a sudden and heavy rainstorm covered the ground with a few inches of water, the plains were literally "converted into a sea."

Nor was lack of geological relief necessary for the image. Across from St. Joseph, "after the first six miles the prairie was very rolling like the waves of the sea"; but farther west there was an "immense ocean of moun-tains and prairies."[108] "In fact," noted Father De Smet, "nearly the whole of this territory is of an undulating form, and the undulations resemble the billows of the sea when agitated by the storm."[109] The variety of the prairie's surface corresponded to the various moods of the ocean. Cyrus Shepard gave it the proper adjective. "We are now encamped on the open prairie which stretches before us like the vast ocean and is truly a sublime object."[110]

On the prairie, said another traveler, the wagons looked like a fleet of vessels under full sail.[111] The cultural introspection that accompanied the awakening to manifest destiny made the wagons into ships – the traditional vessels that carry history in the making. "White-topped craft . . . over the green billows," cried a New Yorker on the plains. "One who has never ex-perienced it can hardly appreciate the bounded pleasure under the broad sky, upon the free earth. Our crowd acted under the same impulses. We sing of 'The sea, the sea, the open sea, / The broad, the boundless, and the free.'"[112]

Much of the soil between Independence and the Platte derives from loess, which conforms to the underlying landform. Where it is quite deep, its appearance is determined by the laws that govern homogeneous, wind-blown materials, and it tends to resemble wavelike dunes. The Nebraska Sand Hills are also of eolian origin, although the pioneers saw them only along the Platte, where they are dissected by the river and its tributaries. "The banks of the Platte are high sand-hills, scantily covered with grass, and present many fanciful shaped cones and broken ridges, which I can compare with nothing else in form than high drifted snow heaps," noted Mr. Delano.[113] Waves were apparent, too, in the sand hills.

Was this great prairie ocean a lifeless sea? A forty-niner tells us that it was not: "Independence rock at a distance looks like a huge whale."[114] The whale was a reassuring sign of life in the briny deep of the underlying shale, which indeed is of marine origin. The prairie sea was a joyous and yet sublime—fearful, that is—experience for the pioneers in their prairie schooners. There were billows where the terminal moraines of the second glaciation marked the edge of the prairie, where the ripples of eolian deposits made swells and troughs and bacon went uncooked for want of trees, where the flatness of the plains was like the sea of the ancient mariner or like the flood after a rain, and where mountains, if not whales, were island landmarks on the trackless ocean.

Solitude

When Joel Palmer left Independence in 1840, he and two companions galloped through a large company just outside town and in three days caught up with the Adams-Meek party near the Kansas River. A strange scene was in progress. The group had halted to discuss their dogs, a vote had been taken, and a committee was moving among the wagons shooting the dogs whose owners would not carry out the general order of execution. As a wave of reaction swept among the emigrants, the mass slaughter ended as quickly as it began, presumably when the committee encountered people who defended their animals with the threat of arms. This curious behavior, which involved delaying a train of more than 150 wagons for a lengthy midday parley, was ostensibly to reduce the noise of the emigrant party in order to slip past hostile Indians![115]

What was behind this neurotic episode that led the emigrants to the brink of shooting their own dogs? Was the prairie really otherwise silent? Some thought so.

> Here we left the last traces of civilization, and seemed, for a time, to be beyond even the borders of animated existence. Not even the song of a bird broke upon the surrounding stillness; and, save the single track of the emigrants winding away over the hills, not a foot print broke the rich, unvaried verdure of the broad, forest-begirt prairies; and in the little islet groves that dotted the plain—the wooded strips that wound along the course of the rivulet—and the blue wall that surrounded, not a trunk was scarred, not a

twig broken—It was a vast, beautiful, and perfect picture, which nature herself had drawn, and the hand of man had never violated. No decoration of
art mingled to confuse or mar the perfection—all was natural, beautiful, unbroken. The transition had been sudden, as the change was great. Everything
was calculated to inspire the mind with feelings of no common kind.[116]

The association of stillness with the pictorial landscape is reasonable
enough, since pictures do not make sounds.

The absence of landmarks and familiar sounds made A. Delano feel
lonely: "As we looked over the broad expanse of prairie, till earth and
sky seemed to blend, we could not repress a feeling of loneliness."[117]
The sheer emptiness engendered a delicious melancholy. The "motion-
less torpor and tomblike stillness of the landscape" led to the conclusion
that "a lovelier scene was never gazed upon, nor one of more profound
solitude."[118] Solitude was aesthetically associated with sublimity (Usher
and Wordsworth, for instance, believed that solitude was a prerequisite to
the sublime experience), and thus anything that reduced incidental noise
made this amazing environment even more sublime.[119] The emotions
aroused in the English landscape garden were supposed to depend on the
solitude and privacy that surrounded the ruin or the brink of a waterfall or
the pastoral lawn. Americans were fortunate in this respect, wrote Andrew
Jackson Downing in 1847; they need not wait a lifetime for seedlings to
grow but had merely to hew out the walks and drives from the forest to
leave the natural boundary around their "seclusion and privacy."[120] An
environment totally deficient in cover might well be a landscape where
people became neurotic or hysterical.

If privacy was impossible on the plains, the vastness of the landscape
with its associated ideas of solitude and loneliness might substitute. If vision betrayed this illusion, the echoless quality of sound on the prairie,
muffled by the grass carpet and lost in the wind, would compensate. One
must, of course, *want* to hear nothing.

In the transition zone between the forests of Missouri and the plains of
western Nebraska, trees occupied the low places. Since they were lower
than the horizon, one did not need to see them, particularly if solitude
was a pleasure. "The truth is that solitude is not so solitary if there is a
tree in it," a student of landscapes reminds us, "and if there is a group of

trees we feel it to be almost peopled."[121] A wall of trees was a barrier that aided the illusion of solitude on the lawn of the garden park in a settled region; a party in the plains needed no trees to experience solitude.

The sameness of the scenery could make a man believe himself lonely even though he was attached to a party. "This day we crossed a beautiful prairie and through a little grove. There is no variety of scenery here; it is one thing over and over. If I could see a big rock or a buffalo I should think I had company," wrote Loren Hastings.[122] The landscape had bewitched him into thinking himself alone just as it bewitched others into hearing only silence. A slightly sharpened aesthetic would make him feel that "there is a charm in the loneliness – an enchantment in the solitude – a witching variety in the sameness."[123]

Such fancies led toward the generalization that the plains were empty – but it seldom reached that extreme. An "if," "but," or "except" was always tagged on. The one sound or the one living thing was presumably the exception that proved the rule: the flute in the grove that made its melancholy loneliness more imposing, the "lone elm" that nearly every traveler saw between the Kansas and Platte Valleys. "The only living thing we saw was green nutritious grasses," remarked B. F. Dowell.[124] Nutritious for what? He did not say. Another traveler saw a great arid plain without so much as a shrub, but covered with buffalo in tremendous numbers.[125] What were they eating? Where were their water and camp followers – their symbionts and parasites? Some travelers saw only birds. "Here the traveler is struck with admiration by the musical notes of many birds which from the vast extent of silent prairie around seem to have collected in this spot."[126] And, "We started on over rolling prara with but little to relieve the monotony except the great number of plover and prara hens that start up at every rod."[127] "The wolves gave us their usual music last night," wrote Joseph Sedgby, using a familiar figure of speech – or was it familiar?[128]

The trouble with the one exception that framed the silence and solitude of the prairie was that it tended to proliferate. If one looked too closely for the exception, others appeared. Deer, antelope, and birds; only "these moving objects relieve the death-like torpor and silence which generally prevail."[129] In stormy weather, J. Thornton wrote, there was no sound – and he listened – but the pattering of the rain. The next day the weather cleared and the great prairie was "quiet." "The silence unbroken by ought save the peculiar soughing noise – for note it can scarcely be called – of the grouse. . . . Soon the ear was saluted with confusing sounds of the lowing of cattle, the neighing of horses, the braying of mules and asses, the tinkling of bells, the tramping of busy feet."[130]

At dusk the plains landscape lost its vastness and the horizon seemed to come closer.[131] At night the space contracted even more. A wall of black was the backdrop for a ring of fires that gave the appearance of "a rustic village."[132] People sat listening and wrote in their journals about the sounds they flung into the darkness: the shuffling of mules and horses, men and women singing and fiddling, children laughing and crying, the walking to and fro. With the smoke and the tents, mused J. Quinn Thornton, the evening sounds were reminiscent of a Methodist camp meeting.[133] John Lewis heard only "the rumbling of the stream and the footsteps of the guard."[134] Rufous Sage perceived the night sounds and solitude, the hoot of the owl, the whistling of the wind, the bellowing of bison, and the howling of wolves as uniting "to invest the scene, so magnificent in itself, with a savage wildness, at once incitive of terror and admiration."[135] The "scene," of course, could be seen only by daylight. Perhaps those who had refused to allow their dogs to be shot were remembering – and fearing – nights when the darkness closed around them.

Some travelers clearly understood that the sense of solitude was the combined effect of the apparent lack of animation with familiar sounds. "On leaving Laramie," Rev. Spaulding noted, "the whole face of the country is changed in appearance – East of that Meridian the principal objects that strike the eye of the traveler are the absence of timber, the immense expanse of prairie, covered with a rich verdure of grass. Countless herds of buffalo and bands of flying antelope give animation to the country. The absence of mountains in the distant horizon, and the songs of birds in the morning, gave to it a solemn feeling."[136] It is difficult to understand how he could have failed to hear the spring songs of birds between Independence and Fort Laramie. Others said that they "awoke this morning to be saluted by the noise of the prairie hen and the songs of the innumerable birds"; "The green woods where we were encamped were again vocal with happy choristers"; and "thousands of birds were chanting their mating hymn."[137] Perhaps some members of the westbound parties were unable to hear the singing birds because sound and silence had been transmogrified through solitude into a function of space, the inconspicuousness of life in the plains rendering its sounds inaudible.

Sublime sounds were those associated with vastness and power that, like the rocky shore of the ocean or Niagara Falls, seemed to fill the auditory horizon. It seems unlikely that men who were hearing silence so acutely and finding biology so minute would find the prairie's animals sublime. Yet there were times when individual species appeared in sublime numbers. One night Samuel Hancock heard "more wolves than I ever saw. They made the night hideous with their yelling. . . . It seemed to me as if all the wolves for a thousand miles around had congregated."[138] They deafen your hearing, said a German traveler named H. B. Sharmann.[139] And there were nights when the universe seemed overrun with mosquitoes and the only thing a person could do about it was laugh. "These companions of our sleeping hours, were much attached to us — and not unlike the birthright virtues of other races in its effect upon the happiness of the human family. It can scarcely be imparting information to my readers, to say that we passed a sleepless night. But it is due to the guards outside the tent to remark, that each and every one of them manifested the most praiseworthy vigilance, watchfulness, and industry."[140]

The sheer mass of the prairie's creatures shifted the emotional response to its vastness. Rather than an empty hall of unimaginable size, some saw the opposite extreme, a cloudburst of life. Everyone was deeply moved by the immense herds of buffalo as they roamed beside, toward, and even through the wagon trains, and today's reader can only guess from the breathless words in the journals the thrill of taking part in a hunt. The prairie, which had seemed empty of life, became once again a teeming ocean.

Far as the eye could reach the prairie was literally covered, and not only covered but crowded with them. In very sooth it was a grand show; a vast expanse of moving, plunging, rolling, rushing life — a literal sea of dark forms, with still pools[,] sweeping currents, and heaving billows, and all the grades of movement from calm repose to wild agitation. The air was filled with dust and bellowings, the prairie was alive with animation — I never realized before the majesty and power of the mighty tides of life that heave and surge in all great gatherings of human or brute creation. The scene had a wild sublimity of aspect that charmed the eye with a spell of power while the natural sympathy of life made the pulse bound and almost madden with excitement; Jove but it was glorious![141]

The perceived silence and emptiness of the plains also increased the emigrants' awareness of the sounds they made themselves, the self-conscious sounds of men setting out to make history, reflected back into their own ears by sheer willpower. It was a bigger, emptier environment than they had imagined.

The Natives

Although there were Americans Indians inhabiting the land along the Oregon Trail, the large parties of emigrants did not have enough personal contact with them to acquire a concept of native life — at least not between Independence and South Pass. Small parties, individuals, and missionaries learned much more. Yet, the concept of "Indians" as innocent pagan children in a theatrical environment persisted. It was not uncommon for curious travelers to wander from the wagon train and be robbed. Most of the parties lost livestock in spite of their vigilance. But the great tide of people rushed west so rapidly that the experience of one group apparently was not communicated to the next. Guidebooks came into wide use after about 1847, but these perpetuated misinformation as well as communicating experience.

Someone should study the idea of the "noble savage" in a broader context than as a self-indulgent affectation or a form of literary folklore. It would be enlightening to know how actual experiences on the plains affected the myth of the noble savage. The widespread sense of the virgin purity of the new landscape seems to have been linked with the innocence of its inhabitants, and each was exploited in the name of progress and religion. In his famous book *The Oregon Trail,* Francis Parkman remarked that he was sorry to see civilization advance onto the plains. A modern scholar has accused him of belonging to "the slightly decadent cult of wilderness . . . a mood of refined hostility to progress . . . a romantic love of the vanishing wild west . . . a delicious melancholy for sophisticated and literary people."[142] All of this may be true, but such condemnation

Figure 26. *Medicine Circles,* 1837. Painting by Alfred J. Miller. The Walters Art Museum, Baltimore, Maryland.

involves a failure to recognize that there are—and were then—several kinds of progress.

The devastation brought to the social organization and physical existence of the American Indian was but a part of the violence being done to the whole landscape—with which the indigenous culture was intricately connected. In this respect the westward migration was anti-ecological. We have long accepted the American Indians' unavoidable fate, and the western emigrants in the 1830s and 1840s were almost unanimous, if they thought about it at all, in forecasting the doom of the Native American. Whether that fate was unavoidable or not, it is nonetheless true that the "cult" of literary people approached a comprehension of the prairie and its inhabitants as a dynamic complex. Native people's interplay with the environment gave their lives a fragile pattern of great beauty and continuity. If this understanding was arrived at by emotional rather than scientific means, it has nonetheless been vindicated by recent anthropological and ecological research.

It is true that many travelers had never seen an American Indian before and would never come to know one well. They were motivated as much by a widespread sentiment for all life as by the spirit of Hiawatha. A. J. McCall, for instance, managed to catch an injured rabbit to cook with the evening's antelope, "but as I took him in my arms and found he had a broken limb, which with his great watery eyes and palpitating heart pled so eloquently in his behalf that I was fain to restore him to his hiding place."[143] Rational reflection would have led to eating the rabbit, which could not have lived long anyway. Most of the travelers on the Oregon Trail seem to have viewed the natives as curiosities; in camp they were thieves, and in the distance they animated the landscape.

Many of those traversing the plains in 1846 saw the noble savage as the true owner of the land. The free-living "aboriginal inhabitants" were "luxuriating in the blooming wilderness of sweets which the Great Spirit had created for their enjoyment, and placed at their disposal."[144] This helps to account for the inclination of the travelers to pass through one of the most beautiful countries they had ever seen without thinking of settling it. Population pressures were not yet such that rationalizations were necessary for taking what was given the American Indians by both God and treaty.

The indigenous people were an important part of the plains aesthetic. "Bisons constitute the poetry and Indians the romance of a life upon these vast prairies," mused J. Quinn Thornton.[145] The sight of a wandering native elder aroused in Henry Smith Williams dreams of the man's past in a pleasant wilderness. "Here in the solitude of the mts. and with the utmost contentment, he was willing to spend the last days of his life among the hoary rocks and craggy cliffs, where perhaps he, in his youthful gayiety, used to sport along crystal streams which run purling from the mountains."[146] Essentially there is nothing untrue in this; yet it is an interpretation that, so far as Williams was concerned, could not have been improved by anything the native could have told him. Only a few minor modifications had been necessary to transfer the flourishing legends of the Mohegans in New England to the plains. Samuel Parker found the Native Americans interesting too, but observed that on the plains one could hardly call them "children of the forest."[147]

The American Indian as an integral part of the environment was an important discovery. Father De Smet, for one, recognized the relationship.

> In the plains there are none of the evergreen ridges, the cold clear springs, and the snug flowering valleys of New England: none of the pulse of busy man . . . none of the sweet villages and homes of the Old Saxon race. But there are there the vast savanahs, resembling moulten seas of emerald sparkling with flowers, arrested, while stormy, and heaving, and fixed in eternal repose. Nor are there lowing herds there, and the bleating flocks that dependence on man has rendered subservient to his will. But there are there thousands of fleet and silent antelope, myriads of the bellowing buffalo, the perpetual patrimony of wild, uncultivated red men. And however other races may prefer the haunts of their childhood, the well-fenced domain and the stall pampered beast – still, even they cannot fail to perceive the same fitness of things in the beautiful adaptation of these conditions of nature to the wants and pleasures of her uncultivated lords.[148]

If the nobility and innocence of the savage appear to be momentary projections of a passing tourist, the journals of Father De Smet and George Catlin are exceptions. Both spent years among the Plains Indians, one Christianizing them and the other painting them, and both men knew them well.

De Smet was not trying to make farmers out of the Indians, as the Protestant missionaries did; he wanted only to save their souls, and his faith did not blind him to the realities of their own society. He did not believe that the West would ever be civilized, but feared that the country would instead become "a mixed and dangerous population of malefactors."[149] The love he bore the Indians was not full of gloomy damnation but was cheerfully directed at "children." He dreamed of the Indian: "O! Soon the silent wilderness / Shall Echo with his song of praise."[150] It was a form of exploitation, of course, as well as an impossible fantasy.

George Catlin, a young Philadelphia lawyer, went west to paint portraits in 1832. He was not attempting to change the Indians at all, but rather to find them in untarnished nature – and his dreams were even more fantastic than De Smet's. He too believed the plains could not be cultivated. His letters from the West are smattered with "picturesque" and "romantic" mountains and crumbling bluffs. If, as we are told, a characteristic of Rousseauism is reverie, then Catlin could take a place with Chateaubriand as the perfect disciple.[151] But living among the Indians had given him a unique perspective. "It is generally supposed, and familiarly said," he wrote,

that a man "falls" into a reverie; but I seated myself in the shade a few minutes since, resolved to force myself into one; and for this purpose I laid open a small pocket-map of North America, and excluding my thoughts from every other object in the world, I soon succeeded in producing the desired illusion. The little chart, over which I bent, was seen in all its parts, as nothing but the green and vivid reality. I was lifted up upon an imaginary pair of wings, which easily raised and held me floating in the open air, from whence I could behold beneath me the Pacific and the Atlantic Oceans – the great cities of the East and the mighty rivers. I could see the blue chain of the great lakes at the North – the Rocky Mountains, and beneath them and near their base, the vast and almost boundless plains of grass, which were speckled with the bands of grazing buffaloes!

The world turned gently around, and I examined its surface; continent after continent passed under my eye, and yet amidst them all, I saw not the vast and vivid green, that is spread like a carpet over the Western Wild of my own country. I saw not elsewhere in the world, the myriad herd of buffaloes – my eyes scanned in vain for they were not. And when I turned again to the wilds of my native land, I beheld them all in motion! For the distance of several hundreds of miles from North to South, they were wheeling about in vast columns and herds – some lay dead, and others were pawing the earth for a hiding place – some were sinking down and dying, gushing out their life blood in deep drawn sighs – and others were contending in furious battle for the life that they possessed and the ground that they stood upon. I cast my eyes into the towns and cities of the East and there I beheld buffalo robes hanging at almost every door for traffic; and I saw also the curling smokes of a thousand stills – and I said. "Oh, insatiable man is thy avarice such! Wouldst thou tear the skin from the back of the last animal of this noble race, and rob thy fellow man of his meat, and for it give him poison!"

Many are the rudenesses and wilds in Nature's works, which are destined to fall before the deadly axe and desolating hands of cultivating man; and so amongst here ranks of *living,* of beast and human; we often find noble stamps, or beautiful colours, to which our admiration clings; and even in the overwhelming march of civilized improvements and refinements do we love to cherish their existence. Such of Nature's works are always worthy of our preservation and protection; and the further we become separated (and the face of the country) from that pristine wildness and beauty, the more pleasure does the mind of enlightened man feel in recurring to those scenes, when he can have them preserved for his eyes and mind to dwell upon.

And what a splendid contemplation, too, when one (who has travelled these realms, and can duly appreciate them) imagines them as they might in the future be seen, (by some great protecting policy of government) preserved in their pristine beauty and wildness, in a magnificent park, where the world could see for ages to come the Native Indian in his classic attire, galloping his wild horse, with sinewy bow, and shield and lance, amid the fleeting herds of elks and buffaloes. What a beautiful and thrilling specimen for America to preserve and hold up to view of her refined citizens and the world, in future ages! A nation's Park, containing man and beast, in the wildness and freshness of their nature's beauty![152]

The four paragraphs quoted above discuss a cosmic voyage, the biogeography of the buffalo and grasslands, field observations of buffalo behavior, comprehension that the commerce of buffalo robes for whiskey was beginning to replace the fur trade, recognition of the love of wild nature as a product of a highly civilized society, awareness of the disappearance of wilderness, admiration of the noble savage, understanding of the ecological interrelationship between the Indian and the grassland, and recommendations for preservation of a representative example of the whole complex. This painter's fantasy is a combination of cartographic and pictorial motifs. His apostrophe to "insatiable man" was in keeping with the widespread agitation for social improvement of his time. To Catlin, as to few others, the Native Americans were worth preserving for aesthetic reasons, and this meant saving some of the landscape of which they were a part.

History Being Made

The silence of the prairie was punctuated, for those who were aware of it, by the sounds of progress and destiny. If the natural solitude yielded pleasure, it also was monotonous; against it the doings of men were like a birth for which nature had been prepared. Along the Platte below the forks there was "nothing worthy of note. . . . The prospect of the country on the right and left being shut out by the bluffs – nothing save the cracking of whips and voices of the drivers . . . broke the monotony of nature's silence."[153]

When the emigrants climbed the nearest hill to measure their progress, they looked back along their route and saw the beautiful, fresh prairie being penetrated by civilization, and this made nature seem all the more enchanting. Looking along the trail one saw the vegetation in "dark winding lines[;] and when we add to this the long train of wagons with several hundred footmen scattered promiscuously on either side, and now and then a horseman galloping over the plains; the broken embankment, the clumps of trees, with here and there a lone one, we have a sight at once beautiful and rare to those who, have never crossed this western world of prairies."[154] It looked, in other words, like a picturesque and beautiful English landscape park, a prognostication of its future under civilized man. But this was only having the cake. Eating it too was seeing – was being – the pioneers.

In Kansas, spirits were high, teams strong, the weather cool and bracing. Heavily loaded wagons were later to be lightened at South Pass as fatigue and the exertion of the trip increased at the rugged portages from the Platte Valley around narrow canyons where rivers were cross-axial to mountain ridges. If the traveler had the thrill of feeling that he was the first ever to enter the untrodden prairies of Kansas, he also enjoyed the social excitement of discovering signs of those who had preceded him – the little ruins of history along the trail. The little ruins became towers in Wyoming, where the wagons were cut down to two wheels and possessions were pared to the bare minimum.

Figure 27. *Scotts Bluff,* 1958. Photograph by Paul Shepard.

When J. Bruff arrived at the mouth of Deer Creek along the Platte in Wyoming, he looked up to see the Red Buttes, but at his feet lay a diving bell.[155] Monuments of human litter marked every obstacle in Wyoming. At the mouth of Horse Creek there were beans, flour, bacon, and trunks; a little farther on, scores of dead cattle that had drunk the alkaline water in the local pools littered the ground.[156] All these were duly described like paintings in a cathedral recorded by the Grand Tourist.

Certain places along the route had bits of history attached to them, like Scotts Bluff. In the 1820s, two companions had abandoned Scott when he became weak from hunger, but he had crawled for some distance before he died. His body was found later near a cliff that was named after him. The cliff looked something like a building, and when seen as Israel Hale saw it, over a foreground of bacon, we see three lines of the new historical landscape braided into one: architectural resemblance, legend, and litter.[157]

Stories of Scotts Bluff, Brady's Island on the Platte, and Johnson's Creek, at the south end of which he was murdered, passed from campfire to campfire and into the guidebooks. Violent death was objectified in a landscape filled with bleached buffalo bones. Anglo-Saxons had never lived in a landscape where there was more than enough calcium in the soil and where rodents, for want of nutrients their diets otherwise lacked, did not immediately convert old bones to protoplasm. Of bacterial decay, it was as Jim Bridger had said: nothing corrupts in the mountains.

Nature produced abundant curiosities, but sometimes humans were even more interesting. Loren Hastings was greatly excited by the Devil's Gate, but two days after seeing it he met an eastbound family along the trail. "The woman rode with one foot on one side of her pony and the other foot on the other side. This is the greatest curiosity I have seen yet, it knocks everything else into the shade."[158] A man would long remember the spot where he saw a woman riding astride.

Human death was a sure and fascinating sign that events of moment were taking place. Cholera was common as far west as the Nebraska line, and beyond that there were accidents with fatal results from gangrenous broken legs and arms or accidental gunshot wounds. Back in the East, people were recreating in the new rural graveyards; here men were full of the optimism and exuberance of space and altitude and adventure. When John Lewis stopped to bury a friend on the twentieth of May, there were three other new graves nearby to remind him that cholera was a threat to all. "This was a little serious time," he said; but on the morning of the twenty-first he "arose . . . in fine spirits" and rode west.[159]

The emigrants' spirits were resilient, but death affected them deeply nevertheless; sometimes a whole train would stop for a funeral. Their feelings at such times profoundly involved the environment. "Death in the wilderness—in the solitude of nature, and far from the busy abodes of man—seemed to have in it a more than usual solemnity."[160] One journalist proclaimed: "Society is so dear to man, that even to see the grave of a departed one in the wide uninhabited plain or desert, suggests solitary feelings."[161] Most travelers mentioned the new graves with their markers or covering of rocks along the trace; some even made a daily count of these little monuments and quoted the inscriptions on them. The little markers did not last long; they vanished with winter storms or were torn apart by wolves. More fortunate were the dead like Scott, whose marker seemed indestructible. "Now these wild and picturesque bluffs in the neighborhood of his lonely grave, bear his name."[162] Death lent piquancy to the landscape.

On Independence Rock the pioneers wrote their own epitaphs: "On this rock is inscribed the names of some of the most distinguished voyagers and scientific travelers who ever traveled in any country, some of whom now lay beneath the sod with this alone for a monument, and forever it will become the mighty tombstone of thousands who have crumbled to dust."[163] In other words, "this rock is hardly worthy of notice, except for its many inscriptions."[164] Independence Rock was more than a tomb, it was a real historical record full of names "famous in the history of this country," quoted J. Q. Thornton from Frémont's journal – and, he added, a symbol of "our gallant and enterprising countrymen."[165]

The inscriptions were also messages of hope from those who had gone ahead, leaving behind the names of their former homes to inspire those who followed. So the names of the eastern states were painted on Independence Rock where the Sweetwater River joins the Platte in the Wyoming desert, little offertories to the genius of the place and a sign of familiar men and known places to those who could read. It was "the great registry of the desert."[166] Thus, a man rode miles across the bottoms of the Platte to Chimney Rock, which he said reminded him of a church, carved his name, and then "broke off a piece of the rock for a relic."[167]

One could leave a message even without leaving the trail. On the upper Platte in 1849 there were signatures everywhere, on the blocks and cliffs, on skulls, stumps, logs, trees, rocks, and gravestones.[168] In Kansas, there had been fewer rocks to carve on, but there was a landscape of messages all the same. "I think I never laid eye on a more charming place," wrote A. J. McCall. "The ford was steep and difficult and caused a delay of nearly three hours. We found the trees and stumps on the banks covered all over with the names of hundreds of emigrants who had preceded us, the dates of their passing and the state of their health and spirits, together with an occasional message for expected followers. Such records in the midst of a wild solitude like this can not but make a strong impression upon every new comer."[169]

There were men who would not bother to leave their names on a rock or a tree because "Sic transit gloria mundi"; the rains would obliterate them.[170] But not many travelers overlooked the signs others had made – whether legend, litter, signature, or bones – for these were visual assurance that civilization was making its mark on the great West.

Nature's Meadows and Parks

Overland travelers in the 1840s all thought that Kansas was beautiful. Their unanimity of opinion is marked by a repetition of imagery and phrasing in their journals and diaries. On the first night out of Independence, a party "encamped in a beautiful grove of timber through which meandered a small stream"; the next day they stopped "on the border of a beautiful forest where we found plenty of grass and water." On the third, they found themselves "in a commodious valley, well watered by a beautiful little stream which glided smoothly through the scattering grove."[171] It was the landscape of the virgin dream: "Before us were the treeless plains of green, as they had been since the flood – beautiful, unbroken by bush or rock, unsoiled by plough or spade."[172]

The prairie in May was a particularly rich prospect, noted Edwin Bryant. "The beauties and glories of spring are now unfolding themselves, and earth and sky seem to vie with each other in presenting the most pleasing influences to the eye and upon the sensibilities. Vegetable nature in this region has arrayed herself in a gorgeous garniture, and every object that raises itself above the surface of the ground, is so adorned with verdure and all the variegated and sparkling array of floral coloring, as to challenge the admiration of the most unobservant eye."[173]

A. Delano was likewise impressed with the beauty of the landscape: "In the afternoon the country was less broken, and afforded many beautiful views. We were on a ridge with a broad valley on each side, and many little creeks making down into the Namahas, and their courses were marked by timber sparsely growing on their banks. All the grass was green and luxuriant, and it seemed, as we ascended one rise after another, that each view was still more charming than the other. I did not wonder that the aborigines were attached to their delightful country."[174]

The statements and hundreds more like them recorded in the travel journals are not merely topographical descriptions. They are an expression of the amazement of forest-edge man at a paradise. No wall of forest stared back at pioneers across a hard-won clearing that by a relentless ecesis continued to advance toward the house. Here was rolling country like that which delighted seventeenth- and eighteenth-century Englishmen. One could see through or around the little groves in the distance. The delicate ecological balance between grass and trees tipped toward one on slopes with a little warmer ground surface temperature, and toward the other where the winter snows remained the longest, making an aesthetically pleasing landscape of diversity. "The beauty of the place and

Figure 28. *The Plains,* 1958. Photograph by Paul Shepard.

variety of its landscape scenery served in great measure to alleviate the weariness of delay," noted Rufous Sage. "The country was most agreeably interspersed with hills, uplands, and dales – amply watered and variegated with woods and prairies, attired in all the gaudy loveliness of wild-flowers." There were sounds of bees and birds and the incense of flowers, and it "seemed more like the breath of Eden than the exhalations of earth."[175]

Eden it seemed to others, too, or perhaps the dwelling place of a supernatural being from the classics. The mixed cultural context of the emigrants' vision is perhaps nowhere better exhibited than in the journal of the young missionary Cyrus Shepard. "[We] have this day passed some of the most rural and enchanting places that my eyes ever beheld, such as wide spread plains and gentle swells of land clothed in living green and embellished with numerous flowers (which appear to bloom to blush unseen) and verdant groves of valuable timber on either hand over spreading the bottomlands – while passing these delightful scenes almost untrodden by foot of civilized man a person of visionary cast might fancy them the abode of some sylvan deity or imaginary being unseen by mortal eyes."[176]

Although the "valuable" wood was being wasted, this was an enchanting place, pristine. There was a Golden Age quality to the landscape and the promise of idyllic pastorality. Instead of the peaceful cows that occupy such scenes in landscape paintings by Claude Lorraine, Ruysdael, or Constable, Shepard saw equally picturesque buffalo. "A more pleasant sight I never witnessed[;] the prairie here extends from the river in an almost level plain to the distance of about three miles where it is broken by high ragged bluffs – On this plain (clothed with a most luxuriant verdure and bespangled with thousands of brilliant flowers glowing in vernal beauty) were often to be seen hundreds of these huge unshapely creatures in a drove spread over the verdant landscape grazing on its soft herbage and heightening the scene beyond description."[177]

Instead of sheep or goats there were antelopes: "There was a broad bottom covered with rich green, bounded by a hill miles in extent, and the stream was fringed by a luxuriant growth of trees. Antelopes were running about in all directions, and the river was covered with ducks, swimming lightly about, while the opposite side was variegated with dead and green patches of grass, which covered the swells of the background as far as we could see."[178]

Human emotion was part of the pastoral dream. The appropriate concordance of landscape features invited thoughts of young women. Usually these first appeared in the middle of Kansas as a mention that there were young, unmarried ladies present. "For their sakes may the gods grant us the most propitious weather, and may the bountiful hand of nature, the beautiful romantic scenery, the dancing rill, serve to enchant and delight."[179]

Pastorality was a type of agriculture as well as a human dream finding its way into art. The mid-grass prairie was like parts of rural England, especially Scotland, as it was interpreted poetically. A. J. McCall was inspired by it to quote Robert Burns. It was "[t]he most beautiful country I have yet seen, passing through splendid groves of noble oaks and hickories and dipping into ravines coursed by murmuring streams reminding me of the sweet landscape in and around the classic land of Burns:

The braes of Doon! So fond, so fair;
So passing fair, so more than fond
The Poets place of birth beyond,
Beyond the grassy banks of Ayr."[180]

The prairie seemed to offer the perfect landscape for pastoral agriculture. "The most enthusiastic votary of agriculture and pastoral life, could
here," it seemed to Bryant, " . . . realize the extent of his desires – the full
perfection of rural scenery, and all the pleasures and enjoyments arising
from the most fruitful reproduction in the vegetable and animal king-
doms."[181]

The land did not even seem to need development. It sat prepared and
awaiting settlement: "The scenery around us presents greater pastoral
charms than I have witnessed in the oldest and most densely populated
districts of the U.S.; houses alone are wanting to render the landscape
perfect. . . . The power and taste of Omnipotence had here been manifested, preparing for his children a garden as illimitable in extent as it is
perfect, grand, and picturesque in appearance."[182]

Some were surprised at entering not a "great American desert" but an
agricultural paradise: "We are not traveling through forests, nor a solitary
desert, but so far as boundless meadows are concerned, the country has
the appearance of being under good cultivation. We see no fields of grain
secured from the beasts of the earth by fences, nor habitations of civilized
men, but meadows adorned with a great variety of plants."[183]

Where moisture was critical the trees were sometimes spaced geometrically, forming savannas. Howard Egan "traveled through a beautiful
country, the Loop Fork on one side and a ridge on the other with groups
of trees that resembled orchards in an old settled country. The pretyest
location I have seen this side of the Mississippi River."[184] S. R. Dundass
also saw geometry in the landscape: "The Plain was variegated with hills
and bluffs; a shade of timber marked the course of the creek running out
on the side we occupied, much like an old orchard. We fancied that the
trees were in rows; some certainly were. They were a species of oak with
low round spreading tops like the apple tree."[185] The oaks that looked
like an orchard were a part of the rationale that made Scotts Bluff into
a great tombstone. There was no legend associated with the orchard of
oaks, only a vague visual resemblance, and yet it was a surer sign of the

future than Scotts Bluff, one more proof that a vast, fertile landscape was a token of its own future habitation.

Edwin Bryant agreed that Kansas was indeed the Eden of America, but he was much too interested in progress to let it remain so. "When that epoch arrives, he who is so fortunate as to be there a traveller along this route, may stand upon one of the high undulations, and take in at a single glance a hundred, perhaps a thousand villas and cottages, with their stately parks and pleasuring grounds; their white walls seen through the embowering foliage."[186] Bryant's reference to the villas and the parks and pleasuring grounds carried the future in one bound beyond mere perfect agriculture to English civilization's best landscapes, the gardens of gentlemen. This was not only the fruitful garden, the pastoral landscape with its meadows and forest edge, or the ultimate agriculture with its grain and orchards, but the planned pictorial environment to which a great civilization devoted some of its finest talent and space.

Terms ordinarily used to describe the garden appear in profusion in the journals. A spring was a "fountain of the natural beverage so welcome to the thirsty and weary traveller"; "We encamped this evening in a beautiful situation near a chrystal fountain and shady grove."[187] The prairie was a lawn: "And merrily did we cross the Savannah between the woodland, from which we had emerged, and Council Grove – a beautiful lawn of the wilderness."[188]

Even the birds contributed to the civilized aspect. A. J. McCall was so struck by the apparent enjoyment and contentment of the cows chewing their cud "that I was fain to lie down myself upon the soft grass and enjoy the scene with them. There were a few birds twittering among the trees scattered along the little stream that ran hard by. So far we had seen few singing birds; they were created of civilized man, and are only found among his haunts."[189]

Said James Clyman: "Even a friendly Indian would be a relief to my solitude, but no person appearing I moved off down stream some two or three days after I came into a grove of large old cottonwoods where a number of village Martins were nesting. I laid down in the Shade and enjoyed their twittering for some hours it reminded me of home and civilization."[190] Americans who had fought forest and brush for generations were especially impressed with the ornamental character of the vegetation. The hills were "covered with stately groves, as tastefully arranged as if planted by the hand of man," with grass and flowers around them instead of underbrush, wrote Rufous Sage.[191]

Underneath these words is the imagery that Western man has accumulated of the paradise garden and the legendary wealth of the East. Those who were not so well educated were more likely to think in terms of the Bible and popular literature than the landscape park and pleasure ground. In either case, strange things were seen in Kansas. David J. Staples could not believe the landscape was natural: "We have traveled over a rolling prara some of the most beautiful landscape views I ever saw it looked as though some wealthy monarch of the East had spent a fortune in laying it out."[192]

The travelers were almost unanimous in their enthusiasm for the beauty of the first part of the Oregon Trail, which ran from Independence west along the extreme limits of the old Nebraskan glaciation, then north and west across the Kansas River and parallel to the Big Blue River. It was a country of relatively recent glacial drift, all rounded and smoothed with two layers of fine, windblown material. The prairie with its woodland margins was extremely fertile. In the spring the whole countryside seemed to sparkle with its latent wealth. It looked like the humanized landscape of New and Old England without fences or houses, like the great landscape park of a country gentleman.

The trail left the ice-contact topography about halfway up the Big Blue River, just inside the Nebraska line. The loess covering continued, but here it overlay the mixed debris of glacial outwash rather than drift. The outwash lined the Platte Valley as far up as the Laramie Range in Wyoming.[193] Many continued to believe the country beautiful past the old ice front, between the Blue River in Kansas and the Platte in Nebraska, but then the first doubts began to appear—or to reappear after being overwhelmed just outside Independence. "The land over which we have been traveling for the two or three last days is barren when compared with other parts of the prairie." The herbage was scantier, although there were deer, prairie hens, and turkeys.

The doubts that appeared on the loess plain were soon dispelled by the appearance of the Platte and its valley. Here, along the south bend of the central Platte, the valley is twenty miles wide and the river flows over the

deep deposits of sand and gravel that cover vast areas of the Great Plains.
The river is somewhat anomalous here in that it appears to be an upbuild-
ing stream channel, braided and anastomosed like the material deposited
by a stream whose gradient is so small that it is incapable of transporting
much material. The little islands of the braided channel would elsewhere
be a key to aggradation, but not here, where the gradient is six and a half
feet per mile. The sandy deposits beneath the river drain away its waters
to a water table lower than the stream surface. With loss by evaporation,
this reduces the stream and accounts for the braiding.

The valley of the central Platte is wide and green, with sand-and-gravel
formations capped with loess rising on either side.[194] S. R. Dundass called
it "one of the most beautiful in the world, extending on each side of the
river for several miles in an unbroken plain, covered at this season of the
year with a rich growth of Prairie grass; a slight Bluff ridge rises some
miles from the River beyond which it again becomes level."[195]

But it was not only the wide, fertile valley after the high loess plain
that was beautiful; the braided channel had a beauty of its own. "It is . . .
very shallow and interspersed with numerous small islands whose verdant appearance renders it the most romantic scene I ever witnessed."[196]
To Father De Smet the islets looked like a moving flotilla of ships as the
current flowed around them. "In the middle of the Nebraska," he said,
"thousands of islands, under various aspects presented nearly every form
of lovely scenery."[197] Like the Eden of Kansas, they seemed to be freshly
created, continued De Smet.

> Abstraction made of its defects, nothing can be more pleasing than the per-
> spective which it presents to the eye. . . . [Its islands] . . . have the appearance
> of a labyrinth of groves floating on the waters. Their extraordinary posi-
> tion gives an air of youth and beauty to the whole scene. If to this be added
> the undulations of the river, the waving of the verdure, the alternations of
> light and shade, the succession of these islands varying in form and beauty,
> and the purity of the atmosphere, some idea may be formed of the pleasing
> sensations which the traveler experiences on beholding a scene that seems to
> have started into existence fresh from the hands of the creator.[198]

Add to this the scattered trees, the tents of the itinerants, and the sunset
and moonlight, and the Platte Valley became sublime. "The sunset clear,
and the green valley washed by a beautiful river dotted with small islands

and shaded by a few scattering trees along its shore presented a view so enchanting, so full of sublimity as fully to indemnify us for the fatigue of the day. . . . As the moon shone on the vast green plain, the tents and herds spread out on its face reminded us of the ancient and patriarchal or pastoral life so beautifully described amid the recorded facts of Bible history."[199]

The Oregon Trail ran along the south shore of the Platte, following the south fork a few miles above its junction with the north, and then crossed the stream and a tableland to join the north fork in west-central Nebraska. This "Cheyenne Table" is Tertiary rather than glacial in age, lying over impervious Brule clay of the Cretaceous, and is capped here and there with windblown material. These surface features are aligned northwest–southeast and are believed to be the result of the drainage pattern formed on longitudinal dunes. The valleys are cut into the clay substratum of this lineated landscape, and the Oregon Trail paralleled them. The day's travel between the south and north forks over this landscape impressed the emigrants. It was their first departure from the Platte Valley since the trail had crossed from the Big Blue River in Kansas.

Along the Platte the trail led into semiarid country with rainfall ten to twenty inches less than is necessary to grow trees. Compared with the green landscape parks of Kansas and the pastoral Platte Valley, this country seemed even more desertlike, especially by midsummer. It was to J. Q. Thornton

a high, open, and rolling, or rather hilly prairie, presenting a very desolate and forbidding aspect. Much of the way was sandy and in some places we saw immense numbers of lizards. . . . Many persons in camp were quite unwell. . . . The low lands in many places show a white efflorescence of salt; and the country in the prospect is broken, barren, and naked. Herds of bison frequent many portions of the region; and savages, cool treacherous, and cunning, range upon the rear of these roving bands, or hover around the emigrants encampment at night, like wolves prowling about the fold of the flock. . . . [It is] the most dreary country we had previously seen.[200]

The contrast was greater between the dry uplands and the wet bottoms, and the emigrant moving between the forks of the Platte was once again put in mind of the Great American Desert.

Where the trail approached the north fork of the river it entered a large tributary canyon that has eroded regressively into this upland, cutting across the parallel lineation of the topography. Within two or three miles the trail dropped almost five hundred feet to the valley floor at an altitude of about forty-three hundred feet. As the train descended from the plains, the bluffs of the upper Platte rose up around the trail, sheltering Ash Hollow. Some found the tableland beautiful though difficult. "The road was very uneven and difficult, winding from amongst unnumerable mounds six to eight feet in height, the space between them frequently so narrow as scarcely to admit our horses. . . . The mounds were of hard yellow clay, without a particle of Rock of any kind, and along their bases and in the narrow passages, flowers of every hue were growing. It was a most enchanting sight; even the men noticed it, and more than one of our matter-of-fact people exclaimed, 'Beautiful, Beautiful!'"

But the lack of woody vegetation was nonetheless significant. "On the afternoon of the 31st we came to green trees and bushes again, and the sight of them was more cheering than can be conceived, except by persons who have traveled for weeks without beholding a green thing, save the grass under their feet."[201] How could it have been "beautiful, beautiful!" and then inconceivably improved by the presence of trees? Landforms and vegetation are not usually viewed separately.

The "cheering" green trees and bushes were not in ordinary landscape, however, but in Ash Hollow, a place of rare beauty. "A crystal stream flowed from a deep recess at the base of the bluff that overlooked the green little vale below. We travelled leisurely though this attractive spot; and felt more pain than pleasure, when we emerged from its delightful shades and found ourselves again on the monotonous valley."[202] Ash Hollow, where the walls tend toward the perpendicular because the rates of rock decay and removal are more nearly synchronized in the arid climate, was a basin of perfume. The smell of roses filled the air. "The majestic sandbluffs on either side, assuming a variety of appearances, and the extensive plains between the bluffs and river, covered with beautiful figures and roses, present a delightful scenery to the eye," enthused Rev. Spaulding.[203]

With its great ash and cedar trees and ripe wild fruit, Ash Hollow's similarity to a garden was irresistible. "As a whole it presents to the eye a pretty flower-garden walled in by huge piles of argillaceous rock, and watered by murmuring streamlets whose banks are ornamented with shade trees and shrubbery."[204] And again, this garden not made by man was an Eden. "In some of the low vales, there were beautiful little fresh roses, which bloomed amidst the desolations around. How ornamental are the works of Nature—She seems to decorate them all as if each spot was a garden, in which God might perchance walk, as once in Eden!"[205] Rufous Sage, noting the fruits and flowers and the "pines" on the conical hills near Ash Hollow, concluded: "I could die here, then—certain of being not far from heaven!"[206]

The Platte River from Ash Hollow to the Sweetwater is entirely different from the river that runs from the forks to its mouth at the Mississippi. In the high plains the river has cut as much as seven hundred feet into the earth, down through the eolian and alluvial deposits into the Cretaceous clay of an old seabed. The Laramide uplift that formed the Rockies and tilted the plains came in bursts; hence, the valley between the water and the bluffs on either side is a series of sculptured terraces with a thin veneer of alluvium. The rush of running water from the tablelands carved the sandy bluffs themselves. At the Wyoming line the Platte crosses the northern end of the Laramie Range.

The treeless valley plain was not monotonous to all. Even beyond Ash Hollow the travelers "encamped in a rich and beautiful bottom surrounded except on the west by steep bluffs and its beauty much heightened by some twenty or thirty trees principally ash, which . . . gives rise to agreeable sensations that ever remain unknown to those who are unaccustomed to travelling in a country destitute of timber[.] Bless O my soul the living God. For the ten thousand gifts bestowed upon us."[207]

The bluffs along the Platte were continuous after Ash Hollow and appeared to be closer to the stream. William Frush found the site pleasing: "This bluff and others surrounding forming a great basin between them and affording a very Romantic Scenery."[208] There were still a few islands with willows and cottonwoods that "presented a cultivated appearance; the green foliage of the willows, in contrast with the white sand, represented circular and serpentine walks of shrubbery in the distance."[209] The serpentine walk was right out of the eighteenth-century landscape garden.

The handsome cedars high on the bluffs gave way to pines near Fort Laramie, but those too appeared to have been planted by man. "A handsome scenery is in view of our camp . . . at the foot of the mountain. In the southwest there is a straight level bench and on the edge a handsome row of pine trees. Now if Dr. M. should see this place he surely would build upon it, for the place is already fitted to suit his fancy and indeed it would suit the fancy of almost any one."[210]

Beyond Fort Laramie, mountains were almost always in sight and the vegetation was more varied. "There was a great change in the country, hilly, brooks of water, partially wooded, and better feed for horses. . . . It was a pleasant change from the monotonous plain."[211] In spite of the wild disorder of the channels, where the river seemed to have forced its way through the mountains, the order of the park prevailed even here, however. The country had a "varied appearance." There were "ravines and ridges of gray and red sandstone with walled sides crowned with green summits on which occasionally appeared a lonely cedar or pine; while the various objects seemed to arrange themselves in order to diversity a sight of so promiscuous and so vivid a contrast of colors that the scenery was strange and singularly beautiful."[212]

Instead of the cattle or roe deer of the English park, the buffalo furnished the placid bovine animation that grouped to form pictures. The Platte wound its way "at times through fine timbered bottoms, and occasionally through beautiful unwooded valleys occupied by herds of buffalo quietly grazing."[213] In places, the trail left the valley and entered uplands covered by sage and unpleasant cacti. Along the Platte was a "pleasant tract of land beautifully diversified with gentle rises and declivities, clothed with a luxuriant verdure and adorned with a profusion of the richest blossoms. Leaving this enchanting scene (which is greatly heightened by the gently flowing and windings of the Platte, which is now skirted on either bank with narrow groves of fine cottonwood, ash and box elder . . .) we entered a rugged uneven country of rough barren hills and deeply indented ravines abounding in prickly pears that . . . prove quite an annoyance."[214] No sooner did one get used to Eden than one was forced to make short detours into the desert—as though to be reminded of what lay outside.

Travelers praised the beauty of the valley along the Sweetwater River, which runs east from the south tip of the Wind River Mountains and joins the Platte at Independence Rock. "The rocky cliffs closed into the road presenting quite a picturesque scenery. . . . [A]nd when entering the level bottom through which the crucked stream winds its way, there is a scene no less beautiful."[215] Pierson B. Reading and his party "[m]ade today six miles and camped in a beautiful valley surrounded by high mountains forming a park."[216]

A characteristic landscape scattered throughout the Rocky Mountains featured high mountains surrounding grassy bottomlands. These were the "parks" of the American trapper, alpine or alluvial beaver meadows with clear, cold water, abundant game, green grass with flowers, and scattered groves of trees with a mountain background. Attempts to approximate this landscape are widespread in the gardens of the world, although usually without the mountains. Finding such landscapes in the Wild West of America was a surprise to travelers. Insofar as they were only passing through, they were more objective, and more prone to fancy, than residents would have been. Pictorial and other aesthetic impulses were released from utilitarian bonds. The travelers judged these landscapes based on knowledge from the whole of their cultural past. The paradox of the dream gardens in the absence of civilization was resolved as being the work of God or of a personified nature. Travelers pretended that the manor house was just within that distant grove.

Perceiving the works of humans and God in the undisturbed prairie of Kansas and Nebraska prepared the way for the visitors to discover more of these works in the elaborate architecture of the river channel.

Architecture in the Wilderness

Plant and animal life decreases westward across the Great Plains, and the biomass is much lower than that of the deciduous forest environment. The conversion of solar energy, soil, and organic material diminishes with temperature and rainfall in the arid rain shadows of the Rocky Mountains. Living communities are never absent, but they take on new patterns in space and time as they are reduced in biomass.

The social organization of mammals living in an open environment where survival depends to a large extent on vision is highly integrated for defense and, among the larger forms, mobility. The normal dispersal of forage in the high plains kept the large herds of buffalo on the move and made many of the Plains Indians seminomadic. Water holes were important, especially during the dry periods, and also contributed to the

Figure 29. *Chimney Rock,* 1958. Photograph by Paul Shepard.

tendency for life to appear concentrated in discrete spots. The subjective effect of these dispersion patterns on westbound travelers, as noted in the travel diaries, seems to suggest that they considered the prairies and plains uninhabited and reacted accordingly. Yet buffaloes and insects and birds could suddenly appear, and the pictorial and gardenlike landscape formed a thousand miles of pleasure grounds, meadows, and ornamental groves.

In this receptive attitude the travelers reached the Platte River, their senses stimulated to a keen and perceptive level by the healthy routine of outdoor life. They found lush meadows like those that had covered the tall- and mixed-grass prairies, and the water and trees seemed no less ornamental. Islands like the tiny mounds in the Platte had long been a picturesque part of landscape parks large enough to have a lake, and the tradition carried forward into the wilderness. Everywhere the travelers looked they saw architecture and images of life back home.

"Our camp-ground for the last night," reported J. Goldsborough Bruff, "is a fine position for a prospect – on the top of a pretty high plateau, the broad and silvery Platte, sprinkled with numerous small sail vessels – The willowy foot of Gravel Island, a little ways above, the broad expanse of blue plains on the north side of the river, and below, looks like the ocean, bounded by the dim blue mountains."[217] This mild speculation was only the beginning. Others already thought this landscape "fairy-like and highly pleasing to the eye." Some twenty-five islands in a single field of vision had "fantastic shapes," like ships, gondolas, elephants, camels, and flat-boats.[218]

Herds of buffalo left signs reminiscent of cattle, and if no buffaloes were visible the illusion was so much the stronger: "Here we had hoped to meet buffalo, but not one was to be seen; although the face of the earth was covered with buffalo heads and bones, and the incredible amount of dry buffalo manure (bois de vache) would make one feel that he was standing in a cowyard, rather than in the wilderness. The grass was sheared close, leaving a poor show for our animals."

A man who knew the urban end of the beef industry found something familiar in the view: "The scenery of the country on the Platte is rather dull and monotonous, but here are some objects which must ever attract the attention of the observant traveler; I mean the immense quantity of Buffalo bones, which are everywhere strewed with great profusion, so that the Valley, throughout its whole length and breadth, is nothing but one complete slaughter yard."[219]

The road was busier than any highway in the populous East. "The Platte Valley is delightful, broad flats, more than two miles wide, with bold bluffs skirting them on either hand. There is a broad and well beaten highway on each bank of the river, both more crowded than any high road in the world at this writing."[220] The travelers tended to project meanings into the road and the animal trails that were far outside their actual function in the prairie. Near the Pawnee Fork of the Arkansas River on the Santa Fe Trail in Kansas, Thomas Farnham found the road over the flint hills "as hard as a McAdams pavement."[221] Generations of buffalo moving through the Platte Valley had left a network of paths that looked "like the once oft-trodden streets of some deserted city."[222]

Humorous remarks comparing the prairie dog towns to human towns have little significance, perhaps, except as they impress us with the general ethos, the ultimate criteria behind speculation on the new landscape. An empty prairie dog village suggested to one traveler, for instance, that they had all gone visiting; another concluded, on who knows what evidence, that "their government is purely Democratic in which the females have an equal voice."[223]

The vegetation became increasingly restricted as the trail wound west, and artifacts appeared in rapid succession as the geomorphology of the landscape became more obvious. The north fork of the river, for instance, had "the appearance of a grand canal."[224] And "[f]rom the Black Hills to the skirt of the river bottom were two ridges, which resembled immense even embankments, for railroads or canals."[225] The hills themselves (the Laramie Range) "seemed to be a mighty wall, elevated as a boundary line between two hostile countries."[226] High upon the bluffs that lined the Platte appeared terracelike beds of flowers, as though a pleasure garden had been built on a housetop.[227]

Along these bluffs, "everything had more the appearance of civilization than anything that [P. C. Riffany had] seen for many days, the trees, the shrubs and bushes, grape vines, the grass-resembling blue grass – the singing of the birds in the trees, the sound of the ax cutting wood for breakfast."[228] All around there were homelike sounds, artifacts, and vegetation, details of a vague architectural view of the world: "our home was the wild uncultivated field of Nature . . . whose walls the hills and forests were, whose canopy the sky."[229]

From the Cheyenne tableland west of the river in western Nebraska, where the trail turned northwest, Pumpkin Creek flows east to the Platte. A neck of upland between the two streams has been regressively eroded from both sides. An observer moving slowly up the Platte sees this ridge end-on as he or she arrives at the mouth of the creek and then passes along the north face of the bluff, some three or four miles from it. Several short spurs lead from this ridge at right angles toward the river; at their extremities they have been dissected into huge boulders, pedestals, and other disconnected remnants. The rock, rising about seven hundred feet above the valley floor, is sandstone and compacted alluvium of various sizes and resistances. Differential erosion on these rocks has produced a great variety of sculpturing. Within a distance of ten miles westbound travelers encountered Courthouse and Jail Rocks at the point of land nearest the junction of Pumpkin Creek and the North Platte River, then Chimney Rock just beyond the tip of the first spur, Castle Rock on the second, and finally the largest and least dissected of these outlying remnants, Scotts Bluff.

Chimney Rock is not actually an obelisk, as its name suggests; it is shaped like an inverted funnel, with only about one-third of its height in the pinnacle and the rest in an inverted cone pedestal. Such a formation could not exist in a humid climate; it is specifically a product of semiarid or arid weathering, where the debris that wastes from the rock is broken down or removed as fast as it is produced, so that the large block looks clean around its base. Where not sculptured by the river itself, remnants such as these usually have an inclined slope of rock at their base, thinly mantled with debris. Completely detached pieces like Chimney Rock have a sloped pedestal. Soil creep, the gentle movement of the whole surface down the slopes in humid and semihumid climates that masks the bases of hills in the eastern United States and Europe, does not occur in semiarid climates where the soil is thin or discontinuous. These hills do not have broad, concave "entrants" where they merge with valleys. In the West, roots of individual woody plants often hold the rock or soil in place at the lip of a slope, thus increasing its verticality.

Many travelers saw nothing more than a chimney in Chimney Rock, either of some strangely shaped house or like the gaunt stack of a burnt-out structure. "Many curious shapes and forms may be seen among the bluffs. Some abrupt elevations look like houses with steeples to them. One we saw sixteen or eighteen miles ahead of us, which resembled a house with a chimney in the middle of it."[230]

Others saw in the formation general types of familiar architecture; many, like Capt. Nathaniel Wyeth, saw Chimney Rock as "a work of art."[231] In connection with the perception of the prairie and plain as an ocean, many wrote in their journals that it resembled a lighthouse, "a striking landmark on this prairie sea."[232] It was a "beacon of the plain" to some; and more specifically like Boston's Beacon Hill to others.[233] Some thought it looked like a cathedral; it was a "grand and imposing spectacle . . . of the eccentricity of Nature, and at the same time looked like a church steeple."[234] This idea was quite popular among the many naïve observers and found its way into the most elementary journals. John F. Lewis, for example, saw a "tall pique from a beautiful mound . . . [that] resembles the steeple of a church somewhat."[235] Others were reminded of a shot tower.

But Chimney Rock was not the only architectural feature in the vista. Seen against a background of broken cliffs with many vertical fragments, it was but part of a larger spectacle. "Chimney Rock looming up in the distance like a lofty tower in some town. . . . The rock much resembled the chimney of a glass house furnace. . . . The hills in the vicinity present a fanciful appearance – sometimes like giant walls, of massive gray rock, and again like antiquated buildings of olden time."[236]

The less impulsive observers, remembering that the chimney was a mere semblance caused by erosion, offered more cautious comparisons. "As we advanced towards these hills, the scenery of the surrounding country became beautifully grand and picturesque – they were worn in such a manner by the storms of unnumbered seasons, that they really counterfeited the lofty spires, towering edifices, spacious domes, and in fine all the beautiful mansions of cities."[237]

Here the emigrants saw a brick kiln, and there a rock of "imposing and symmetrical architectural shape not unlike the capital at Washington."[238] In the bluff beyond these individual rocks, "with a little imagination, we fancy a dome and porticos, halls and pulpits. . . . The country seemed to be more broken and barren, but in appearance more beautiful."[239] Regardless of what they thought the formations resembled, excitement ran high among those who saw them. Journals and diaries run on and on with enthusiastic description. The bluffs several miles away were given a perspective by the long spurs, which, broken and irregular, projected a distant city almost to the stream. At the top of the ridge were outlying buildings: Chimney Rock, Courthouse, and Castle. Behind them was everything a man might imagine in a new world:

> The sand hills were so washed by the rains of thousands of years as to present at a distance, the appearance of Cities, Temples, Castles, Towers, Places, and every variety of great and magnificent structures.
>
> With a cloud across the sun the splendid panorama of the sand hills was mellowed, and the prospect was softened, until it seemed one vast, brilliant picture wrought with a mysteriously magic touch. Beneath the rising cloud was a vast plain, bounded only by the distant horizon. Here like beautiful white marble, fashioned in the style of every age and country.[240]

It was "a beautiful illusion." The awareness of its geological origin was solidly grounded in the new geology with its sense of time and process, but "the rains of thousands of years" gave the formation a sublime appeal. It was a short step from the merely architectural shot tower to castles and palaces "fashioned in the style of every age," by a "mysteriously magic touch."[241] Interest in medieval life had been growing since the mid–

eighteenth century. Ann Radcliffe, Charles Brown, and Sir Walter Scott helped give it architectural content in their novels. Archaeologists were exploring the Near East, Africa, and Mexico. Perhaps all this prepared the travelers for the pleasure grounds of Kansas, the pastoral central Platte, and the gardens of Ash Hollow.

Chimney Rock looked like one of the Egyptian pyramids, a "solitary tower" like "some ancient structure of the old world," and "a big castle on a small mountain."[242] But behind it in the distance were "pillar, dome, spire, minaret, temple, gothic castle, and modern fortification."[243] Castles and forts appeared everywhere. "The appearance of the country is beautiful and the hills on the left are washed into blocks, presenting a square front, not unlike old barracks of a fortress."[244] If the fortresses brought to mind troops across the river in the sand hills to the north, one could see entire armies from the ridge: "a vast prospect of low conical hills far below us, ornamented with occasional groves of small pines, which from their linear and curvilinear shapes, appear in the far distance like immense armies drawn up in battle array."[245]

A curious aspect of this pleasant and conscious process of perceiving the landscape as architecture was that persons so knowledgeable in geology that they could identify the minerals and rocks surrounding them, who realized that erosional processes were the cause of the architectural landscape, were nonetheless unable to resist such illusions. There was tenacity about the feeling that Scotts Bluff was a city. The "solitary castle" with turrets, battlements, and wings "would deceive the most practiced eye were it not known that it is situated in a wilderness hundreds of miles from any habitation."[246] One man who was not convinced that the formations were natural until he rode six miles across the plains to examine Chimney Rock explained:

> While viewing the noble monument at the distance of a mile or two I could not help imagining that it might be the work of some generation long extinct and that it was erected in commemoration of some glorious battle or in memory of some noble chieftan. But on arriving at the spot I could discover no marks of hammer, axe or chisel, no cemented joints by which it should be cemented in one solid mass. It is not the work of human hands. It must have been a freak of nature to display her art, astonish man with the variety and grandeur of her works and show the power of Deity.[247]

Their perceptions of this lost city in the desert affected the travelers' perspectives of their own journey as well. It is not unusual to find in the journal entries for any part of the trip such notes as, "the water of this spring was as grateful to us as nectar to the fabled deities of heathen mythology."[248] But as the upper Platte bluffs appeared, the allusions began to shift. Springs that had been called fountains in the gardenlike prairies became desert oases. On leaving the oasis, one wrote, "I must turn my back on the *El Dorado* of my fond anticipations, and hurry forward over the dreary wilderness which lay beyond."[249] Cooking their meals on bois de vache, some were reminded of the Arab's camel dung. Father De Smet, quoting Washington Irving's *Astoria,* compared the Platte forks to the Asian desert.[250] The Arkansas River, wrote Thomas Farnham, who was following the Santa Fe Trail, was "the American Nile."[251]

The illusion caught up with the train itself, and the wagons and emigrants seemed to become a part of the dream. "[T]he scene on either hand was truly delightful—there in company about two hundred animals of burden, vis. horses and mules, eighteen or twenty head of horned cattle and upwards of sixty men—the appearance of these while on the march reminds of the vast caravans in Oriental nations of which I have read accounts."[252] Although Cyrus Shepard wrote this passage shortly after leaving Independence, it is an excellent example of the analogy of which travelers felt a part as they set out into the plains. It was as though they were reenacting Marco Polo's journey. In the six hundred years since, there had been new deserts and new explorations of remote cities, and all combined in the mixed references that went along with the western pioneers as cultural baggage.

Summary

In the diaries of westbound emigrants on the Oregon Trail before 1850—some of them unpublished, weather-beaten, written in blunt pencil—are descriptions and accounts of landscapes new to the Western eye. From what perspective did these itinerants (not settlers) on the high plains between Independence and South Pass see the environment through which they passed? Most of them probably grew up in the woods or mixed forested and open landscapes of the eastern half of North America or Europe, in a culture shaped by a temperate-climate habitat. What resources

Figure 30. *Jail and Courthouse Rocks,* 1958. Photograph by Paul Shepard.

did they bring to bear on this novel world of short grasses and tree-lined streams, with a different climate and feel to the air, new smells and sounds, and unfamiliar rock formations? To what images, ideas, printed materials, or myths could these farmers, ministers, and other ordinary people refer to ground and give meaning to their experience?

The diaries call into question the popular imagery of unremitting hardship and monotony by revealing an almost playful spirit and joie de vivre. Recurrent themes in these records indicate the context within which the accounts took form. The impulse to dramatize what they saw signals the degree to which the Romantic era in the arts had permeated the popular mind. In many ways their reactions were unexpectedly intense.

Although those who kept journals may have been more literate than some of their companions, they did not bring to this experience the cultural baggage of educated travelers. Though they had imagery in the mind's eye to call upon when they arrived, it is unlikely that many of these men and women had seen pictures of the Great Open Spaces that would have prepared them in advance. As might be expected, then, there was much speculation about the uncultivated, treeless land and its resources along the Oregon Trail. All asked the same question: How do you account for open country unless it was cleared?

They answered according to their backgrounds. People who had "made" open land through heavy work found their imaginations carried toward fantastic histories and explanations. The landforms and geology along the track were more open to observation than those in the East and thus seemed to invite analysis. The Great Plains was a new environment to these forest-edge people, particularly visually. Even so, travelers carefully observed the utility of the land's streams for navigation, the fertility of the soil, its suitability for agriculture, and the presence of minerals. The Protestant missionaries, along with some others, strongly supported the view that uncultivated land was immoral.

The immorality of uncultivated landscape extended both to the Indians and to the guides and mountain men who led the trains west. Some travelers saw the landscape allegorically, others as outright evidence of the workmanship of God. A limited background in geology and other natural sciences was a part of the ordinary traveler's experience. To some, the new geological features extended the scientific support of scripture. Pseudogeological theories to explain every new observation along the way abounded. Beliefs in divine origin, enthusiasm for geology, speculation on unusual landforms, and abhorrence of "uncultivated" lands and humans combined to draw out the emigrants' curiosity and stimulate observation and speculation.

The immensity of the prairie struck the travelers with wonder. Aesthetic theory could not account for it because it seemed to combine the vastness of the sublime with the beauty of a lawn; it was at once a wilderness and a place cleared of timber. The travelers enjoyed the violent prairie storms, the fires, and the mountains as seen from the plains. Where the Platte lay across the axis of mountain ridges the landscape was seen as particularly sublime and picturesque, as were the dark cedars on the bluffs and the omnipresent silence. There were suggestions that landscapes should be painted and observed for pleasure from high points.

Even among inlanders seafaring was not far from the experience of the general public in the 1840s. The metaphors of sea travel were perhaps inevitable. The rolling prairie resembled the ocean, making the wagons look like vessels under sail. These pioneers saw themselves as voyaging to a new land in their "prairie schooners," swept along on seas of billowing grass, with no expectation of landing until they reached the eventual shore. These products of the Romantic era felt themselves to be living the allegory of life's voyage.

The silence and emptiness of the plains and the kinesthetic effect of the open country made isolation and loneliness a major theme of the journals. Although in the company of others, the pioneers had a sense of being alone that was reinforced by the vast distances that lay before them. This feeling had its own kind of excitement and indulgence. There was an intense self-consciousness of human sounds, particularly at night when the great spaces of the plains were invisible. This interplay of senses in forming attitudes toward the landscape was particularly evident in the plains.

These travelers, unlike their successors, were not looking to settle this land, and they showed a considerable amount of sympathy for the Indians. The theme of the free and noble savage, like that of the sublime and picturesque, had trickled into the popular consciousness in spite of the previous two hundred years of conflict. Two men particularly notable for their recognition of the Indian as a part of the environment were Father Jean P. De Smet and George Catlin. Catlin made a noteworthy recommendation for preserving a part of the natural community.

The sense of loneliness in a vast wilderness encouraged the pioneers' awareness of their mission and group self-consciousness. Legends and stories of particular places grew out of the litter of dead animals and the sights and sounds of the wagon train. Graves, signatures on the rocks, stories associated with particular places, even the impressive view of the wagon train itself from a high vantage point were all subjects of attention. A self-conscious, emotional sensibility about being a part of history-in-the-making emerged as the journey continued across this unfamiliar landscape.

The travelers found the prairie of Kansas extraordinarily beautiful, primarily because of its pastoral and parklike appearance. "Garden" was a commonly used term of description. Gardens and parks were associated with wealth, and the conscious illusion developed that humans were responsible for this beauty. The landscapes along the Platte Valley lent further support to this fantasy by their similarity to humanized landscapes. The dry uplands only accentuated the beauty of the valley and stimulated the fiction that these were gardens.

The gardenlike prairies prepared the travelers to perceive other evidence of civilization. In the weathered rocks of the semiarid plains were landforms new to Western imaginations. The bluffs along the Platte River, because of their composition and the climate, weathered into forms that looked architectural. Their appearance constantly brought to mind built structures, especially the fantastic architecture of monumental buildings, forts, and castles. Individual rocks were given names that were widely known among the travelers. Many seemed to resemble familiar buildings, while others were simply gothic, classical, or exotic in style. The pleasant illusion was encouraged by the contemporary enthusiasm for discovery and improvement; the presence of mysterious buildings contributed to the reenactment of great journeys of discovery in the past.

The bluffs along the Platte River often seemed to resemble historic ruins. The aesthetic of ruins had been for more than a century a central feature of the historical imagination, with its concept of the cycle of empire. Ruins greatly stimulated the imagination and the sublime image of the vast civilizations sunken in the cycle of time. Ruins also enhanced the sense of history in the making. Along with the gardens, the ruins confirmed the continuity of the existence of an ethereal civilization rather than an eternal wilderness in the plains. It was difficult in that open country not to believe them to be real ruins.

The architectural fantasy displays a persistent conviction about the completeness of a landscape, a pervading belief in its humanization, so difficult to dislodge that a thousand miles of the virgin continent was not enough to do so. It fed on first one and then another landform, on the grassland climax and the special distribution of woody plants, drawing from literature and history everything that might continuously realize the wish of civilization in the wilderness.

The Nature of Tourism

AMONG THE MOST SENSITIVE OBSERVERS OF MAN AND
nature are the seasonal ranger-naturalists of the National Park
Service. Put upon by waves of holiday flotsam surging into the
parks, the rangers continue to translate something of the cosmos
with an astonishing display of altruism. With such firm and gentle
dispensation do they work that the acid cup rarely overflows.
When it does, usually at the end of a day filled with foolish
questions and futile explanations, the opprobrium appears that
is otherwise checked with magnificent patience. A ranger of my
acquaintance was handed a bouquet almost in the shadow of a
no-picking sign. Asked to identify the flowers, this green-suited
erstwhile schoolteacher flung them down and twisted them into
pulpy fragments under his heel.

The implication of such behavior is not only that the tourists
are mistaken, but also that they are boobs. Sympathetic colleagues
and cynical tourist industries would undoubtedly agree. Historically there is some justification for this conclusion. Before travel

155

was so corrupted, the original tourists to Rome were either scholars or young aristocrats, or both together, one as tutor to the other. The young sixteenth-century gentleman was sent for the "benefit of wit, for the commodity of his studies, and dexterity of his life." This design and its humanistic, didactic formula deteriorated in the following century. Men and women of the aristocratic and mercantile classes usurped the Tour to Rome to absorb culture and get a change of climate. The Grand Tour became fashionable. Americans of the upper social strata patronized the fashion even though it cost them an ocean crossing.

Numerous factors contributed to the rise of popular tourism in the United States, not the least of which were the discomfort and the epidemic diseases that riddled the growing cities in summer. In 1826 the Erie Canal provided easy passage to Niagara Falls, which was reputed to have numerous inherent qualities and to radiate religious, hygienic, and intellectual blessings. Chauvinistic arguments for Grand-Touring America instead of Europe bloomed with the railroads.

As native poets and painters discovered the virtues of rural New England, their patrons and the socially elite came humbly after. The mob followed, further distorting the elevating intent of the original Tour. Contemporary magazines are full of popular imitations of Coleridge, Wordsworth, Byron, and Bryant directed at New England landscapes.

Once in the field, most of the ordinary tourist's time was devoted to securing accommodations, conveniences, and safety. The only trouble with Yosemite Valley, according to a visitor in 1864, was the difficulty of finding out who won the election in Cincinnati. The most acute outer reality was composed of rates, schedules, and meals. When the passengers began wildly leaping from the train as it arrived at Niagara Falls in 1856, an observer "looked upon them at once as a select party of poets, overwhelmed by the enthusiastic desire to see the falls." As it turned out, "they were intent upon the first choice of rooms at the 'Cataract House.'"

Undoubtedly, the busywork of attending to trifles helped to avoid the unabridged emptiness between tourists and nature. Bryant's cathedral of the forest was theoretically as edifying as St. Paul's, and the crowd attended the outdoor temple as perfunctorily as it went to church on Sunday. The landscapes of "wild" nature in the heritage of ideas coming to us from Rousseau and the English artists and aestheticians were essentially rural.

Most of Europe has been subject to more than two thousand years of humanization through grazing, burning, cultivation, forestry, and "varmint" control. Even in the eighteenth century little evidence remained of European wilderness. Tourism was compounded of several factors, one of which was the idea of natural beneficence and the nobility of "wild" things. American tourists were unfortunate enough to have real wilderness close at hand. Neither the painters of the Hudson River School nor poets such as Bryant and Thoreau strayed too far from the farms and villages of the principal river valleys. For them the Catskills and White Mountains were wilderness enough – and too much for the rank and file. It is not generally recognized that the flood of national sentiment for the preservation of Yosemite and Yellowstone had as much to do with their particular similarities to old humanized landscapes as any other factor.

Weaknesses in aesthetic and scientific discrimination made the tourist a ready prey to scenery vendors and fakers. Toll trails and a kind of promotional facade appeared in the landscape. As William Dean Howells put it with reference to Niagara Falls, "Their prodigious character was eked out by every factitious device to which the penalty of twenty-five cents could be attached." Kaaterskill Falls, epitomized on canvas by Thomas Cole and Asher Durand and in the novels of J. F. Cooper and Washington Irving, were typically visited by fast coach in 1850. The carriage drew up before the Falls Hotel and the bar was opened immediately. As the tourists straggled out to the falls a boy was sent upstream to open a floodgate. It cost a quarter to have the falls turned on. When the crest had passed, the travelers returned to the bar and the coach, and thence to the Catskill Mountain House, where dinner was always formal.

Travel was fraught with incredible haste long before automobiles entered the picture. Horace Greeley rode the sixty miles from Mariposa to Yosemite on one August day and had to be lifted down from his horse. As early as 1872 a visitor complained, "The Valley, in the height of its short season, is a confused scene of hurry, pushing and scrambling."

Paradoxically, there were long, vexatious hours in the tourist's day that were not earmarked on the five- or eight-day tour program. Partly as a result of this, there was much measurement of the "curiosities" in height and volume, with favorable comparison to the better-known natural wonders of Europe. Calibrated walking sticks and plumb lines were part of a gentleman's equipment, as the Claude glass had been a century earlier. Tourists patronized "sybaritic" baths at the Cosmopolitan House in Yosemite, played cards, danced cotillions, or bowled on the logs and stumps of Big Trees, and talked about whether it was more chivalrous or more dangerous to chase butterflies on horseback. A howitzer was kept for making echoes. After motors had overwhelmed the sounds of the landscape, making these pleasures vestigial, the howitzer was replaced by an evening ritual in which a spectacular stream of burning faggots was pushed from a mountaintop.

Everyone is aware that improved transportation has not reduced the haste of the vacation. By the opposite route of the search for easy thrills, we approach the attitude toward nature advocated by St. Anselm in the twelfth century. Sin, he asserted, is proportional to the number of senses involved. As Edgar Anderson recently pointed out, few of us hear a landscape any more. Taste and smell are likewise handicapped. The day is here when the air-conditioned automobile carries us across Death Valley without discomfort, without disturbance to our heat receptors, and without any experience worth mentioning. We do not touch the burning sand.

The pursuit of comfort and amusement may be weighed against the degree of the encounter with nature. There is a choice to be made between capricious pastime and recreation. In a thoughtful essay, a Canadian geographer, Roy Wolf, suggests that the whole matter revolves about the question, "What relationship do I choose to assume with the environment?" The answer must be made from qualitative opposites: amusement and recreation, one an emotional debit, the other a credit. Whether we spend our spare time on a roller coaster or hiking in a forest may greatly influence our psychological equilibrium. To Wolf's conclusion it might also be added that the choice determines what happens to the environment. Incredibly, we campaign against litterbugs by trying to convince them that they should not exist – an approach entirely without success in the annals of pest control.

The history of tourism shows that we cannot account for the boobism of the tourist entirely as a machination of the twentieth century. All this century has done is narrow the lag between a vague desire for greater comfort and its realization. Perhaps the full swing of the pendulum will evoke a loathing out of satiation from which tomorrow's tourist will reject amusement. If and when such a millennium arrives, it may be too late. The improvers will have saturated the scene, leaving no landscape worthy of leisure.

The same park rangers who speak privately of tourists as "churnheads" return to their interpretive work annually, poorly paid and demanding though it is. It seems unlikely that many of them could do so with a conviction that they serve only as nuts and bolts in a booby machine racing nowhere. Is it fair to ask what are the redeeming qualities of tourism?

It should be noted first that the bulk of the summer travel in the United States is prodigious. It is unfortunate that almost nobody except builders of filling stations, chambers of commerce, and a few fitful figure-minded agencies has given the matter much attention.

The basic goodness of spare time is taken for granted by recreational agencies and labor unions. Ever since industrialization split the work week from the seven-day week there have been occasional objections to this assumption, of which Mr. Wolf's is a cogent example. The concept of leisure itself is fundamental, and from it any meaningful philosophy of tourism must extend. Leisure is reputed to have given us science and the arts. But a very few individuals are responsible for advances in these fields. Can we assume that the most meaningful aspect of leisure for all the other people would be merely appreciation or advance in amateur science and art? Perhaps even more significant to the plebeian is the effect of leisure on the whole range of his values, a spectrum that may be assigned to his religion. Josef Pieper has given us a modern restatement of leisure as "the basis of culture" – not, that is, as recuperation for more productive work, but as the antithesis to work. It is the only reason that labor is tolerable or meaningful. Yet leisure is not idleness. To Pieper, it is not synonymous with spare time, as it is to the labor union, but instead is a matrix for the evolution of the cultus, the basic religious body. The cultus is related to God through sacrifice, and from its rituals come the behavior and values of a society. Pieper compounds the Greek concept of leisure with Christian orientation in a fruitful way. It can be concluded that the use of leisure exhibits the essence of a particular society's relationship to the universe. The greatest contributions to civilization are made principally in leisure, not by "intellectual work" but by contemplative, intuitive, religious, or romantic orientation stemming from a release from travail.

Applied to the relationship between humans and the landscape, it is apparent that the process envisaged by Pieper could lead to a world perception unfettered by a rigid thesis of nature for man's use. The ordinary citizen lives in the corridors of a narrow experience and knowledge. Its walls are his routine. In such circumstances his recognition of broad patterns in nature is not a rational product but a gift, unhinged from the necessary scheming in work or amusement. It is very fortunate that most tourists do not go afield, notebook in hand, but go instead with an undefined desire to see stimulating curiosities. This is the first step toward recognition of themselves as part of nature.

We smile at the giddy antics of the self-styled nineteenth-century "pilgrim" to the falls or to the West who suffers inconveniences in wild nature. But today the sacrifice is merely expressed in a different form—the splurger who pays outrageously for trinkets, meals, and gimcracks. The Christian ideas of suffering and sacrifice remain central to the idea of Western tourism. A unique feeling associated with some encounters in nature was labeled "sublime" on the Grand Tour. It was a word transferred from religious to terrestrial description in the seventeenth century. Subsequently, God returned to the landscape. Persistently, though partly in fun and in part allegorically, a kind of equivalence appears in tourism between prayer and sensual reception, sacrifice and inconvenience, and worship and travel. There is an almost crusading zeal in the tourist. Of course, there were those who merely used the associated clichés and followed the stereotyped guidebook patter, but there was also John Muir, who actually believed that God was visible in the landscape. The sublime was the awful and cosmic moment when one perceived in a landscape a relationship to God.

The pervasive and fascinating study of geology was a related influence in the evolution of tourism. The "pilgrims" flocking into Yosemite Valley, to Niagara Falls, or to the Yellowstone plateau gathered about peculiar geological phenomena; and so it has been since Richard Lassells interrupted his tour through Italian cities to peep over the lip of Etna as Petrarch had climbed Mont Ventoux. Almost everyone in the first half of the nineteenth century deliberated the stinging questions that geology raised about the Scriptures. Discussions concerning the Old Testament date of 4004 B.C. for the creation of the world, the location of the Garden of Eden, the Great Flood, fossils, holocausts, cataclysms, and the permanence of hills and ocean basins buzzed like angry bees. The naturalist was an amateur, and everyone was something of a naturalist. Each considered the inconsistencies between Bible and landscape from personal observations and reading.

Perhaps today's amateur naturalists are more apt to look at a book about mountains than at the mountains themselves. If they observe the mountain and read the book, the effect may be much more efficacious than one would expect from a kind of laboratory demonstration. For one thing, they reenact the discovery of the mountains as geologists perceived them, a procedure no different from rehearsing the discovery of the solar system as it was perceived by astronomers. The sublimity of these experiences reminds us that part of Galileo's "technique" was prayer. Perhaps because of our enthusiasm for history, or perhaps for more atavistic reasons, we never tire of putting ourselves on the stage to re-create great events. The traveler, too, recapitulates a cultural experience, giving his leisure a purpose, and a liveliness and excitement otherwise absent.

William Gilpin, an eighteenth-century English vicar, wrote a book telling how to enjoy the English landscape. Since there was no completely wild nature remaining (that is, sublime wilderness), it was necessary to do two things while hiking through woodland. The first was to imagine yourself to be lost, which might possibly release an instinctive fear.

The second necessity, according to the vicar, was to imagine that you were the first ever to set foot in that place. This precept may embody the most important aesthetic aspect of tourism: its reenactment of exploration. The relationship of hunter and fisherman to nature is also a re-creation of an earlier challenge. A myth of need and hunger is supported in the act of eating the catch. Gathering, husbandry, and hunting are recapitulations of a different class from the portrayal of discovery—which was itself a product of leisure. Whether this makes any difference in the perceptive value of its execution is doubtful.

The late Aldo Leopold believed that such mimo-drama had "split-rail" value, a virtue diminished by the use of gadgets. Split-rail values do not necessarily lead to perception, as when little boys play Cowboys and Indians. But they may catalyze meaning for the traveler in a landscape. When the airlines were young, passengers were given guidebooks for reading the landscape below. In those days, every passenger was a Wright brother. Flying for the traveler has since become too high, fast, and monotonous; it is no longer an adventure. Perception may require an agent, whether a book or a personal interpreter. The federal government has assumed this obligation in the national parks with its publications, museums, and ranger-naturalists. There are various levels of the interpretation of nature, the most elementary being the identification of forms. Thousands of bird-watchers over the United States keep "life lists" and concentrate on recognition. Genuine perception proceeds beyond this, first into the life history of the identified organism or geological form and then into its relationships within a larger field. The last is much more difficult to perform, but it yields the only significant comprehension of patterns.

There are reasons why the interpretation of the landscape should be easier than it was a century ago. One is that more travelers live in cities. This may seem to be a paradox, but the city man, who is normally further removed from nature, is willing to accept a skillfully presented scheme of nature woven on a framework of pattern and process, even though he may not be convinced that it is important. The farmer will only accept parts. Another reason is that we know more about these patterns than we did a few years ago. A course in ecology was given recently to college seniors, none of whom were biologists, using the landscape as a focal point. Orientation and textbook emphasized process, pattern, and order versus disorder.

It is noteworthy that this course could be given in a liberal arts college, which represents the best surviving arena of the leisurely ideal. Visual habits in the normal workaday world of the public almost preclude the possibility of seeing whole patterns in nature. Christopher Fry pointed out several years ago that we learn very early in our lives the meaning of certain "signs" in our environment. While these may be important in our orientation, they are not looked at very closely after childhood. Most of us retain a small portion of childlike vision toward the part of the world that is economically unimportant, though we seldom bother to exercise it. For this reason we are much more likely to look closely at a landscape painting than at a landscape and we become better critics of the canvas than of the view. The acme of this form of blindness is expressed in Santayana's explanation of Romanticism: "The promiscuous natural landscape . . .

has no real unity, and therefore requires to have some form or other supplied by the fancy." Recent work in animal behavior has validated Fry's remarks with respect to "signs."

The best modern alternative to college life as a greenhouse for perception is the vacation – degraded, perverted, and streamlined though it may have become. The sportsman, observing the pattern of stream life in which moves the fish, is himself moving in a sphere that has no immediate connection to the conduct of business. The beauty of this activity is that it is completely useless. It has the merit of a low amusement but high reenactment quotient. Metamorphosis comes with the desire for an interpretation of the life of the fish. The whole watershed then assumes a new significance. Sometimes the sportsman appears before legislative committees urging antipollution laws, although neither the passage of laws nor any other particular objective need be the end of perception.

Tourists follow a classical pattern. They move through novel landscapes with minimal sign value. Detachment from daily niches increases the potential for understanding relationships. If amusements are avoided, one may even become curious. Going west is like replaying the history of the pioneer and the discoverer. Even in a city, if it is strange, wilderness with the charming possibility of becoming lost presents itself. The journey is at once a pilgrimage and a retreat. In this plastic and receptive mood the tourist is essentially a new and different person. Travel is broadening not because of the nature of travel but of the traveler.

In 1873, Grace Greenwood prophesied a time when Yosemite Valley would contain "horse railroads and trotting tracks, hacks and hackstands, Saratoga trunks and croquet parties, elevators running up the face of El Capitan, the Domes plastered over with circus bills, and advertisements of 'Plantation Bitters.'"

Some observers may feel that this, essentially, has already come to pass. Others may wonder why it has not. When the ranger rudely rebukes the tourist with her precious but plucked flowers, it could mean that she reveals the dual nature of the traveler in the most provoking way.

They Painted What They Saw

ABOUT THE YEAR 1820 TWO MEN STOOD ON A HIGH TOWER overlooking the countryside near London. One was an American gentleman of some intelligence, the other his English host. They had climbed the tower so that the American might see the beauty of Britain in the early summer. The field, fenced by hedgerows, gave way in the distance to treetops, so that the highly cultivated land actually had the aspect of a broken forest, becoming more and more compact toward the horizon.

"Do you call this beautiful?" the Yankee asked. "In America we would consider it to be one of the most desolate scenes that the mind can conceive. It resembles a country that has never been cleared of wood."

The opinion was typical of a way of seeing nature that is contrary to the modern way. "Desolate" has been, in fact, the adjective most often used to describe the New England forests damaged by the big hurricanes. So in little more than a century the American attitude toward the forest has completely changed.

Unfortunately there are not many examples as vivid as this of the artistic evaluation of nature by the public. And it is only slightly more difficult to determine what emotions the surroundings stirred in a reflective person a hundred years ago than to find out the same thing today.

There are, however, two important forms of visual evidence: the parallel evolution of landscape gardening and landscape painting during the past five centuries. Both are a series of clues calling for a good deal of interpretation, landscape painting in particular. Measuring the notions of nature that a man puts on canvas requires, to begin with, a background familiarity with the human eye. The color spectrum is, after all, only a small octave out of a whole keyboard of wavelengths. Then there is a surprising variety of psychological and subjective tricks or habits. We are often unaware of a perceptive distortion by which, for instance, we derive the visual impression of a whole form from a series of broken lines. In addition, there is the immense technical problem of translating with brush and pigment a three-dimensional image onto a flat surface. Finally, the painter himself is subject not only to the caprices of his own personality and the storms of his hormones, he is also something of a slave to the whole heritage of landscape painting, to which he may have been exposed little or much.

The tradition of nineteenth-century American painting originated largely in England, but the English landscapists themselves had been inspired by Frenchmen painting in Italy and by the vision of men in northwestern Europe. Painting influenced the appearance of the English countryside; large stretches of England were actually landscaped during the eighteenth century after the manner of paintings by Claude Lorraine, Poussin, and Rosa.

The nineteenth-century American landscape artist was generally restricted to those subjects which fashion made paintable. This restriction was in a sense the acid test of his perception, for much of the traditional European subject matter was unavailable. There existed instead a whole series of frontier landscapes without counterpart in Europe. It is still a test, as artists who go into new kinds of landscape — as those, for instance, of the Deep South and the Far West — soon realize. In the artistic interpretation of the indigenous scene, new attitudes toward the surroundings are most strikingly revealed, since there are only fragments of artistic formulas to serve as crutches.

The American painter of the early part of the last century dwelt amidst a harsh set of vistas, chiefly those of land-clearing activity. Historic England – and English painters – had never known such a relentless sunshine as this; the Italian painters had never known winters so cold, or Dutch painters such torrential rains. Even the aspect of the vegetation was new: except for scattered glacial drift and the rich alluvial bottomlands, the thin soils in this harsh New England climate were associated with rocks of low fertility. High rainfall leached out the nutrient materials and long, cold winters slowed the organic decay and the chemical processes upon which the regeneration of soil life depends.

Such were the specific characteristics of a region in which the measures taken to ensure human survival constantly threatened the stability of the natural landscape. The practice of forcing grains and new crops out of this soil speeded its waste. Continued need for capital demanded incessant clearing and the planting of the old. The agricultural landscape of Europe had been hundreds of years in developing. In contrast, America was a place of changes in which vast disruptions were producing equally violent oscillations. Thus the interpreter of the American countryside faced a situation for which his artistic Old World heritage had not prepared him. He found himself amidst new earth forms controlled by a climate of extremes and in the habitat of peculiar plants and animals; and superimposed upon this setting was an economy that proved so ruthlessly extractive that some of the land spoiled a century ago is still unreclaimed.

The history of European art and the strange landscape of the New World were not the only influences at work on the American artist. The wilderness was disappearing; the continent was no longer uncharted. The industrial revolution and the growth of cities were undermining the sympathy with nature that eighteenth-century pastoral England had brought into focus. Science marched on, but its findings only isolated things in the landscape and seemed to separate humans from their surroundings. One mechanical device, the camera, was a revelation to the artist. The moral, the message, or the emotion derived from nature, which the landscape painter, like the poet and even the landscape gardener, had sought to ex-

press, was neglected, and transition to city life by both patrons and painters helped demolish interest in the traditional subject matter. To painters
the new technological environment became one composed primarily of
color, form, and experimentation.

The artists moved with commerce up the great rivers. In this romantic
view, memories of Italy as partially digested by French painters, then by
Englishmen, and taken in capsule form by tourists are reinterpreted in
the New World. The pondlike effect obliterates the actual dynamic quality
of the river. The Lombardy poplars are not American; here, imported or
imagined, they are symbols of a transplanted culture and will gradually
be swallowed by the native vegetation. The mullein plant, on the other
hand, is a verity; the artist has looked with care at the intimate features
of nature. The large tree is a cliché, and the smaller trees and the distant
forest are what persons thought they saw and what they loved. The stone
wall is as much a part of this peculiarly American landscape as is the Old
First Church in the distance. Walls and fences are tokens of independence
and ownership, and suggest perhaps a postrevolutionary social feeling.
But the rustic sentimentality is out of eighteenth-century England – an
unrealized dream of some immigrant gentleman. The rural ideal did not
involve hard work in the form of cultivation; water provided a means
of transportation; the town had the amenities. The sheep represented a
marketable crop and food and clothing. Boulders, instead of hindering
agriculture, were convenient resting places.

It was possible, as John Trumbull did in 1810, to go to Norwich Falls
in Connecticut, where Cooper had placed a climactic scene in *The Last of
the Mohicans,* and do a portrait of the place, an analysis of its character the
way one would analyze a person. Trumbull was a painter of heroes and
battles; his work hangs in the Capitol. He probably painted no more than
three landscapes in his busy career. The fictional heroes and events, no
less than the historical, gave place to elements of American identity – for
we identified with the Irving and Cooper characters.

His painting of Norwich Falls may well be the only painting of a waterfall in which the falls are invisible (figures 31 and 32). Mr. Trumbull,
George Washington's friend, scrutinized the work of stream erosion and
found it monumental. It had in fact produced a ruin dedicated to itself
while contemporary Englishmen were still erecting artificial ruins in their

Figure 31. *Norwich Falls* (or *The Falls on the Yantic at Norwich*). Painting by John Trumbull. Oil on canvas, 27 x 36 in. Yale University Art Gallery, Mabel Brady Garval Collection, New Haven, Connecticut.

gardens. To exhaust the analogy, the garden ruins were often representative of morality, a sort of lesson in the ultimate futility of all human effort, while in Connecticut, runoff—due to clearing—speeded erosion and eventually ruined the uplands and choked the streams with debris. The ecological fact that caught Trumbull's eye (though he would never have called it that) was the cliff from which the last of the Mohicans threw himself. Romantic enough but, more important, a symbol of the clash between two cultures. This is a multipurpose tombstone. The big rock is granite, a sort of symbol of low soil fertility in New England. On its surface is an acid-tolerant plant succession that the artist, who usually painted historical subjects and portraits, observed with great fidelity. Of

Figure 32. Site of *Norwich Falls,* 1953. Photograph by Paul Shepard.

all the aspects of the lived-in landscape around him Trumbull chose the element of embroidery, a romantic point of interest that might also have the eye of Salvator Rosa. But he would scarcely have cared for Kansas.

According to John Marin himself, the back of Bear Mountain offered great retinal possibilities. Although the possibilities he saw are very different from those offered by the painters of the Great Age of landscape painting, there are certain comments on our environment in this picture, however inadvertently expressed. The watercolor was composed from a series of sketches embracing a panoramic 104 degrees, a far greater angle than the nineteenth-century painters ever used. It is a definite representation of nature, for everything in the painting has a basis in fact, though facts the size of mountains have been omitted. It is the comment, the impression, of a person in a hurry, of a man in an automobile who is

Figure 33. *Bird Mountain, Castleton, Vermont,* 1855. Painting by James Hope. Oil on canvas, 35 x 54 ⅛ in. Gift of Maxim Karolik for the M. and M. Karolik Collection of American Paintings, 1815–1865, 48.429. Courtesy, Museum of Fine Arts, Boston. Reproduced with permission. ©2002 Museum of Fine Arts, Boston. All rights reserved.

interested in a succession of fleeting landscapes rather than in a single one. As in the days of early settlement, the human may move into a landscape, have done with it, and then move on to unexploited fields. Fortunately, the effect of the painter, in so doing, is not so devastating as that of the farmer-woodsman.

Wolfgang Born has said that the intense pride in the new land stimulated the growth of an American "documentary" style, a style that irritates many critics today. Yet looking at James Hope's painting of Bird Mountain, one senses the love the artist must have felt (figures 33 and 34). It is beautiful even though – or because – the forest has just been cleared; and the livestock, the atmosphere of rural calm, have drastically altered the aspect of the land. The locomotive, a new and exciting creation, whistles

Figure 34. Site of *Bird Mountain, Castleton, Vermont,* 1953. Photograph by Paul Shepard.

across the scene. The abstract form of the terrace in the center is in reality a graveyard; death has been banished by the painter. The picture is unusual in its combining of historical ideas, of ideal and picturesque and abstract and factual concepts. The changing fields and forests could only represent a new country. Did the clearing actually go right to the water's edge, after the pattern of the Old World where the rains are gentler? And if so, what devastation must have followed! This is a landscape people live in, for it holds them in its lap.

Some nineteenth-century American painters went west, sought out the green spots that most resembled New England and the East, and produced work new only in the gargantuan proportions of the canvas. As Klitgaard has pointed out, however, in "Through the American Landscape," contemporary painters are still struggling to interpret the great arid landscapes with as little help as possible from the old Romantics and the indoor modernists alike.

Yet even to paint a landscape as a sort of retinal stimulation is to formulate a judgment on nature, a judgment more formal than that of the American tourist on the English tower, and no less important.

The modern approach is quite unlike that of the New Englanders whose quiet joy in the countryside is expressed in their detailed painting. The course of its analysis is full of pitfalls, but it can perhaps be best approached through a survey of what those early New Englanders thought. Their records have been gathered, their historical environment is reasonably well known, and time has lent us perspective in the study of the nineteenth-century New Englanders and their works.

Dead Cities in the American West

THE TOWERS OF BABYLON AND THE WALLS OF JERICHO follow Western travelers no matter where they go. They are a part of a body of resources from which Christians and Jews continue to draw rich imagery. They have become symbolic in somewhat the same way that the mundane world is visually reduced to a workaday body of signs. What happens when an antique imagery, cast in the desert, is returned to semiarid lands as cultural baggage?

Perhaps there is no better example of the evocative power of geomorphic forms than the response of westering pioneers to the novel lithology of eroded remnants and angular cliffs. To many of the thousands who followed the Oregon Trail before 1850 the escarpments and sedimentary bluffs along the Platte River in western Nebraska were the structures of a ghostly architecture. The Reverend Samuel Parker wrote in his diary in 1835:

Encamped today near what I shall call the old castle which is a great natural curiosity. . . . [It has] the appearance of an old enormous building, somewhat delapidated; but still you see the standing walls, the roof, the turrets, embrasures, the dome, and almost the very windows; and the guard houses, large, and standing some rods in front of the main building. You unconsciously look around for the enclosures but they are all swept away by the lapse of time—for the inhabitants, but they have disappeared; all is silent and solitary.

These speculations were more than the whimsy of a saddle-sore preacher. The journals of mountain men, farmers, speculators, and soldiers are replete with similar comparisons. Their wonder is directed toward rocks called Steamboat, Table, Castle, Smokestack, Roundhouse, Courthouse, Jail, and Chimney. Why should these particular rocks have looked more like buildings than any back east? And why should they have made such an indelible impression on the traveler? These are problems in human ecology, of the genesis of attitudes toward the landscape, of the fusion of experience in nature with historical ideas of process and natural change; and they reveal a projection into new situations of values evolved in an old, familiar, and different environment.

Proceeding northwest along the terraced banks of the Platte at a longitude just beyond 103 degrees, a few minutes south of the forty-second parallel, the traveler was about six weeks out of Independence. After crossing the upland between the Platte forks, he had followed for almost two weeks the "shores" of what Washington Irving described as the "most beautiful and least useful" river in America. Because the Platte was a kind of linear oasis the itinerant was scarcely aware of the progressive alteration in vegetation and landforms. The travelers hailed from several states, particularly eastern and midwestern. They were heterogeneous groups, numbering sometimes in the thousands. They were alike insofar as they shared the geological provincialism of men reared in the subhumid forest landscapes of America and Europe. They shared also the historical background and values of Protestant Yankees and Hoosiers of the 1830s and '40s.

At Scotts Bluff the itinerant had climbed more than three thousand feet above Independence. He had traversed the northern high plains from the oak-hickory forest to the margin of semiarid highlands, from regions of more than thirty inches of rainfall annually to under fifteen. Leaving the savannahs of the western boundaries of the forests, he had crossed the tallgrass prairie and the shorter mixed grasses to the place where the up-land vegetative cover ceases to be continuous – a significant point where the influence of weathering and mass wasting of geomorphic structures results in a change in the vegetation. The traveler had also entered a re-gion of greater daily temperature range, more numerous cyclonic storms, and less relative humidity, with their varied and subtle effects on human perception and response.

The climatic stage was set. Plodding up the valley of the Platte, with its arm of forest, meadow, and savannah, the unaware traveler penetrated new biotic and geomorphic surroundings. Shortly after he had entered what is now Scott's Bluff County, Jail and Courthouse Rocks appeared on the left horizon some fifteen miles away. As the column passed slowly to the right of these structures, more came into view, and finally an escarp-ment appeared parallel to the trail about five miles from the river. This mountain, "Wildcat Ridge" on present maps, is more than thirty miles long and sends three spurs north almost to the river's edge, the western-most being Scotts Bluff.

The first fifteen miles or so produced a galvanizing impact on the ob-server. There had been intimations of things to come, such as buffalo trails that looked to one pioneer "like the once oft-trodden streets of some deserted city." The valley with its pleasant greenery had itself been suggestive; Rufous B. Sage observed that "everything had more the ap-pearance of civilization than anything that I have seen for many days, the trees, the shrubs and bushes, grapevines, the grass – resembling blue grass – the singing of the birds in the trees, the sound of the ax cutting wood for breakfast." Then, as the westbound party drew abreast of the bluffs, a wave of astonishment swept through it. John Bidwell wrote in 1841, "the scenery of the surrounding country became beautifully grand and picturesque – they were worn in such a manner by the storm of un-numbered seasons, that they really counterfeited the lofty spires, towering edifices, spacious domes, and in fine all the beautiful mansions of cities" (figure 35).

Figure 35. *The Stone Walls, Upper Missouri.* Painting by James Meyer. From James Meyer, *Scenery of the United States,* 1855.

Numerous observers discovered lighthouses, brick kilns, the Capitol, Beacon Hill, shot towers, churches, spires, cupolas, streets, workshops, stores, warehouses, parks, squares, pyramids, castles, forts, pillars, domes, minarets, temples, Gothic castles, "modern" fortifications, French cathedrals, Rhineland castles, towers, tunnels, hallways, mausoleums, a Temple of Belus, and hanging gardens that were "in a tolerable state of preservation, and showing in many places hardy shrubs that, having sent down their long roots into partial openings of the supporting arches, still smiled in beautiful green, amid general desolation," according to J. Quinn Thornton. Taken at a glance the rocks "had the appearance of Cities, Temples, Castles, Towers, Palaces, and every variety of great and magnificent structures . . . splendid edifices, like beautiful white marble, fashioned in the style of every age and country," reported Overton Johnston and William Winter. Where more palpably than in America could such a jumble of architecture actually look like a city?

A. Delano saw ancient and exotic ruins:

> Here were the minarets of a castle; there the loopholes of bastions of a fort; again the frescoes of a huge temple; there the doors, windows, chimneys, and the columns of immense buildings appeared in view, with all the solemn grandeur of an ancient, yet deserted city, while at other points Chinese temples, dilapidated by time, broken chimneys, rocks in miniature made it appear as if by some supernatural cause we had been dropped in the suburbs of a mighty city—for miles around the basin this view extended and we looked across the barren plain at the display of Almighty power, with wonder and astonishment.

But the cities were not often American ones. What cities came to mind?

J. Q. Thornton: "The mind was filled with strange images and impressions. The silence of death reigned over a once populous city, which had been a nursery of the arts and sciences, and the seat of a grand inland commerce. It was a Tadmor of the desert in ruins."

What people had lived here?

Edwin Bryant: "No effort of the imagination is required to suppose ourselves encamped in the vicinity of the ruins of some vast city erected by a race of giants, contemporaries of the Megatherii and Ichthyosaurii."

John K. Townsend: "Noble castles with turrets, embrasures, and loopholes, with draw-bridge in front and the moat surrounding it: behind, the humble cottages of the subservient peasantry and all the varied concomitants of such a scene, are so strikingly evident to the view that it required but little stretch of fancy to imagine that a race of antediluvian giants may have here swayed their iron scepters, and left behind the crumbling place and the tower, to all of their departed glory."

What had happened to them?

There was a room, suggested J. Q. Thornton, where "that monarch might have sat upon his throne, surrounded by obsequious courtiers and servile slaves, while the lifeblood of men better than himself was being shed to make him a holiday." Perhaps because of this degeneracy the city had been overwhelmed. Another suggested that it had been occupied by "a people who had perhaps gone down into the vortex of revolutions . . . leaving no trace of their existence, save those remains of architectural grandeur and magnificence." From the position of the ruins some travelers reconstructed the probable course of catastrophe, a series of pitched battles, slaughter, pillage, fire, and the "bodies in promiscuous piles about the gates."

The illusion was so difficult to resist that a present reader of these journals discriminates with difficulty between a speculative visual play on forms and their animation by ghosts from the European and biblical past. The mirage "would deceive the most practiced eye were it not known that it is situated in a wilderness hundreds of miles from any habitation." There was a continual protestation of bemusement and flashes of embarrassed self-consciousness. Rev. Sam Parker declared, "One can hardly believe that they are not the work of art. Although you correct your imagination, and call to remembrance, that you are beholding the work of nature, yet before you are aware, the illusion takes you again, and again your curiosity is excited to know who built this fabric, and what has become of the by-gone generations." Israel Hale rode twelve miles to inspect the incredible Chimney Rock (figure 36): "I could not help imagining that it might be the work of some generation long extinct and that it was erected in commemoration of some glorious battle or in memory of some noble chieftan [*sic*]. But on arriving at the spot I could discover no marks of hammer, axe or chisel, no cemented joints by which it should be cemented in one solid mass."

The first half of the nineteenth century had been an era of geological discovery. Many who had little education but for one reason or another were interested in minerals and rocks felt the impact of this science. Among them, and certainly among the more educated groups, geology was providing exciting new vistas of the earth's surface and the origin of landforms. By 1835 anyone who thought about the new geological information at all was aware, however vaguely, of the process of change. It was a time of electric tension at the popular level between an old assumption of a static world and the discovery of a new one in which time seemed to carve itself upon the landscape.

The advances in geology strangely influenced certain aesthetic theories, particularly those involving the picturesque and sublime ruin. From the evidence at hand the ruin seems to have a respectable and venerable iconography. It had, for instance, Christian and pre-Christian symbolism. With the Renaissance and its new veneration for classical antiquity,

Figure 36. *Chimney Rock,* 1837. Painting by Alfred J. Miller. The Walters Art Museum, Baltimore, Maryland.

and the emergence of nationalism with its celebration of the indigenous past, the ruin became enmeshed in several historical strands. Perhaps the ruin's most provocative effect was as testimony to the ravages of time. It is unfortunate that, while most aesthetic histories probe the importance of the ruin in the eighteenth and nineteenth centuries, with its sense of the sublime progression of time, there has been very little study of its ecological context.

The Chimney, noted William Watson, "is composed of soft sandstone, and like the surrounding bluffs, is in a state of decay; and nothing that I saw on the route put me so strongly in mind of my approaching dissolution." There is no question that the city in Wildcat Ridge was in ruins. One rock had "the appearance of a vast edifice, with its roof fallen in, the great doorway partially obstructed, and many of the arches broken and fallen." The structures were all magnificent "but now lift up their heads amid surrounding desolation; befitting monuments of man's passing glory, and of the vanity of his hopes," sighed J. Q. Thornton. The description of the cycle of empire postulated by several itinerants was exactly the view of cyclic history that Thomas Cole, the landscape painter, had impressively depicted in his five large paintings of *The Course of Empire*.

Perhaps no aspect of the pioneer experience at Scotts Bluff was more cogent than the combination of geomorphic circumstances. The arm of the familiar deciduous forest community that follows the Platte may, as already suggested, have marked the transition into a novel environment. But the geomorphic situation was suddenly, shockingly evident. Because of its cut-and-fill nature, much of the Platte Valley is without bluffs; in Scotts Bluff County the river has cut bluffs and they are sufficiently distant from the trail to be seen as a whole. Semiarid climatic conditions begin to prevail at about this longitude and there seem to be fundamental changes in the relationship of mass-wasting or erosion factors. The result is that the forms of the hills are no longer rounded, and their slopes lose the S-shaped profile so characteristic of a humid climate. A theoretical line, the critical slope, is much decreased, with the result that, with the passage of time, the mountains retreat rather than lose height and steepness.

The peculiar situation in Scotts Bluff County is partly due to the location and direction of a tributary called Pumpkin Creek, which flows east into the North Platte. For some distance it parallels the larger stream and, like it, has cut deeply into the conglomerates, sandstone, and compacted alluvium of various sizes and resistances. Wildcat Ridge is a neck of upland towering between the two valleys. Regressive erosion into this ridge has separated it in several places, leaving isolated outlying remnants and sculpturing it with the aid of other climatic agencies into a maze of forms that show the differential erosion of the various materials. Architecturally, a single cliff is only a facade compared to the fully sculptured three-dimensional forms cut here by these two streams and their tributaries.

The clear air and absence of trees made perspective exceedingly difficult for men whose visual habits had developed with the size and distance clues of a humid landscape. The three long, dissected spurs running north from the ridge lent additional depth to the scene, creating the impression upon observers of standing in the city rather than looking at a flat picture. The box canyons into which they looked, Horseshoe Flat and Cedar Valley, contained nothing to dispel the architectural image, their floors neatly terraced by the stream.

In this way the ceaseless process of geomorphic change had staged a scene that caught the imagination. The landscape forms in the distance seemed associated directly with an aesthetic that had developed around ruins, and psychic experiences may have been heightened by novel physical circumstances. But alone these do not account for the extravagant response of plains-weary pioneers any more than they do for that of the modern traveler who is drawn to those same rocks today by subtle forces that cannot be identified. There was more to the experience than contemporary aesthetics. It seems possible that Wildcat Ridge and Scotts Bluff and other cliffs along the Green, Snake, Missouri, or Platte Rivers operate as signs in part of the biological syndrome associated with "imprinting." When a gosling just from the egg attaches itself for life to the first-large-object-moving-away as its "mother," it is imprinted for life. This is the fixing of associations at a crucial period in the developing brain. To apply it here, rocks of certain angular shapes may always mean "man-made structure" to European Americans because of an indelible association of form with human works perceived at a crucial moment in the mental growth of the observer. A somewhat similar phenomenon is the interior of the forest as a metaphor of a temple, of which there are many examples in literature. J. Z. Young has suggested that large structures, notably cathedrals, are, because of their permanence, ultimate symbols of the most human of qualities—the striving for perfection of communication. It is interesting to note that thousands of people moving up the Platte in the 1840s left their names, destinations, and the date carved and written on every available surface along the Oregon Trail.

The refinements of the illusion of architecture and the interpretations that make vivid reading of these pioneer diaries emerge richly from the lush eclectic heritage of the American and European past. For example, the imagery associates these structures with nobility and with a violent destruction. Revolution against autocracy and despotism, more precisely the American Revolution, was fresh in mind and yet distant enough to have acquired the sheen of legend. Although professing to oppose them, then as now, Americans seemed strangely receptive to the forms and pomp of feudalism and royalty. Other cultural aspects can be only briefly mentioned. Undoubtedly the medieval European background from the forest myths of children's stories to the gothic novel continued to occupy a cultural vacuum, which the new life failed to nourish. In addition, among the mythologies of our Mediterranean and Near Eastern heritage are those of classical history with its associated architectural forms. The advent of modern archeology lent power and charm to the notion of the cycle of empire, a cherished view of history in the eighteenth and nineteenth centuries. A prebiblical myth involved the rebuilding of ruined cities in the desert by heroic measures. W. H. Auden probed it briefly in *The Enchafed Flood,* indicating the effect of its imagery on the literate mind of the nineteenth century. The mystery of the Lost Tribes was a living issue. Here is a striking coincidence. To what extent and in what ways did the expressions of human experience in the American West fall back upon an imagery that had originally come from the desert, persisting as metaphor and fable in European life until it once again found its way to the desert? It is a factor in the inception and pursuit of our national concept of reclamation and the tenacious idea that only good can come of unlimited irrigating, reclaiming, and repopulating the deserts of America. No complete explanation of the formation of Americans' ideas of their West could afford to omit the significance of the landform as a compelling force.

English Reaction to the New Zealand Landscape before 1850

THE NEW ZEALAND LANDSCAPE POSED A SPECIAL PROBLEM in the perception of the Pacific by Europeans. Its climatic and geomorphic variety, its unusual biota, its size and distance from England, its relationship to Maori culture, its complex of landforms and biotic features combined the familiar and the exotic and offered new experience for English eyes. Though foreign, these landscapes were laced with familiar features similar to those of the humid temperate environment of home.

Travelers and settlers in New Zealand joined in the discovery and description of the Pacific. Much of this work was routine and topographic; letters and books reported the soils and lay of the land and documented resources with the appraising eye of the practical man.

But at least half of those whose diaries survive in the Turnbull and Hocken Libraries responded in additional ways to the environment: they reported the landscape in terms of an iconography of scenery, with a language of natural theology, with a sense of man in nature that did not end with the inventory of usable resources. These reports reveal feelings rooted in a tradition of landscape aesthetics informed by neoclassical ideas of art, natural history, and empirical science. These feelings were attached to visual clues referring to features of the man-broken forests of northwestern Europe and to the pastoral traditions in the interpenetration of European man and nature. Together with a strong evangelical bent, this was the framework within which the English traveler and emigrant came to grips with a new world.

The itinerant Englishman was also a traveler with a mode, style, and language available to him from the traditions of tourism. Like the American pioneer going west on the Oregon Trail in the same years, he was curious and speculative about the environment; he collected mineral specimens for his cabinet, he listened to bird songs, and he climbed the nearest hill for the view. His ideal world was fruitful and productive, but the fruitfulness was part of a context greater than the cultivated field; it was an arrangement of patterns involving many aspects of nature.

The new arrivals delighted in scenes recalling home. They remembered the domesticated English countryside whenever they saw small fields under cultivation or openings resembling meadows, where there were cottages with flowers around them, and where rural industry and productivity formed an animated genre. The cottage garden evoked "old English feelings," said Felton Matthew in 1840, feelings that he was eager to redirect to his new country wherever signs of home shed an ambience of familiarity. Only a few isolated clues were necessary, he said; there was nothing in much of the New Zealand landscape "to remind the spectator that he is looking upon a foreign country."

The human-centered landscape of domesticity with hedges and clovers always recalled home, whereas only some parts of the undisturbed areas seemed familiar. Harbors, forested nearly to the water's edge, were compared to English lakes. Creeks were like trout streams. Most of the bush vegetation was too different in detail to be confused with English woodland, but there were similarities. Edgar Allen Poe had said that the beauty of a landscape increased by half closing one's eyes. So, a forest grove might suggest an English rookery. A closer look spoiled the illusion: the finer details of trees were different, "nests" resolved into parasitic plants, and rooks themselves turned into tuis. A distant and general view was possible where the bush edge was seen across an open place, such as a body of water or a paddock. Seen in this way the bush could be beautiful, though a forest without a sward, according to Mrs. S. H. Selwyn, compared poorly to those of England. The pleasant green of cleared settlements near Wellington, laced with small streams, reminded Tyrone Power of English turf. Clearings were welcome as cheerful, homelike relief from the gloomy strangeness of the bush, especially as these clearings acquired crops and hedges, domestic animals, and English weeds.

Panoramic views reminded the settler of certain provinces in England. This was like Cornwall, but hillier; only Devon had such grand scenery; here was a Canterbury scene; there was open land like the downs of Wiltshire or Dorsetshire; the new land was fertile like the vales of Somersetshire; or wild and fertile like a combination of Derbyshire and Devonshire. This sort of comment applied to the general scenery although the species of plants were exotic and foreign. The typology was largely physiographic, referring to general vegetation and geomorphology rather than to details. Hills and plains, forest and grassland, occurred in both New Zealand and England, although the specific clues suggesting a resemblance were not always identified. There was an unarticulated, spontaneous perception of slope, physiographic texture, horizon lines, and patterns of bush and open land, and of village and wild land. Less clear but evident was the nineteenth-century interest in scenic "types" on a common climatic basis and a cataloging of comparative landscapes whose chief advocate was Alexander Humboldt.

There were comparisons to European scenery: rivers like the Rhine or the Arno, the Rhône, and Saône; mountains like Mont Blanc or Monte Rosa; village scenes reminiscent of Italy, Portugal, or Asia Minor; forests like the Black Forest or the Indian jungle. Particularly to the settlers from Scotland the fern and scrublands of the Bay of Islands resembled moors and heaths, while harbors looked like lochs. These diverse and seemingly arbitrary places were nothing more than those foreign parts of the world best known to Englishmen, perhaps from books more than actual travel.

Such likenesses with their suggestion or analogies and equivalences were actually based on scanty clues and occasional visual forms that seemed to give the scene heightened significance.

Thomas Cholmondeley observed in 1854 that every farm servant's "beau ideal of a new country" was the gentleman's park. He noted that Englishmen preferred pastoral country in the image of "some great gentleman's seat," with its fine domestic grasses, its clumps of graceful trees, and lack of underbrush. This was not only the farmer's view, but also a general attitude of gentry and educated men.

In New Zealand a partly cleared area—that is, a scene "studded with woods"—suggested a park, particularly if the remaining vegetation was "like ornamental shrubbery" and the cleared area was in grass or young wheat so as to suggest "a fine English estate." Rolling hills and meandering rivers in such a partly cleared country were likewise suggestive. Open ground near a lake with a skirt of pines looked like "English pleasure grounds." In the New River area of the South Island the extensive open country with clumps of trees seemed to be a gentleman's park "on a magnificent scale." In such circumstances, some observers could scarcely believe that the scenery was not the result of human activity. The idea was attractive not only because the park landscape had become a sign of gentility, but also because it lent to a raw new country a mark of artistic achievement suggesting a previous civilization. The European landscape aesthetic did not allow for naturally open country. It was easy to imagine meadows as the tokens of a past society of great wealth and taste, of which the Maoris might only be the barbaric successors or the degenerate survivors.

The most abundant references in the immigrant literature to the native landscape were disparaging. These remarks referred mostly to its uninhabited and unimproved aspect. The "heath" was gloomy and the mountains and forest, like "Caesar's Britain," were frightful without humans. It was not only uninviting, rugged, and repulsive, said W. Mann, but unproductive and accursed. The bleakest, most barren, and most uninteresting lands were the scrublands, sandy coastal plains, interior volcanic plateaus, and the sparse tussock grasslands. The forests evoked gloom except when seen from the outside, which was possible only across water, from a clearing, or from a mountaintop.

In some instances this seemed merely to be the voice of the utilitarian, to whom land was beautiful which was most fruitful, as Dr. Johnson had once said. From this perspective it was "a grief" to see this wasteland, desolate and uninhabited, barren and sterile in the absence of man's hand. This dissatisfaction was not based on the appearance of the land so much as the knowledge of its unproductive state. But it was more than a negative response to the land's appearance; the wilderness in this view was immoral. The evangelist was indignant, for he knew that barrenness was a curse and that barrenness in nature was a sign of the absence of the Christian. It was a place, said Sarah Mathew, without the signs of Deity – such as flowers; or, as William Marshall put it, a landscape seemingly barren because of the failure of the settlers to retain God in their thoughts. Where treeless, the countryside was "sterile." The more nearly desertlike the scene, the more compelling the sense of a "world blasted by sin," as Richard Taylor described the grassland near Tongariro. Puritanical Protestants of the nineteenth century contrasted nature with grace; wild nature was the outer of a series of concentric zones surrounding the European village. These zones were the wild forest, tamed woodland, outer pastures, cultivated lands, gardens, meadows, and village nuclei. In the village was the home with its family patriarch, the church with its minister, and the individual's recognition of a heavenly hierarchy. However, this conservative, feudal concept of the universe was far from untouched by newer opposing views that were less pessimistic than the Calvinist doctrine.

The heathen and the wild land were interrelated. In the evangelical view, wilderness and paganism were part of the same context. As Bernard Smith has shown, the ignoble savage was a product of science and evangelicalism, the contradiction of the innocent and naturally noble child of nature. No wonder Sarah Mathew saw in New Zealand's "wilds . . . a counterpart of the inhabitants that possess it." Where are the valleys in corn, lamented Thomas Chapman, "the flocks lying in the green pastures, and the temple of the Lord?" The missionary knew that his converts, in changing their way of life, would modify the landscape as well as their personalities. His conviction was reinforced that sin in man and sin in nature were counterparts of the same unsatisfactory but redeemable state.

The bishop, wrote C. J. Abraham, "never misses an opportunity to point out to the natives the moral superiority of the shepherd's life." The fern is like the savage, said Taylor; both are going down before civilization. The native and the country would rise together, uplifted by civilization, industry, and rational ideas, according to John Lilliard Nicholas; or, as George Angas, the painter, put it, elevated from barbarism by colonialism and Christianity. In this view native agriculture and crafts were inferior to keeping sheep and cattle, the pastoral scene more elevating than the rough clearing of a gathering economy.

The model of redemption in the landscape was the English countryside. The land needed English grasses and English trees. It seemed a great pity that the land lay uncultivated, that there were noble forests and fertile plains without anyone to till them. Traveling through the wilderness, Taylor invariably found the scenery improved at villages; Pahia, he wrote, was a civilized spot in a dreary wilderness. Others found "charm" in cultivation surrounded by woods and mountains, homesteads that broke the monotony, the beauty increasing where there were villages and men were busy "leveling the land for God."

Here, said Charles Hursthouse, were "home beauties stealing over the wild grandeur." These solitudes need the English oak to make them beautiful, said J. L. C. Richardson. Such was the association of nostalgia with morality, aesthetics, and utility.

There were additional evangelical uses of the wilderness. In the biological sense, only an occasional sandy coastal plain or acidic, volcanic upland could be termed a desert. And, although the travelers and settlers at this time had scarcely seen the semiarid area of the South Island, which climatically approaches desert, there was no hesitation in applying the term to any wilderness. Like the Flemish painters of the sixteenth century who put their Christian saints in the "wilderness" of green meadows and groves of trees, the Englishman had a northerner's view of the desert as any countryside removed from Christian settlements. In Scriptures, however, the semiarid desert is the prototype of wilderness.

The central area of the North Island was like the wilderness in Scripture, said Ashwell. It was "a desert land and uninhabited," wrote Colenso. Years later, J. L. Campbell wrote in Poenamo that civilization was to make "the desert place glad." Taylor, finding Kihikihi an oasis in a dismal state of nature, preached from Luke 16:17 and referred to St. John in the wilderness. He was inclined to compare his position to that of Moses when the throng assembled like a "multitude in the wilderness."

The metaphorical use of the desert, with its tacit contradiction of all that is normal and Christian, involved the immediate environment in evangelical semantics. The "wonders of creation" were interesting to Ashwell because they suggested the "wonders of redemption." The evangelist looked beyond Wesley to the Puritanical perspective, the notion of the complementary book of Scripture and book of Nature, and further to an ancient world of emblems, of the Physiologicus. In the early Middle Ages, nature was a world of anthropocentric symbols where mere things stood for moral truths, where nature's cryptograms functioned only to illustrate the Word. It had been modified as a result of early natural science, compatible with revealed religion in that it simply increased the number of such signs, as study of any object in nature might reveal more general truths. Nature had been symbolic in a time of symbolic painting, but remained so even when painting (and vision) focused on nature. But by the nineteenth century, its symbolism had become less doctrinaire and more literary.

Richard Taylor of Wanganui was a master of this sort of vision. Although he was capable of a rather technical geological analysis of the exposed bedding in a cliff, he often described his surroundings – to which he was very sensitive – in allegorical terms, characteristically using these figures in his sermons. He improvised on the grander aspects of scenery in this way. Volcanism he found frightening in contrast to the plains and forest that showed a God of love. Tongariro reared its head above the world like Christ; the Wanganui was like faith; Egmont rose above the clouds like God's word above the darkness; the wilderness was like the natural heart; the garden like the new man. Even details had this function: the crust over the fumaroles was like a pavement of love over hell, its strength equivalent to one's faith. The glow-worm was a gleam of faith in the surrounding gloom. Descriptions were usually of vast, geomorphic structures and in this way borrowed from the "passion of the sublime" which, historically, had its roots in religious contemplation of the earth and the heavens.

In sharp contrast to the view that wild nature was cursed with the fallen Adam was the conviction of the virtue in nature. Early explorers in the South Pacific transported this theme from the geographical mythology of the past, finding islands in a state of paradise. This pleasant illusion was shaken repeatedly by natural science and anthropology in the eighteenth and nineteenth centuries, but, a theme as old as the golden age, it persisted in the human mind.

The area of the Bay of Islands, said William Marshall, showed us what the earth might have been were it not for the curse. The tropical aspect of the bush and the prodigality of growth evoked the image of paradise. William Yates observed that New Zealand, having no lions or tigers, was preserved by Providence for man. Indeed, the absence of "beasts in the dim forest" and, in contrast to America and India, of dangerous reptiles, was one of New Zealand's most paradisiacal aspects. The lack of desirable animals could, said Hursthouse, be remedied. We can add the good, he suggested, whereas America will have great difficulty getting rid of the bad.

Yet in 1840 there was relatively little said of paradise; neither the climate nor most of the countryside suggested Eden. The Maoris, though more "noble" in appearance than Australian blacks, were far from innocent in the eyes of most Englishmen.

The theme of an intrinsically virtuous nature was broader than the image of paradise. From the time of the Cambridge Platonists and Lord Shaftesbury at the end of the seventeenth century, the religious-compassionate faith in nature expanded from Deistic convictions to an epitome in Rousseau, Goethe, and the English Romantic poets. In America, an editor devoted all his time to publishing Wordsworth for the local market. Such a sentiment did not flourish in New Zealand, although individuals who were strongly evangelical often expressed their experiences of certain wilderness scenes as both good and religious. In the Bay of Islands Augustus Earle found that the countryside – wild, magnificent, fresh from the hand of nature – inspired thoughts of God. Some believed that clearings and houses detracted from its beauty. Even the vast, stony volcanic landscapes were beautiful handiworks of God. These occasional, qualified remarks carry suggestions of romantic thought, characteristic of English and American poetry and fiction of the time, particularly in Coleridge, Wordsworth, and Byron. Lines from literature were quoted and amateur attempts made to describe the wilderness. In New Zealand forest scenes evoked reference to "children of the mist," "German diablerie," and "theatrical scenes." Ulysses and Jason were mentioned, Shakespeare's Jacques, Burns's "Halloween," and a cave suggested Coleridge's "Kubla Khan." But on the whole, literary references were impoverished. The writers were not illiterate; they were just not seeing nature in literary terms.

Yet these writers were "romantic" about the landscape, insofar as that term has been used to mean an emotional or irrational response. They described their pleasure in bird song and, when birds were silent, commented on the dreary lack of animal sounds. The "monotonous" lack of "animated life" referred particularly to the absence of indigenous mammals.

Many travelers experienced the combination of unique fauna, wilderness, and exotic surroundings as what might be called the paradox of noisy solitude. (A similar experience was common among westward-moving Americans crossing the plains on the Oregon Trail in the 1840s.) Observers frequently noted that they were surrounded by "silence," "solitude," "the absence of sound," "stillness," or "quiet." But the remark was usually qualified by "except for:" and followed by a description of many sounds. In the bush the silence was broken only by the calls of certain birds, pigs and dogs, the splashing of water, the wind in the foliage, and the noise of the travelers themselves. Generally, the bush was probably quieter than the village, but it was seldom described as silent without qualification. Perhaps there are psychological reasons for this sort of response to environments structurally and acoustically unfamiliar.

A closely related experience was a profound sense of loneliness, most likely to afflict those who stood on high places contemplating panoramas of wild countryside. They wished to share the scene with their spouses or, in the mood of the nineteenth-century tourist, regretted that, besides themselves, there were none but savages to see it. It was not only a matter of quiet contemplation but, as Sarah Mathew said, "We might fancy ourselves the only inhabitants of the world." Taylor urged himself on the long, hard track between Wanganui and the Taupo area with the thought that, fatigued as he was, his was the first European foot on that particular trail. Angas's pleasure in exploring a cave in its virgin purity was in knowing that "ours were the first human eyes to behold" it. William Gilpin had written in the previous century, in the course of wandering and sketching in England, that to get the greatest pleasure from such trips one must imagine oneself to be the first person ever to behold the scene. Imagining that one was lost was also one of those romantic dramatizations of the self.

Although the perception of the scenery did not stress the virtue of the wild in poetic terms, it was literary in another way. After we have hedged and planted, noted Hursthouse, there will be but one thing lacking, "the charm of age, the vestiges of the past, the spot endeared by old associations and traditions." A bright future for the colony seemed ahead, but it was a promise in which the past seemed more attenuated. Although their lives were the product of a stream of English tradition, it was not a family or political history that was lacking so much as the visible relicts of a society. The landscape was itself a result of the interworking of human and natural history, but only ruins lent venerable dignity to a countryside. At home and in Europe, particularly on the Grand Tour, remains were everywhere: Great Reminders of the accumulating experience of a nation and the melancholy turning of the Wheel of Time. Even certain old trees, crossroads, passes, and hills had their associated history. The Americans were especially sensitive to the shortage of such tokens in their own country and went about the remedy in much the same way as the early New Zealand English.

First, there were some actual ruins of rather impressive dimensions: the Maori terraces and ditches. While these were interesting in themselves, with a knowledge of the legends associated with them they became much more exciting. Godfrey Mundy found them appropriate, "with their legendry [*sic*] associations of strife, and massacre, and cannibal feasts," as sites for vineyards and olive groves. Even better, they looked like Roman tumuli in England. J. Logan Campbell argued bitterly that the English should keep the Maori names for mountains, rivers, and all the landmarks, and so add to their dignity.

Second, there were suggestive geomorphic and biotic forms. Here a river channel looked like the work of man and there hills formed a "grand amphitheatre." The simile embraced cliffs, erosion residuals, and caves. A distant "castellated outline," a remarkable rock with a cupola on its summit like St. Peter's, isolated pillars like Druidical altars, volcanic rocks suggesting ruined castles, "turreted" points of the sort found near "mouldering battlements," an island looking as though it had Gothic windows, cliff tops reminiscent of bastions along the Rhine were typical examples. Angas, reminded of Coleridge's "Kubla Khan" by a cave, called it a natural temple.

The Canterbury grasslands, observed Cholmondeley, are ruins of forestlands. Hursthouse spoke of the forested mountains of the South Island as country in which Audubon might meet the moa and Owen stumble over the ichthyosaurus: the ruins, as it were, of the biological past. The intense amateur interest in geology and natural history stimulated a reconstruction of events that focused on the cliffs and other exposures that looked architectural. A serious interest in geological process was not out of keeping with an interest in ruins, for geology itself had emerged from seventeenth-century speculation on mountains as "the ruins of a broken world." Moreover, the man of taste and education found such forms aesthetically as well as intellectually interesting; ruins had been built in English gardens and had a significant place in landscape painting and the romantic novel. And so Joseph Banks and many after him found the natural arches along the coasts and other ersatz architecture "picturesque."

The third and most curious remedy for the dearth of local ruins was the view that New Zealand was now like "Caesar's Britain." The fern, said Taylor, was rapidly going down, England having long ago passed through its fern stage. He was plunged into melancholic meditation by the sight of abandoned English cottages. Angas described the moonlight on the ruins of an unfinished mill as a picturesque scene. But the young Cambridge graduate, Thomas Arnold, expressed it most clearly when he envisioned the New Zealand scene two centuries hence, "should English civilization and power be overthrown," when ruined embankments, bridges, and fragments of locomotives and dynamos would testify to the earlier glory. In short, today's world was full of tomorrow's ruins.

Just as solitude was a condition for either a profound religious or an extremely romantic experience, certain scenes categorically regarded as Sublime "affected the mind" in a way that could be interpreted either aesthetically or religiously. The Sublime had been defined in detail in the previous century by Edmund Burke, in dealing with "the effects of visible objects on the passions." In contrast to the Beautiful, which corresponded to pastoral scenery, the Sublime excited the "emotions of self-preservation." From an older reference to cosmic and heavenly things, in the seventeenth century it was transferred to the description of terrestrial phenomena: those scenes that produced in the observer feelings of awe or horror—horror as an aesthetic—vast, obscure, powerful natural forces, and pictures of them. In the north of Europe sublime landscapes had been painted by Adrian Van Diest and in the south by Salvator Rosa. From the time of James Dennis, travelers had sought out sublime experiences that had, in fact, made possible the aesthetic enjoyment of mountain scenery.

From this point of view William Colenso's climb along the brink of a cliff, leaving him horror-struck and with swimming brain, might be expected among the waterfalls and precipices of the hills along the Mohaka River. Seashore cliffs, with the "hollow moaning of the waves, dashing among submarine excavations formed in the black craggy rocks," were a spot of "solitary horror" in which J. S. Polack said his prayers. Others found not only the shore but also the terrible cauldrons and horrible springs of the thermal areas delightfully repugnant. Mount Egmont was vast and grand. To most the interior of the forest was gloomy, and the newcomer, Richard Hodgskin, decided that he was "afraid to venture in very far."

A night scene in a Maori village, with a dozen fierce, tattooed men in the red glow of the fire, caused Augustus Earle to comment that Rosa could not have created a finer example of the horrible. From prayers and real danger the sublime experience graded into pictorial scenes or rhetoric.

Longinus defined the Sublime as a form of elevated speech or colored oratory. Exaggeration and vivid language characterize the rhetorical sublime. Those who get their information from other written sources usually, in retrospect, describe such scenery as indescribable and then proceed to use a flood of contrasting adjectives. It is a substitute for rather than a record of sublime experience and the foundation of travelogue writing. The tourist industry in 1960 referred to New Zealand as a "world in miniature," a phrase employed by G. B. Earp in his *Hand-Book for Intending Emigrants* in 1849. The rhetorical description, though turgid with the enumeration of natural wonders, seldom describes a specific scene, but rather a generalized bird's-eye view.

The painterly vision of New Zealand was second only to evangelism as a general attitude toward the new environment. Pictorial perception of the surroundings is a kind of abstraction with its own mode and history. Henry and Margaret Ogden, in their *English Taste in Landscape in the Seventeenth Century* (1955), believe that its development was marked by a breakdown of the distinction between topographical and ideal painting in such a way that aesthetic values were transferred from the ideal to the topographic and from it to the scenery itself. The newly excited interest in nature influenced painting. Itinerant Flemish limners, then the Dutch, worked in England through the seventeenth century. An emergent pictorial attitude followed several distinct lines in the eighteenth century. The "prospect," usually a panorama from a high place, had great prestige. Its paramount models were by Claude Lorraine, whose broad Virgilian pastoral scenes with their classical figures and idyllic wistfulness inspired Cozens, Wilson, Palmer, and other English landscape painters. In the foreground was the shadow of a nearby tree. Beyond was a middle plane with figures and architecture and two background planes, the nearer usually a body of water or a valley, the farther a range of mountains.

When John Nicholas visited Whangaroa Harbour in 1814 he found "matchless scope" for the pencil of the artist. For "doing justice to the sublime scenes" he needed, he said, the power of a Barry or a Radcliffe. Like many others he drew sketches in his journal. At the Three Kings Islands he thought of Claude Lorraine or Salvator Rosa. Canterbury, in its open parts, lacked "variety in the foreground" according to Hursthouse, and Tyrone Power criticized the scenery near Wanganui because of its lack of cultivated lands.

The most detailed descriptions of New Zealand landscapes, except for geological and botanical documentation, were written of panoramas from ships or high places. Men frequently climbed a mountain to observe the scene. William Marshall called such a scene a "glorious painting." Godfrey Mundy described the scenery of the Bay of Islands first with the fern and shrubs at hand. He then proceeded to the estuary with its islands, and on to the plains of Victoria with the Waimate station. "Beyond these the swelling ferny hills, rising gradually into mountains of wilder and grander form, lose themselves in the showery clouds common to this climate." He was painting a picture with words, not in the order that a painter constructs a landscape but in the manner of a connoisseur looking at a painting.

The panoramic view, regardless of the state of cultivation or settlement, tapped a familiar aesthetic need for the assimilation and enjoyment of New

Zealand nature. Its neoclassical ideas of pastorality, virtue, and allusion to empire and culture were harmonious with the aspirations of pioneers and their image of a new country. Even a terrain that seemed monotonous in its vegetation could seem interesting for its physiography. Such a varied prospect called forth "Christian optimism," a visual expression of the plenitude of God's creation for man. The evangelical attitude of the nineteenth-century Englishman followed the righteous Christian view of nature, diluted by two centuries of connoisseurship and the growing tendency to discuss art abstractly.

The details of a scene could also be dealt with in an abstract way. Uvedale Price, at the beginning of the nineteenth century, wrote an observer's guide to "the Picturesque" that included features of the landscape of interest to artists because of their rough textures or the broken or irregular play of light and shadow. Henry Thoreau in America had argued against this when he pointed out that this rendered a dead horse hanging from a hook as aesthetic as a live one in a pasture. It made many homely details worth sketching that had no place in the neoclassical form of graceful mythological scenes. Old Crome and the "Norwich School" in England, and before them the Dutch landscape painters, had prepared the English eye to enjoy old bridges, bosky trees, shaggy animals, and the general hodgepodge of peasant life.

Two aspects of the New Zealand scene in particular became aesthetic through picturesque vision: the forest and the Maori village. Angas ascribed the picturesqueness of the forest interior to the epiphytic plants clinging to the "noble trees of gigantic growth." It was this same luxuriance and the diversity of form of these plants hanging from the trunks and foliage that Hursthouse found picturesque. The tree fern, the roots on the forest floor in ravines where the rock was exposed, and the play of light through the foliage high overhead contributed to the effect. It is interesting to note that it was just these features—the gloominess, the ominous net of plants between the forest floor and tree crowns, and the mass of surface roots, which trapped water and made walking difficult—to which others objected, or which they found distressing, desolate, and repulsive.

A similar antithesis focused on the Maori village. The sculpture and architecture of the *pah* were far from beautiful by classical standards. Village lanes were muddy and cluttered with pigs and dogs. Sleeping huts were often flea-ridden and smoky, their exteriors rough and temporary. It was possible to regard such a scene as barbaric and filthy, or else as picturesque. As E. J. Wakefield said, "Picture to yourself this scenery." It was charming to imagine oneself as being in such a picture, an encampment in the woods that, "could it have been flashed by some magic mirror before the eyes of the relations and friends of those who formed the foreground, they would have gazed upon it with intense interest." The Maoris harvesting potatoes, corn, and kumera resembled peasantry at work in their vineyards. In its reference to Italian peasants the picturesque tended to slip from purely pictorial qualities back to a literary association.

In a different direction, a newer and even purer visual abstraction emphasized light and color. At the beginning of the century Allison had proposed that color had aesthetic values quite independent of the subject matter. As the connoisseur had learned to sort out the visual enjoyment of chiaroscuro, it would be possible in the nineteenth century to do the same with color, then with line, form, and so on. These were some of the steps in the acquisition of modern visual sophistication to which the tourist of the century, as well as the connoisseur, owed his facile commentary and detached point of view. The forests are "nothing but green," complained Hursthouse, and need "fifty more gaudy flower-bearing trees like the scarlet Rata." He found that the color improved with settlement and the introduction of domestic flowering plants.

The aesthetic pleasure in light and color was extended by interest in the weather and the sky. In the voyage across, every atmospheric event was keenly observed; in the new landscape, sensitivity to the novel features of the sky developed.

This combination of abstract visual qualities, the picturesque, the traditional panorama or bold prospect, and scenery similar to Italian Renaissance landscape painting, to Flemish and Dutch paintings on English walls, and to their English imitators, provided a complex footing for "pictorial vision" in New Zealand. Its elements varied in relative importance according to individual experience. It was not only a basis for judgment but also a guide for vision itself.

The romantic sentiment that had swept Europe and the older settlements of America in the first half of the nineteenth century endowed wild land with a moral imperative. Even on the prairie frontier of America in the same years that Wellington was being settled, praises to God and nature were united. At its most urgent this mixture of feeling, faith, and discovery was more to the observer than a matter of taste, reflecting convictions about the world and self. The early New Zealander resisted this literary-romantic softening of his Christianity. There is almost no reference to Wordsworth, Byron, Coleridge, Goethe, Chateaubriand, or other romantic writers, and virtually none to Burns, Gray, or Shakespeare. The scarcity of Byronesque poetry and the absence of philosophical naturalism were not marks of illiteracy. The ideal vision of a world undefiled by civilized man was there, but it referred less to the incarnation of deity in the landscape than to the pre-Romantic image of paradise and to idealization of terrain in pictorial rather than literary terms.

There were some exceptions to the dominance of pictorial over philo-sophical romanticism of nature. But in general in New Zealand descrip-tions, there was little of the Rousseau-like reverie, of "intimations" induced by scenery, of the sense of kinship and spirituality in the surroundings found in contemporary English and American writing. To generalize from these diaries, one might say that the authors were theologically fundamen-talist and conservative, yet not Puritan. Positive and immediate reaction to ruinlike forms was characteristic of this time. But ruins did not evoke dreams of the Middle Ages or a cryptogram of the universe in which hu-man societies endlessly rose and fell in a grand cycle of empire. They did not suggest the novels of Ann Radcliffe or Horace Walpole. As vestiges of the past, they were the signs of continuity; natural ruins were a substi-tute for a cultural history. These noble rocks carried a century's intense interest in the interplay of geology and architecture, in rock piles that had once been castles or chapels. This was the legacy of the religious-aesthetic sense of the sublime. Since the seventeenth century it had been associated with theories of the origin of the earth and had linked man and nature in the processes of decay. Indeed, since the Italian Renaissance the ruin had been a major symbol in Western culture that accumulated a whole complex of meanings. It was this aura of the ruin more than any explicit sign value that attached the emigrant's hopes to the new landscape.

The traveler in New Zealand went from scene to scene, from one pleas-ing prospect to the next, between them crossing intervals of barren plains; dull, wet forests; dreary shores; dismal, sandy coasts; and interminable "fir-covered" hills. Landscapes were admired for abstract visual qualities, types of scenery familiar from the great landscape painters, the man-centered biotic community of English country life with its cottages, domestic animals, domestic plants, and field patterns resembling rural and village patterns of home.

The association of such improved pastoral scenery with virtue and Godliness was the most persistent theme in the records written by the New Zealand pioneers. Nostalgia was inseparable from a sense of duty. The necessity of clearing and fencing was inextricably associated with Christianizing the Maoris, and, indeed, with the creation of a beautiful domesticated environment. Because of these intertwined factors, it would be deceptive to refer to this attitude merely as utilitarian in the sense of material well-being. The admiration of a prospect of the "improved" village and its environs is one of the oldest clearly identifiable forms of English landscape aesthetics, dating at least from the sixteenth century. In New Zealand it was newly charged with the spirit of colonial enterprise, humanitarianism, and democratic idealism that exalted the image of the free-holding yeoman not only as an independent God-fearing man but as a figure-with-ground.

The newness of the biota to the English settler—to which in some other parts of the world he was hostile—was ameliorated by two factors in New Zealand. One was the sense of participating in the scientific discovery of the Pacific: Most diaries of the early whites contain more or less systematic observations of a scientific nature on topography, climate, soil, vegetation, and animal life. The other was the structural similarity of the landscape to the English countryside. These likenesses were due to similarities in drainage patterns, topographical texture, or homogeneous diversity; to similar climate or biotic formations, such as the mosaic of open-and-wooded countryside with its vocal, seasonal bird fauna. In this temperate-climate world the itinerant's vision was most selective. Neither continuous plain nor forest belonged to the iconography of scenic beauty or tender home memories. The broken forest is the habitat of temperate-climate humans. If the meadow-with-distant-forest included further signs of humanization—domestic animals, cottages, roads, fences, and so on—it enhanced the scene even further, with an optimum the pastoral rural milieu.

Gardens Revisited

The Garden as Objets Trouvés

THE SIMULATION OF THE ROMAN VILLA DEI PAPIRI IN
Malibu, California, as the J. Paul Getty Museum, with its heterogeneous collection of baroque paintings, medieval manuscripts,
Louis XIV furniture, and Greek bronzes, reminds us that the
impulse to collect may be no less equivocal when the objects are
rare and expensive than when they are selected from the tidal
flotsam and jetsam. Putting aside the possibility that it demon-
strates a form of behavior known from the study of bowerbirds
and woodrats, we should perhaps not overlook the odd behavior
of our nearest nonhuman relatives. Citing Wolfgang Kohler's
study of the great apes, Joseph Campbell notes: "Kohler found
that his chimpanzees would form inexplicable attachments for
objects of no use to them whatsoever and carry these for days
in a kind of natural pocket between the lower abdomen and the
upper thigh. An adult female named Tschengo became attached
in this way to a round stone that had been polished by the sea.
'On no pretext could you get the stone away,' says Kohler, 'and

203

in the evening the animal took it with it to its room and its nest.'"[1] So much for ethology and the likelihood that the phenomenon is larger than just we humans.

Idiosyncratic assemblage and transportation of mobile pieces of the environment was institutionalized in the Renaissance in the form of collections made by wealthy individuals and increasingly given to public show as the owner allowed or was importuned by the egalitarian state. The natural history museum and art collection were historically synchronous and often jointly housed. But there is no doubt that educated people and aristocrats at least as far back as Frederick II in the thirteenth century gathered oddments that crossed their paths or were given as gifts from exotic places.

But neither education nor noble birth is required – nor wealth for that matter. This activity seems, rather, to express a widespread inquiry that may be given no other form, and to have no cultural boundaries. The puzzle it tries to answer remains unarticulated and even unconscious. (I omit from this peculiar behavior the modern museum or collector that, unlike the Getty, sets out to assemble in one place all possible species of dinosaur, postage stamps, or impressionist paintings, or, like the Victoria and Albert Museum in London, all possible examples of everything.)

At the individual level, the irrational assemblage seems to fit Claude Lévi-Strauss's description of the bricoleur, a metapersonality of the atemporal tribe, creating traditional myths from fragments of dreams, shreds of natural history, or remembered events in the same way itinerant repairmen in France make a footbridge or garden gate from the debris of old lumber piles.[2] But the true bricoleur has a clear purpose in mind, while the myths, like the unsystematic acquisition of *objets trouvés,* just grow, empirical but without a formulated intent. If the purpose of the myth is to answer the question, "How did things begin?" any given myth at least has the advantage of a long, pragmatic honing. The individual, picking up scraps of her world, seems to be without an agenda or the benefit of a tested perspective, answering the unasked question by framing a paragraph with no periods, only commas, as though the shape of the puzzle would emerge with the answer.

Collected objects are, initially, carried away from the very place in which they are likely to have context: the beach pebble shaped by the waves, the sunburned bottle from the dump of a ghost town, the opal from the igneous mine tailing. The act is irrational, of course. But then, the peculiar qualities seem to be enhanced by their unconnection. The pieces may be kept in a box or cabinet, or repositioned in the yard. Or, put another way, in locus the *objet découvert* has a kind of untranslated resonance like a bird song, a patterned tonation, vocal but not speech, part of a mysterious closed system, or like the meaningful silence of an old saw blade of a bygone era. It becomes an *objet trouvé* precisely by not sharing that status of the bird song studied ethologically or the blade examined archaeologically. Maybe the gathered objects are comparable to the syllables of elementary speech. Hockett and Ascher theorized several years ago that speech originated with the "opening of a call system."[3] The segments of primate calls were disinterred from inherent sequence and made available to any speaker in new juxtapositions, rearrangements intended to convey new meanings, yet which could be shared in a colloquial way, some kind of vernacular discourse.

In larger perspective, the problem, if not the question, is that the world is far too complicated to grasp. One must seize clues from which simplified and generalized statements may be made. Colloquy in semiliterate society often leads to conventional conclusions, such as, "Well, you may lead a horse to water, but you cannot make it drink." Nor does one need to be semiliterate to feel that a comfortable, trite generality dissolves the novelty of life into a familiar wisdom. I would not suppose, then, that an *assemblage* of old wheels or bird feathers, or a bordering of pansies interspersed with quartz, is intended to be innovative, but instead that these are metaphors like the old saying about the horse, performed differently and subject to a unique, individual witness. It asks for assent within the local culture.

An *objet trouvé* is not sought the way a piece is targeted to fill a niche in a collection. Among ancient hunters it was assumed that the hunted animal presented itself. It was discovered only when it was ready. The found object has a similar phenomenology. It is a compelling presentment, an initiative taken by an incomprehensible world on my behalf. My part of the bargain is to grasp such pieces, wrench them from their setting, take them home, and, by arranging them in some new configuration, bring them into my life.

Then they may speak not of their literal meaning, but something more significant addressed to me and by me. I may say, "I brought it home (or planted it) because it is beautiful"; or "Notice the filigreed way the wasp wove bits of bark into its nest"; or "What could have been the purpose of such a tiny brass hinge?"; but all that is mere conversation, as though describing the symptoms of a viral infection.

It may throw some light on this behavior to consider that we read from culture to nature rather than the other way round. That is, instead of reflecting on and construing architecture while examining the engineering of the wasp nest, we may unconsciously feel the object not to be nature's signal for shaping society but for some very different intention. Art may be said to be an instrument by which members of a society share perceptions, styles of consciousness, modes of preunderstanding. Reality is constructed. The world is an Easter egg hunt, contrived by an unknown artist, shaped, like Wordsworth's flower in a crannied wall, not to show us how to do something nor even to reveal nature's laws, but to give access. We can take the pieces home – seeds from a catalog, an old tire to surround them, a birdhouse – and play a game of composition, miniaturizing the universe. Thus do we incorporate ourselves in it despite the disarray that it seems to be.

Stolen cuttings from a shrub, a boulder left by an ancient glacier, a tree that has endured our careless past all can become part of the culturizing of nature – the scientifically false assumption but phenomenological necessity that all being is a community with common purpose, a mutually signaling society with a strange but shared language of forms, some of which are more revealing than others.

This is the view that nature is a specially coded art, that some natural objects and some man-made forms constitute endpoints in a series that we spontaneously construe as "messages." Testimony to this notion includes the middle ground of things given by nature and completed by the human hand: gems made into jewelry, decorative pieces made from seashells, cut and polished geodes, or, for that matter, varieties of cultivated plants still close to wild forms, bull-roarers, and other fetishes such as saints' bones mounted in gold. In the same perspective, the garden itself is that middle ground between the given and the made, a dialogue undertaken in dialect both provincial and personal. We may script, make pictures and music, and write about nature, but, to my knowledge, the garden is the only place a détente is actually undertaken. When the plants come from horticultural or floricultural programs and are part of a design, the reciprocity becomes fainter. As garden architects, we may laugh at the virgin in her bathtub grotto or the plastic duck behind a chain-link fence, but we should be uneasy about that derision, for the constellation before us affirms that someone engages selectively with a real but inexplicable world rather than retreating into abstractions or rational plans.

I suppose the gardener, in all this casual, playful, and spurious assemblage, is revealed, made vulnerable. Does she prefer bits of colored glass in the lacunae of gaseous, volcanic stone, monochrome flowers planted in antique tin cans, or a geometric alignment of old cogwheels or used bird nests? For some it may be indeed a Rorschach, exposing raw bits of the personality or infantile residues. But for most it must surely be that the world offers little gifts to the eye and mind, realized when they are used to make an environment.

Such a montage is no doubt a personal expression of taste, but it may also be a little cybernetic system in which the collector conveys a message to herself about the nature of the world by rearranging fragments of it somewhat in the manner if not the mission of the archaeologist.

These events probably correlate with something neuropsychological. But that makes no difference. The nervous system is itself part of nature. If it seeks the symmetry of a flower or the sparkle of a crystalline stone, perhaps that is because its genesis and first dialogue was with them.

Phyto-resonance of the True Self

SELFHOOD IS A COMBINED CONSCIOUS AND UNCONSCIOUS construction, aided by the capacity to refer intangible aspects of one's being to conceptual images borrowed from the outside world. In general, only characteristics of the sensible world are represented mentally. Clinical and cultural evidence suggests that a coherent concept of the inner world of the self is compiled by reference, by imagining evanescent aspects of one's being (organic function, emotions, and social relations) as well as the existential reality of the viscera. The environment constitutes a repertoire of connotation, not as a casual reference but as an essential part of the evolution of cognition. Awareness and the manipulation and communication of abstruse reality are achieved by linking them to specific, external configurations—especially visible forms—that can also be reproduced in art.

Animals constitute a major class of connotation, to which certain inner events are keyed. This metaphoric device serves the individual in speech, in mythic and poetic thought, in therapeutic meditation, and in dreams. One application of this resonance is between the image of the animal and the experience of some physical or psychological, peripatetic quality. For example, Eligio Gallegos has been extremely successful with this imaging of animals in the therapist-client setting, in which animals associated in the patient's imagination with the chakras (the body centers of spirit, thought, voice, heart, action, emotion, and base) are invited into low-intensity "conversation" and therefore serve as "voices" for concerns otherwise buried. The procedure implies an active role for the imaged animals, and their corresponding affinity for the feeling and thinking functions traditionally associated with the six energy centers. Such visualization does not require the physical presence of real animals in the meeting. Its emphasis is on performance, in which the animal corresponds to events that "move" us.

I suggest that plants function in a similar fashion and that together they represent a little-known but widely experienced holographic correspondence between the natural world and the mind. The analogous plant-human encounter might have different characteristics. A phyto-resonance—the reciprocation of an internal aspect of the self and an external plant—could act at more fundamental levels than that of animals.

Compared to affective states, what biologists call "vegetative functions" (digestion, assimilation, growth, circulation, metabolism, and so on) are at once more intimate to us, as basic activities, and yet more elusive in the difficulty we have in ordinary experience of perceiving them as part of our being. They do not lend themselves metaphorically to the active voice of animal surrogates. Lacking the humanlike features of animals, plants and plant communities present themselves as externalized elements of the self that are less assertive. Our rootedness in the earth and the spatial qualities of our relationships based on place are imprinted unconsciously, available to a botanically sensitive internal organizer, a resonance to which we are intrinsically predisposed and psychologically committed by our ontogeny.

The history of mythology is rich in signs of plants' affinity for evoking aspects of one's inner life. One need only remember the radiant mandala effect of the rose, the lotus, or the cross section of a tree trunk; King Solomon's "garden enclosed"; the visionary, gemlike, preternatural luminescence of flowers as doorways to "another world"; the syllogisms of symbolic fruits and seeds; and the trees of life and of the knowledge of good and evil. We are inclined by modern culture to see these references as literary or artistic devices. This huge body of symbolic allusion has been tainted by a thousand years of the logic of the parable and homily, or in the modern world of virtuoso performance, by the assumption that natural appearances are merely the raw matrix of creative analogies in art. Poetic references to rootedness, flowering, and fruitfulness are misunderstood as arbitrary rather than essential processes. As figures of speech, literary similes miss the point.

While there are individual plant "presences" and parts to which we respond with allusive insight, such as "stock" and "scion," there may also be a distinctive function of the whole plant association. Freud, for example, speaks of the unconscious as a forest wilderness. This reminds us that plants, more often than animals, are perceived as a collective, from the leaves on a tree or grasses in a field to trees in a forest. In this they seem to connote tissue rather than organs, the organic contexture rather than affect. The landscape appears as the equivalent of the body itself. Its living forms correspond to internal organizations, from cellular to organ systems, to their different activities, to "feeling functions" and emotions. Even the terrain, with its fine-grained, dispersed, continuous, mineral characteristics, may resonate in our consciousness with elemental aspects of the self, with skeletal or even molecular structures.

The unique quality of these metaphors is that plants keep their places and constitute holding ground in nature and thought. There are radial, sessile, marine, and animal forms, and there are plant life stages that move or are moved, but the ordinary distinction that animals are mobile and plants are stationary holds perceptually. The similarity of blood and sap notwithstanding, the exceptions to such generalizations do not vitiate our normal definitions, so that the elements of the self to which the floral world is metaphor tend to be the embedded characters of organs and tissues.

Because of the vegetative structure of the external world we spontaneously perceive ourselves as densely organized, diverse, living, patterned as components, arranged in three- or four-dimensional patterns, self-healing, home to other smaller life that may hide in and move through our tissues, green and innocent to ourselves, brittle and brown in age. It may be that the more useful plant metaphors for the less assertive aspects of the self are the analogy with involuntary functions, or between habitat and the organ system or plant kingdom as the spatial dimensions and sustainer of the living system.

I have noticed with interest that in preparing his participants for meditation on the animal "speakers" of the six chakras, Eligio Gallegos engages his clients in envisioning themselves as germinating seeds reaching for the sun, and I have wondered if this botanical preliminary was not based on establishing the best facilitating environment for the "dialogues" that follow. There is a prior reality to the existence of animals, even of the mind, a herbaceous substrate. Moreover, animals are commonly seen as playing out a role, while plants are silent hosts, yet more powerful in their root growth than any burrowing animal. Although they represent a storied structure of animal spirits, totem poles are wooden, after all, providing the medium of contiguous substance and holding ground for figures. Wood also represents the original growth that made them possible for the carver's knife and ensures their durability.

In studying the history of gardens I found it helpful to think of them as conceptualized miniatures of the cosmos. In this vein, the Garden of Eden is the world before it was stained with death; the thirteenth-century maze is the landscape of lifelong quest and perpetual risk of error and deception, in which the Right Path is scaled down to a ritual or a game; and the seventeenth-century gardens of La Notre or Boyceau are the universe of God the geometrist reduced to small worlds. As gardens, plants function tangibly in these collective images in ways to which animals are not suited.

I now find the alternative to be equally interesting, if not true, that the garden (like the forest or the prairie) is something made large rather than contracted. It is the inner landscape projected. The great outside may therefore be read as it amplifies not only intangible qualities of the self but sets of those inner relationships that are more structural than the boisterous life of desire, anger, and anxiety, which flit through our being like animals. As we move through mazes, formal gardens, or gentlemen's parks we are engaged in ways of thinking that reveal our internalized, cultural notions of faith, logic, and intuition. In gardens, created unconsciously for this purpose, we discover our own mysterious insides, perhaps in different styles at different times in order to meet the contemporary needs of the self-image. In the small, informal garden we deal with plants more individually or in some more intimate, vernacular sense of the inner world of the private self.

At the risk of offending anyone whose aching back and dirty hands testify to hard work in the garden, I suggest that as either cosmic structure condensed or internal terrain writ large, gardens are a spatial and organic metaphor that deals with being rather than doing. Collapsed or projected, the garden metaphor mitigates against the modern impression that cognition, like the body, is essentially androidal – an idea reinforced by the inanimate structures, electronic and mechanical devices, with which we surround ourselves.

Carl Pribham and Joseph Chilton Pearce suggested some years ago the idea that the human brain is functionally a hologram of the universe in the same sense that the body is a metaphrase of a niche in the ecosystem. This idea is consistent with the observation that the human brain is layered, the older or inmost structures at the bottom, like sedimentary rocks. Different parts of the brain and nervous system themselves correspond to aspects of the external world. The mind is implicated in these layers of the brain, as its neural structures represent the evolution of the brains of ancestral mammals and vertebrates. These cognitive centers have available, or are predisposed to acquire, certain external correlates of their own ineffable processes. With the evolution of human cognition, aspects of the outer world became internalized as a code for envisioning or experiencing otherwise inconceivable or alienated aspects of the self. Presumably one may exercise the code in visualization, as in Gallegos's work with animal imagery, but surely the ultimate implication and application, especially in our encounter with plants, is the palpable role of organisms in nature.

What can all this mean in how we understand plants in our lives? (1) It is based on the assumption that the perception of a flower, seed, plant, garden, or prairie spontaneously refers us to fugitive aspects of the self, a reference of which we are normally unaware; (2) that encounter has physiological (or psycho-physiological) consequences, especially in terms of healing; (3) these interspecies interactions between ourselves and plants are ecological as well as psychological, having their origins in the coevolution of our species and plant associations; (4) the beneficial aspect of living in a plant-rich environment may have ontogenetic parameters, as implied in the concept of the *kindergarten* with its overriding concern for the child's development; (5) circumstances of deprivation may exist as well as therapeutic applications that can best be addressed in the art form of the garden; (6) the correspondences between the plant and the human individual have yet to be cataloged; and (7) what the environment provides, in addition to concrete images, is coherence that not only makes the self available to the self but gives it wholeness.

I have used the idea of the person-plant metaphor in the sense that metaphor is defined by Elizabeth Sewell as essentially organic and tacit. If the human self is indeed dispersed perceptually in the landscape, to be discovered there incrementally, a whole new meaning is implied in the phrase "hunting and gathering." While anthropologists no longer think of these activities as strictly gender-bound, the plant-female and the animal-male associations in the long Pleistocene preamble speak to the differences in body-perception of men and women. Now, as our culture assumes that the organic environment is simply a neutral substance for material exploitation, we must inevitably fail—to paraphrase Edith Cobb—to make a world in which to find a self, the way the self was made.

Virtually Hunting Reality in the Forests of Simulacra

IT WOULD BE DIFFICULT TO ARGUE WITH THE ASSERTIONS that our representations of the world are always "interpretations," that concepts shape our perceptions, that the human organism is its own shuttered window. Here I wish to explore the conclusion that reality is therefore invented by words, much the way Benjamin Whorf claimed seventy years ago that colors are a consequence of their differentiation by names. In its current form this idea further argues that such inventions are motivated by a struggle for power and that there is no Grand Truth beyond texts, which are "allusions to the conceivable which cannot be presented."[1] I am also interested in the relationship of this inaccessibility of reality to "virtual reality."

According to the postmodern view, what most of us think of as simulations are only focused chatter about an unknowable external world. Even though they use living materials, the practitioners of "restoration ecology" may now find themselves, in this deconstructionist view, in the same boat with the museum curators making dioramas or habitat groups, who claim to be making artificial re-productions of the past or present world – and who are, therefore, merely engaged unconsciously in a sort of paranoid babble, lost in the vapors of their own imaginations without a compass or a satellite.

A 1973 essay in *Science* asks, "What's Wrong with Plastic Trees?"[2] The essay hardly deals with the question it poses, being primarily the last gasp of a spurious "argument" between "preservation" and "conservation." But the question is important. More recently the curator of the Devonian Botanical Garden, writing in *The Futurist,* points to fabricated lawns and polyester Christmas trees that don't wilt in polluted environments or have to be watered, giving his blessing to the wonderful world of "artificial nature."[3]

For years I have bedeviled my students with the issue of the valid-ity of surrogates for living organisms and the enigma of the mindset in which this kind of ambiguity arises, wherein the nature of authenticity and the authenticity of nature are riddled with qualification.[4] For a time I thought the issue could be clarified by examining the megaphysiology of exchange by natural trees with their environment, health-giving to the soil, air, and other organisms, as contrasted to poisoning the surround-ings by the industrial pollution from making plastic trees. Now I see that such comparisons no longer matter, since what I said to them, my own psychobabble, is itself the subject.

REALITY – YOU CAN'T GET THERE FROM HERE

Looking behind the facades of grafted signification was the intent in 1949 of Marshall McLuhan's brilliant book, *The Mechanical Bride,* which dissolved the rhetoric of magazine advertisements to expose the tacit messages concealed in the hypocrisy, presumptions, and deceit of the corporate purveyors of consumerism and our own lust to be seduced.[5] According to the current literary fashion, however, McLuhan himself can now be deconstructed, and his own agenda revealed as another level of presumptions and the struggle for power.

If McLuhan still lived in the ocean of positivist naiveté, David Lowen-thal, geographer, appeared on the new, dry shore of equivocal reality only thirteen years later. In an essay called "Is Wilderness Paradise Enow?" he argues that the substantive reality of wilderness exists solely in the romantic ideas of it. Even its inhabitants are fictions, the noble savage having been the first victim of the "new criticism." Even the buffalo, Lowenthal says, "is only a congeries of feelings."[6] The buffalo is not some *thing* among other things – the cowbirds, Indians, pioneers, and you and me. It exists only as the feelings that arise from our respective descriptions.

Lowenthal's argument is reminiscent of the psychological conception of life as being locked inside a series of boxes and therefore precluding us from knowing anything but our own internal pulsations: coded patterns of electrochemical stimuli. At the level of cerebral axons, nuclei, and their glial cohorts the assertion that my world is more real than yours seems ridiculous. And suddenly we are back in Psychology 101, where we realize that all contact with "reality" is translated to the brain as neural drumbeats, nothing more; and in Psychology 102, where the instructor titillates the class with the sensational observation that an old tree crashing down on an island makes no sound if there is no ear to hear it. A thrill runs through the class, who will go on to Literature 101 to learn that the other impulses arise in words, a barrier behind which is a vast, unknowable enigma – or, perhaps, nothing at all.

Many of us – including me – may think of a photograph as visual evidence of past reality, so that certain events may then be recalled or better understood. But we are now confronted with the assertion that there is nothing "in" a picture but light and dark patches or bits of pigment – that the events to which we supposed such photographs refer are not themselves in the blobs. If something actually occurred, it cannot be known. The result, in the case of photographs of starving people, is insensitivity to human suffering. This callous aesthetic is the object of Susan Sontag's anathema, identifying her as grounded – like McLuhan – rather than detached with the postmodern solipsists.[7]

Reflected light from actual events, focused through a lens onto a chemically sensitized plate, inscribing images that can be transferred by means of more light, lens, and photochemicals onto paper, does not neutralize the "subject matter," even if a century old. The assay of such a photograph on formal grounds is a form of aesthetic distancing. This surreality of pictures, which denies the terms of their origin, reminds us that, according to the fashion, such a picture is a text, an impenetrable facade, whose truth is hidden.

Likewise Hal Foster observes that recent abstract painting is only about abstract painting. Paintings are no more than the simulation of modes of abstraction, he says, made "as if to demonstrate that they are no longer critically reflexive or historically necessary forms with direct access to unconscious truths or a transcendental realm beyond the world – that they are simply styles among others."[8] As painting becomes a sign of painting, the simulacra become images without resemblances except to other images. Like the events that occasioned the photographs, the original configurations to which abstractions refer no longer have currency. Reality has dissolved into a connoisseurship of structural principles. A twentieth-century doubt has interposed itself between the world and us. "We have paid a high enough price for the nostalgia of the whole and the one," says Lyotard, and so holism of any kind is suspect.

In my view this denial of a prior event is an example of what Alfred North Whitehead calls "misplaced concreteness." Paradoxically, the postmodern rejection of Enlightenment positivism has about it a grander sweep of presumption than the metaphysics of being and truth that it rejects. There is an armchair or coffeehouse smell about it. Lyotard and his fellows have about them no glimmer of earth, of leaves or soil. They seem to live entirely in a made world, to think that "making" language is analogous to making plastic trees, to be always on the edge of supposing that the words for things are more real than the things they stand for.[9] Reacting against the abuses of modernism they assert that life consists of a struggle for verbal authority just as their predecessors in the eighteenth century knew that life was a social struggle for status and the technological war against nature. Misconstruing the dynamics of language, they are the final spokespeople of a world of forms as opposed to process, for whom existence is a mix of an infinite number of possible variations making up the linguistic elements of a "text."

Under all narrative we find merely more layers of intent until we realize with Derrida, Rorty, Lacan, Lyotard, and critics of visual arts that our role as human organisms is to replace the world with a web of words, sounds, and signs that refer to other such constructions. Intellectuals seem caught up in the dizzy spectacle and brilliant subjectivity of a kind of deconstructionist fireworks in which origins and truth have become meaningless. Nothing can be traced further than the semiotic in which everything is trapped. The chain of relationships that orders a functional fish market, the cycle of the tree's growth, breath, decay, and death, the underlying physiological connections that link people in communities and organisms in ecosystems or in temporal continuity – all are subordinate to the arguments for or against existence. The text – the only reality – is comparable only to other texts. Nothing is true, says Michel Foucault, except "regimes of truth and power." It is not that simulacra are good or bad replicas – indeed, they are not replicas at all; they are all there is! In a recent essay, Richard Lee defends this attitude as a "cool detachment and ironic distanciation," an eruption of cynicism caused by our daily bombardment of media fantasy, assaults on the "real," and consequent debasement of the currency of reality.[10] But I think it is not, as he concludes, simply the final relativism. There is no room even for relative truth in a nihilistic ecology.

The deconstructionist points with glee to the hidden motivations in these "falsifications" of a past and perhaps inadvertently opens the door to the reconfiguration of places as the setting of entertainment and consumption. This posture is not only a Sartrean game or artistic denial. It spreads throughout the ordinary world where pictorial, electronic, and holographic creations; architectural facades for ethnic, economic, and historical systems; pets as signifiers of the animal kingdom; and arranged news are the floating reality that constitutes our experience. We seem to be engaged in demonstrating the inaccessibility of reality.

In the past half century we have invented alternative worlds that give physical expression to the denial of disaster. Following the lead and iconography of *National Geographic* magazine, with its bluebird landscapes, and then the architecture of Disneyland happiness, a thousand Old Waterfronts, Frontier Towns, Victorian Streets, Nineteenth-Century Mining Communities, Ethnic Images, and Wildlife Parks have appeared. One now travels not only in space while sitting still but "back" to a time that never was. As fast as the relics of the past are demolished, whether old-growth forests or downtown Santa Fe, they are reincarnated in idealized form.

As the outer edges of cities expand, the centers are left in shambles, the habitation of the poor, or they are transformed into corporate waste-lands that administer distant desolation as if by magic. To console the middle-class inhabitants and tourists, a spuriously appropriated history and cityscape replace the lost center with "Oldtown." In 1879 Thomas Sargeant Perry, having looked at Ludwig Friedländer's book on romanti-cism, wrote: "In the complexity of civilization we have grown accustomed to finding whatever we please in the landscape, and read in it what we have in our own hearts."[11] An example would be the "monumental archi-tecture" of the rocky bluffs of the North Platte River as reported by the emigrants on the Oregon Trail in the 1840s.[12] Were Perry present today he could say that we make "whatever we please" out there and then an-nounce it as "found."

Michael Sorkin speaks of this architectural "game of grafted signifi-cation . . . [and] urbanism inflected by appliqué" and "caricaturing of places." Theme parks succeed the random decline of the city with their nongeography, their surveillance systems, the simulation of public space, the programmed uniformity sold as diversity. Condensed, they become the mall.[13] It is as though a junta of deconstructionist body-snatchers had invaded the skins of the planners, architects, and tour businessmen who are selling fantasy as history, creating a million Disneylands and ever-big-ger "events" for television along with electronic playsuits and simulated places in three-dimensional "virtual reality." Apart from the rarefied discourse and intimidating intellectualism of the French philosophies, the streetwise equivalents are already at work turning everyday life into a Universal Studios tour. It is not just that here and there in the malls are cafés representing the different national cuisines but that the referent does not exist. Who cares about authenticity with respect to an imaginary origin?

The point at which the architectural fantasists and virtual realists inter-sect with intellectual postmoderns and deconstructionists is in the shared belief that a world beyond our control is so terrifying that we can – indeed, must – believe only in landscapes of our imagination.

Amid the erosion of true relics from our past, can we not turn to the museum? What are the custodians of the portable physical relics doing? According to Kevin Walsh, museums now show that all trails lead to us, create displays equating change with progress, and reprogram the past not so much as unlike ourselves but as trajectory toward the present.[14] The effect is like those representations of biological evolution with humankind at the top instead of at the tip of one of the branches. In effect the museum dispenses with the past in the guise of its simulation, "sequestering the past from those to whom it belongs." Its contents, "no longer contingent upon our experiences in the world," become a patchwork of bricolage "contributing to historical amnesia." Roots in this sense are not the sustaining and original structure but something adventitious, like banyan tree "suckers" from the ends of its limbs. "Generations to come," Walsh predicts, "will inherit a heritage of heritage – an environment of past plu-perfects which will ensure the death of the past."

Not long ago I was in a zoological museum in St. Petersburg, Russia, an institution that has not reorganized its exhibits according to the new fashion of diorama art – those "habitat groups," simulated swamps, sea-coasts, prairies, or woodlands, each with its typical association of plants and animals against a background designed to give the illusion of space. There in Russia, among the great, old-fashioned glass cases with their stuffed animals in family groups, with no effort at naturalistic surroundings, I felt a rare pleasure. I realized that the individual animal's beauty and identity remain our principal source of satisfaction. When all members of the cat family, or the woodpeckers, are placed together, instead of feeling that I am being asked to pretend that I am looking through a window at a natural scene, I am free to compare closely related forms. Instead of an ersatz view I have the undiluted joy of those comparisons that constitute and rehabilitate the cognitive processes of identification. Nor does the museum display in St. Petersburg insidiously invade my thoughts as a replacement for vanishing woodlands and swamps by substituting an aesthetic image for noetics, the voyeur's super-real for the actuality.

NEW DRESS FOR THE FEAR OF NATURE

Plastic trees? They are more than a practical simulation. They are the message that the trees they represent are themselves but surfaces. Their principal defect is that one can still recognize plastic, but it is only a matter of time until they achieve virtual reality, indistinguishable from the older retinal and tactile senses. They are becoming *acceptable configurations*. No doubt we can invent electronic hats and suits into which we may put our heads or crawl, which will reduce the need even for an ersatz mock-up like the diorama. These gadgets trick our nervous systems somewhat in the way certain substances can trick our body chemistry – as, for example, the way the body fails to discriminate radioactive strontium 90 from calcium. (Strontium was part of the downwind fallout of atomic bomb testing, which entered the soil from the sky, the grass from the soil, the cows from the grass, the milk from the cow, children from the milk, and finally their growing bones, where it caused cancer.) As the art of simulacrum becomes more convincing, its fallout enters our bodies and heads with unknown consequences. As the postmodern high fashion of deconstruction declares that the text – or bits cobbled into a picture – is all there is, all identity and taxonomy cease to be keys to relations, to origins, or to essentials, all of which become mere phantoms. As Richard Lee says of the search for origins in anthropology, any serious quest for evolutionary antecedents, social, linguistic, or cultural ur-forms, has become simply an embarrassment.

But is this really new or a continuation of an old, antinatural position that David Ehrenfeld called "the arrogance of humanism"?[15] Mainstream Western theology and the Renaissance liberation of Art as a separate domain, with its neoclassical thesis of human eminence, were like successive cultural wedges driven between humans and nature, hyperboles of separateness, autonomy, and control. It may be time, as the voices of deconstruction say, for much of this ideological accretion to be pulled down. But as down-pullers trapped in the ideology of Art as High Culture, of nothing beyond words, they can find nothing beneath "text." Life is indistinguishable from a video game, one of the alternatives to the physical wasteland that the Enlightenment produced around us. As the tourists flock to their pseudohistory villages and fantasylands, the cynics take refuge from the overwhelming problems by announcing all lands to be illusory. Deconstructionist postmodernism rationalizes the final step away from connection: beyond relativism to denial. It seems more like the capstone to an old story than a revolutionary perspective.

Alternatively, the genuinely innovative direction of our time is not the final surrender to the anomie of meaninglessness or the escape to fantasylands but in the opposite direction – toward affirmation and continuity with something beyond representation. The new humanism is not really radical. As Charlene Spretnak says: "The ecologizing of consciousness is far more radical than ideologues and strategists of the existing political forms . . . seem to have realized."[16]

LIFE – OR ITS ABSENCE – ON THE ENTERPRISE

The question about plastic trees assumes that nature is mainly of interest as spectacle. The tree is no longer in process with the rest of its organic and inorganic surroundings: it is a form – like the images in old photographs. As the plastic trees are made to appear more like natural trees, they lose their value as a replacement and cause us to surrender perception of all plants to the abstract eye. Place and function are exhausted in their appearance. The philosophy of disengagement certifies whatever meanings we may attach to these treelike forms – and to trees themselves. The vacuum of essential meaning implies that there really is no meaning. A highbrow wrecking crew confirms this from their own observations of reality – that is, of conflicting texts.

There is a certain bizarre consequence of all this, which narrows our attention from a larger, interspecies whole to a kind of bedrock ethnos. For example, in each episode of the television series *Star Trek* we are given a rhetorical log date and place, but in fact the starship *Enterprise* is neither here nor there, now or then. Its stated mission to "contact other civilizations and peoples" drives it frantically nowhere at "warp speed" (speed that transcends our ordinary sense of transit), its "contacts" with other beings so abbreviated that the substance of each story rests finally on the play of interpersonal dynamics, like that which energizes most drama from Shakespeare to soap opera.

This dynamic is *essentially* primate – their own physicality is the only connecting thread to organic life left to the fictional crew and its vicarious companions, the audience. For all of its fancy hardware, software, and bombastic rhetoric, the story depends on projections of primatoid foundations, a shifting equilibrium like any baboon social dynamic – the swirl of intimidation, greed, affection, dominance, status, and groupthink that make the social primates look like caricatures of an overwrought humanity.

The story implies that we may regress through an ecological floor – the lack of place and time and the nonhuman continuum – to farcical substitutes and a saving anthropoid grace. Should such a vehicle as the *Enterprise* ever come into existence, I doubt that their primatehood will save its occupants from the madness of deprivation – the absence of sky, earth, seasons, nonhuman life, and, finally, their own identities as individuals and species, all necessary to our life as organisms.

In the later series, *Star Trek: The Next Generation,* the spacecraft has a special room for recreation, the "holo-deck," in which computers re-create the holographic ambience and inhabitants of any place and any time. The difference between this deck and H. G. Wells's time-travel machine is that the *Enterprise* crew is intellectually autistic, knowing that other places and times are their own inventions. The holo-decks that we now create everywhere, from Disneyworld to Old Town Main Streets, may relieve us briefly from the desperate situations that we face on the flight deck, as we struggle in "the material and psychic waste accumulating everywhere in the wake of what some of us still call 'progress.'" The raucous cries of post-Pleistocene apes in the *Enterprise* are outside the ken of the ship's cyborg second mate, just as the technophiles on earth will witness without comprehension the psychopathology of High Culture and literary association, with its "giddy, regressive carnival of desire," rhetoric of excess, "orgies of subjectivity, randomness," and "willful playing of games."[17]

What, then, is the final reply to the subjective and aesthetic dandyism of our time? Given our immersion in text, who can claim to know reality?

As for "truth," "origins," or "essentials" beyond the "metanarratives," the naturalist has a peculiar advantage – by attending to species who have no words and no text other than context and yet among whom there is an unspoken consensus about the contingency of life and real substructures. A million species constantly make "assumptions" in their body language, indicating a common ground and the validity of their responses. A thousand million pairs of eyes, antennae, and other sensing organs are fixed on something beyond themselves that sustains their being, in a relationship that works. To argue that because we interpose talk or pictures between this shared immanence and us, and that it therefore is meaningless, contradicts the testimony of life itself. The nonhuman realm, acting as if in common knowledge of a shared quiddity, of unlike but congruent representations, tests its reality billions of times every hour. It is the same world in which we ourselves live, experiencing it as process, structures, and meanings, interacting with the same events that the plants and other animals do.

NOTES

Paintings of the New England Landscape

1. Fisher, "New England Forest," 217.
2. Ruskin, "Arrows of the Chace," 148.
3. Price, *Essays on the Picturesque*, 2:253.
4. Irvine, *Apes, Angles, and Victorians*, 48.
5. Cornish, *Scenery and the Sense of Sight*, 48.

Ugly Is Better

1. Krieger, "What's Wrong with Plastic Trees?"

Place in American Culture

1. Scully, *The Earth, the Temple, and the Gods*.
2. Isaac, "God's Acre"; Isaac, "Religion, Landscape and Space."
3. Eliade, *The Sacred and the Profane*.
4. Modell, *Object Love and Reality;* Lewin, *The Image and the Past*.
5. Cobb, *The Ecology of Imagination in Childhood*.
6. Luria, *The Mind of a Mnemonist*.
7. Bennet, *Journal of Neurobiology,* 47; White, *Human Infants;* Newton and Levine, *Early Experience and Behavior;* Ellis, "Play, Theory and Research."
8. G. L. Johnson, *Proceedings of the Zoological Society;* G. L. Johnson, *Philosophical Transactions*.
9. Spivak, "Archetypal Place."
10. Boyden, *Impact of Civilization*.

11. Neel, "Lessons from a 'Primitive People.'"
12. Jackson, "The Westward Moving House."
13. Auden, "Ode to Terminus."
14. Guthrie, *New York Times Magazine,* 27.
15. Castaneda, *The Teachings of Don Juan,* 18ff.
16. Watts, *Reading the Landscape.*
17. Sandburg, *Selected Poems.*
18. MacLeish, "Where a Poet's From."
19. Rapoport, "Australian Aborigines."
20. McGinley, "In Praise of Diversity."
21. Newcomb, "Beckett's Road."

Place and Human Development

1. Neel, "Lessons from a 'Primitive People,'" 815.
2. Eliade, *The Sacred and the Profane.*
3. Lenneberg, *The Biological Foundations of Language.*
4. Lévi-Strauss, *The Savage Mind.*
5. Fernandez, "The Mission of Metaphor."
6. Laughlin, "Hunting, Biobehavioral System and Evolutionary Importance."
7. Witkin, "Development of the Body Concept."
8. Cobb, "The Ecology of Imagination in Childhood."
9. Shengold, "The Metaphor of the Journey."
10. Margaret Mead, "The Island Earth," *Natural Science* 170:815.
11. Rapoport, "Australian Aborigines."
12. Collier, *On the Gleaming Way.*
13. Campbell, *The Masks of God.*
14. Lévi-Strauss, *Totemism.*
15. Douglas, *Purity and Danger.*
16. Drew, "Wilderness and Limitation."
17. Paul Shepard, *The Tender Carnivore and the Sacred Game.*

An Ecstasy of Admiration

1. Atwood, *The Physiographic Provinces of North America,* 253.
2. Edwin Bryant, *What I Saw in California,* 55.
3. McCall, *The Great Oregon Trail* (May 30), 27.
4. Root, *Journal of Travels,* 9.
5. Ball, "Remarks," 1.

6. Brown, in *Memoirs of an American Gold Seeker* (June 4), 9.

7. Lillard, *The Great Forest.*

8. Webster, *The Gold Seeker* (May 28), 37.

9. Edwin Bryant, *What I Saw in California,* 22.

10. Wilkes, *History of Oregon,* 76.

11. Townsend, *Journey Across the Rocky Mountains,* 57.

12. Cyrus Shepard, Journal (May 30, 1834), Western Americana Collection, Beinecke Rare Book and Manuscript Library, Yale University, New Haven, Connecticut [hereinafter WA MSS], no. 421.

13. Ibid. (May 25, 1834).

14. Webster, *The Gold Seeker* (July 22), 62.

15. Aldrich, *Journal of Route to California* (July 12 and 21, 1849), 17, 19.

16. Sage, *Scenes in the Rocky Mountains,* 36C.

17. Watson, *Journal of an Overland Journey,* 5.

18. Benjamin Franklin Dowell, "Overland Journey by Ox Team from St. Joseph, Missouri, to California, 1850," WA MSS, no. 142.

19. Thornton, *Oregon and California* (May 30), 1:58.

20. Simon Doyle, Journals and Letters, 1849–56 (May 13–16), WA MSS, no. 144.

21. Root, *Journal of Travels,* 8–9.

22. Spaulding, "Early Oregon Missions," 30.

23. Thornton, *Oregon and California* (July 20), 89.

24. Howard Egan, "Journal of an Expedition to the Westward" (June 11, 1847), WA MSS, no. 156.

25. Thornton, *Oregon and California* (June 10), 68.

26. Dundass, *Journal of S. R. Dundass* (May 1), 10.

27. Edwin Bryant, *What I Saw in California,* 55.

28. Spaulding, "Early Oregon Missions," 17.

29. Parker, *Journal of an Exploring Tour,* 47.

30. Ibid., 37.

31. Cyrus Shepard, Journal (May 22).

32. Dowell, "Overland Journey" (June 14).

33. Williams, *Narrative of a Tour,* 6, 9, 14.

34. Thornton, *Oregon and California* (July 12), 134.

35. Cyrus Shepard, Journal (May 7).

36. Alexander Love, "Overland Journey from Leesburg, Pennsylvania, to the California Mines" (June 14), WA MSS, no. 309, p. 26.

37. Dundass, *Journal of S. R. Dundass* (June 14), 26.

38. De Smet, *Letters and Sketches,* 26:223.

39. Ibid., 214.

40. Edwin Bryant, *What I Saw in California,* 117.

41. Thornton, *Oregon and California* (July 9), 25.

42. Ibid. (June 24), 98.

43. Reading, "Journal" (August 23), 178.

44. John F. Lewis, "Overland Journey: From St. Joseph to California" (June 20 and 25), WA MSS, no. 301.

45. Cyrus Shepard, Journal (May 30 and May 26).

46. Sage, *Scenes in the Rocky Mountains,* 31, 36.

47. Edwin Bryant, *What I Saw in California,* 22.

48. De Smet, *Letters and Sketches,* 299.

49. Geikie, *Landscape in History and Other Essays,* 53.

50. Parker, *Journal of an Exploring Tour,* 49, 72.

51. Wm. H. Frush, "Overland Journey across the Plains to Oregon" (July 3), WA MSS, no. 206.

52. Delano, *Life on the Plains,* 108.

53. Edwin Bryant, *What I Saw in California,* 95; Egan, "Journal of an Expedition" (May 11).

54. Delano, *Life on the Plains,* 73.

55. Isham, *Guide to California,* 25.

56. Doyle, Journals (June 14).

57. Sage, *Scenes in the Rocky Mountains,* 60.

58. Bennett C. Clark, "Overland Journey from Missouri to California" (June 6, 1849), WA MSS, no. 81.

59. Samuel Hancock, "The Narrative of Samuel Hancock, Being a Description of his Overland Journey to Oregon in 1845," WA MSS, no. 240.

60. Truesdael, "Letter from Sutter's Mills, Calif."

61. Staples, "Journal" (July 19), 136.

62. Delano, *Life on the Plains,* 99.

63. McCall, *The Great Oregon Trail* (June 29), 31.

64. Dundass, *Journal of S. R. Dundass* (June 29), 31.

65. Farnham, *Travels in the Great Western Prairies,* 17.

66. Cornish, *Scenery and the Sense of Sight,* 52.

67. Edwin Bryant, *What I Saw in California,* 28.

68. Lewis, "Overland Journey" (May 14).

69. Ibid. (June 19).

70. Edwin Bryant, *What I Saw in California,* 22.

71. Thornton, *Oregon and California* (May 20), 35.

72. McCall, *The Great Oregon Trail* (June 4), 29.

73. Spaulding, "Early Oregon Missions," 10.

74. Parker, *Journal of an Exploring Tour,* 54.

75. Edwin Bryant, *What I Saw in California,* 24, 61.

76. Farnham, *Travels in the Great Western Prairies,* 12.

77. Thornton, *Oregon and California* (May 27), 47–48.

78. Farnham, *Travels in the Great Western Prairies,* 34.

79. De Smet, *Letters and Sketches,* 222.

80. Delano, *Life on the Plains,* 35.

81. Sage, *Scenes in the Rocky Mountains,* 31.

82. Delano, *Life on the Plains,* 83.

83. Farnham, *Travels in the Great Western Prairies* (June 30).

84. Townsend, *Journey Across the Rocky Mountains,* 66.

85. Crawford, "With the Oregon Pioneers" (September 8), 18.

86. De Smet, *Letters and Sketches,* 337.

87. Thornton, *Oregon and California* (July 10), 131.

88. Edwin Bryant, *What I Saw in California,* 116.

89. De Smet, *Letters and Sketches,* 238.

90. Egan, "Journal of an Expedition" (June 21).

91. Snider, *Diary,* 231.

92. Egan, "Journal of an Expedition" (June 21).

93. Cyrus Shepard, Journal (May 25).

94. Doyle, Journals (June 3).

95. Edwin Bryant, *What I Saw in California,* 56.

96. McCall, *The Great Oregon Trail* (June 4), 29.

97. Thornton, *Oregon and California* (July 10), 131.

98. Ibid. (June 26), 110.

99. Farnham, *Travels in the Great Western Prairies,* 19–21.

100. Staples, "Journal" (May 27), 124.

101. Edwin Bryant, *What I Saw in California,* 36.

102. Bruff, *Gold Rush* (1849), 48.

103. Egan, "Journal of an Expedition" (June 7).

104. Spaulding, "Early Oregon Missions," 31.

105. Parker, *Journal of an Exploring Tour,* 38.

106. Ibid., 38.

107. Farnham, *Travels in the Great Western Prairies,* 18–19.

108. Hastings, "Diary," 13; De Smet, *Letters and Sketches,* 192.

109. De Smet, *Letters and Sketches,* 214.

110. Cyrus Shepard, Journal (April 27).

111. F. D. Everets, "Journal of the Route to California" (May 26, 1849), WA MSS, no. 193.

112. McCall, *The Great Oregon Trail* (May 8), 12.

113. Delano, *Life on the Plains,* 50.

114. Bruff, *Gold Rush* (July 26), 54.

115. Palmer, *Journal of Travels,* 13.

116. Johnson and Winter, *Route Across the Rocky Mountains,* 10.

117. Delano, *Life on the Plains,* 44.

118. Edwin Bryant, *What I Saw in California,* 38.

119. Monk, *The Sublime,* 136.

120. Downing, "How to Choose a Site," 163.

121. Hammerton, *Landscape,* 297.

122. Hastings, "Diary" (May 29), 14.

123. Sage, *Scenes in the Rocky Mountains,* 15.

124. Dowell, "Overland Journey" (May 23).

125. Farnham, *Travels in the Great Western Prairies,* 33.

126. Watson, *Journal of an Overland Journey* (May 23), 6.

127. Staples, "Journal" (June 4), 126.

128. Sedgby, *Overland to California* (June 24), 28.

129. Edwin Bryant, *What I Saw in California,* 121.

130. Thornton, *Oregon and California* (May 13 and 16), 18, 27.

131. Cornish, *Scenery and the Sense of Sight,* 64.

132. Edwin Bryant, *What I Saw in California,* 29.

133. Thornton, *Oregon and California* (May 15), 20.

134. Lewis, "Overland Journey" (June 3).

135. Sage, *Scenes in the Rocky Mountains,* 49.

136. Spaulding, "Early Oregon Missions," 30.

137. Edward J. Willis, Diary (May 8), WA MSS, no. 527; Thornton, *Oregon and California* (May 27), 47–48; Edwin Bryant, *What I Saw in California,* 21.

138. Hancock, "Narrative."

139. Sharmann, *Sharmann's Overland Journey to California* (1849), 20.

140. Crawford, "With the Oregon Pioneers," 39.

141. Ferris, *Life in the Rocky Mountains,* 25.

142. Smith, *Virgin Land,* 51–52.

143. McCall, *The Great Oregon Trail* (July 3), 47.

144. Edwin Bryant, *What I Saw in California,* 22.

145. Thornton, *Oregon and California* (July 16), 135.

146. Williams, *Narrative of a Tour,* 18.

147. Parker, *Journal of an Exploring Tour,* 48.

148. De Smet, *Letters and Sketches,* 159.

149. Ibid.

150. Ibid., 223.

151. Babbit, *Rousseau and Romanticism,* 227.

152. Catlin, *Letters and Notes,* 1:258–61.

153. Everets, "Journal" (June 1).

154. Ibid. (May 21).

155. Bruff, *Gold Rush* (July 17), 46.

156. Watson, *Journal of an Overland Journey* (June 17), 16.

157. Hale, "Diary of a Trip," 78.

158. Hastings, "Diary" (June 23), 156.

159. Lewis, "Overland Journey" (May 20–21).

160. Thornton, *Oregon and California* (May 28), 54.

161. Dundass, *Journal of S. R. Dundass* (May 13), 14.

162. McCall, *The Great Oregon Trail* (June 14), 37.

163. Doyle, Journals (July 3).

164. Root, *Journal of Travels,* 15.

165. Thornton, *Oregon and California* (July 9), 125.

166. De Smet, *Letters and Sketches,* 162.

167. Sedgby, *Overland to California* (June 28), 30.

168. Bruff, *Gold Rush* (July 9), 36.

169. McCall, *The Great Oregon Trail* (May 17), 21.

170. Dundass, *Journal of S. R. Dundass* (June 12), 25.

171. Bidwell, *Journey to California,* 3–5.

172. Farnham, *Travels in the Great Western Prairies,* 12.

173. Edwin Bryant, *What I Saw in California,* 19.

174. Delano, *Life on the Plains,* 12.

175. Sage, *Scenes in the Rocky Mountains,* 26.

176. Cyrus Shepard, Journal (May 1).

177. Ibid. (May 21).

178. Delano, *Life on the Plains,* 35.

179. Reading, "Journal" (July 2), 161.

180. McCall, *The Great Oregon Trail,* 2.

181. Edwin Bryant, *What I Saw in California,* 53.

182. Ibid., 25.

183. Parker, *Journal of an Exploring Tour,* 54.

184. Egan, "Journal of an Expedition."

185. Dundass, *Journal of S. R. Dundass* (May 2), 10.

186. Edwin Bryant, *What I Saw in California,* 67.

187. Dundass, *Journal of S. R. Dundass* (May 22), 17; Cyrus Shepard, Journal (April 28).

188. Farnham, *Travels in the Great Western Prairies,* 16.

189. McCall, *The Great Oregon Trail* (June 10), 33–34.

190. Clyman, *Journal,* 35.

191. Sage, *Scenes in the Rocky Mountains,* 30.

192. Staples, "Journal" (June 2), 126.

193. Geological Society of America, *Glacial Map of North America* (New York, 2d printing, rev., 1949).

194. Lugn, *The Pleistocene Geology of Nebraska.*

195. Dundass, *Journal of S. R. Dundass* (May 28), 19.

196. Cyrus Shepard, Journal, (May 19).

197. De Smet, *Letters and Sketches,* 157.

198. Quoted in Ghent, *The Road to Oregon,* 128.

199. Dundass, *Journal of S. R. Dundass* (June 1–2), 10–21.

200. Thornton, *Oregon and California* (June 20–21), 89–91.

201. Townsend, *Journey Across the Rocky Mountains,* 63.

202. Dundass, *Journal of S. R. Dundass* (June 28), 24.

203. Spaulding, "Early Oregon Missions," 19.

204. Sage, *Scenes in the Rocky Mountains,* 49.

205. Parker, *Journal of an Exploring Tour,* 74.

206. Sage, *Scenes in the Rocky Mountains,* 62.

207. Cyrus Shepard, Journal (May 25).

208. Frush, "Overland Journey" (June 8).

209. Edwin Bryant, *What I Saw in California,* 106.

210. Hale, "Diary of a Trip" (June 20), 82.

211. Ball, *Autobiography,* 71.

212. Everets, "Journal" (June 22).

213. Ferris, *Life in the Rocky Mountains,* 35.

214. Cyrus Shepard, Journal (June 1).

215. Lewis, "Overland Journey" (July 1).

216. Reading, "Journal" (July 28), 169.

217. Bruff, *Gold Rush* (July 13), 21.

218. Ibid.

219. Bidwell, *Journey to California,* 5.

220. McCall, *The Great Oregon Trail* (July 10), 33–34.

221. Farnham, *Travels in the Great Western Prairies,* 33.

222. Sage, *Scenes in the Rocky Mountains,* 55.

223. McCall, *The Great Oregon Trail* (July 3).

224. Dundass, *Journal of S. R. Dundass* (May 28), 19.

225. Ibid., 92.

226. Delano, *Life on the Plains,* 80.

227. Sage, *Scenes in the Rocky Mountains,* 62.

228. P. C. Riffany (May 24), WA MSS, no. 474.

229. Delano, *Life on the Plains,* 92.

230. Williams, *Narrative of a Tour,* 11.

231. Wyeth, *Correspondence and Journals,* 156.

232. Ball, "Remarks," 69.

233. Hancock, "Narrative"; Parker, *Journal of an Exploring Tour,* 61.

234. Sage, *Scenes in the Rocky Mountains,* 60.

235. Lewis, "Overland Journey."

236. Delano, *Life on the Plains,* 70.

237. Bidwell, *Journey to California,* 8.

238. Edwin Bryant, *What I Saw in California,* 99.

239. McCall, *The Great Oregon Trail* (July 12), 36–37.

240. Johnson and Winter, *Route Across the Rocky Mountains,* 167.

241. Crawford, "With the Oregon Pioneers" (July 24), 10.

242. Palmer, *Journal of Travels,* 18; Ball, *Autobiography,* 69.

243. Edwin Bryant, *What I Saw in California,* 104.

244. Brown, in *Memoirs of an American Gold Seeker* (July 24), 12.

245. Edwin Bryant, *What I Saw in California,* 116.

246. Snider, *Diary,* 235.

247. Hale, "Diary of a Trip" (July 11), 66.

248. Edwin Bryant, *What I Saw in California,* 55.

249. Townsend, *Journey Across the Rocky Mountains,* 64.

250. De Smet, *Letters and Sketches,* 158. See Irving's *Astoria.*

251. Farnham, *Travels in the Great Western Prairies,* 24.

252. Cyrus Shepard, Journal (April 28).

The Garden as Objets Trouvés

1. Campbell, *The Masks of God,* 358.

2. Lévi-Strauss, *The Savage Mind.*

3. Hockett and Ascher, "The Human Revolution."

Virtually Hunting Reality in the Forests of Simulacra

1. Jean-François Lyotard, *The Post-modern Condition,* quoted in Flax, *Thinking Fragments.*

2. Krieger, "What's Wrong with Plastic Trees?"

3. Vick, "Artificial Nature."

4. Eco, "The Original and the Copy."

5. McLuhan, *The Mechanical Bride.*

6. Lowenthal, "Is Wilderness Paradise Enow?" See also my reply, "The Wilderness as Nature."

7. Sontag, *On Photography.*

8. Foster, "Signs Taken for Wonders."

9. I used to think of this attitude as the "Marjorie Nicolson Syndrome." It was from her book *Mountain Gloom and Mountain Glory* that I first got the sense there are those who seem to think that the test of nature is whether it lives up to the literary description of it. Clearly, Nicolson neither invented nor bears the full responsibility for this peculiar notion.

10. Lee, "Art, Science, or Politics?"

11. Perry, "Mountains of Literature."

12. An account appears in Paul Shepard, "The American West."

13. Sorkin, "See You in Disneyland."

14. Walsh, *The Representation of the Past.*

15. Ehrenfeld, *The Arrogance of Humanism.*

16. Spretnak, *States of Grace,* 229.

17. Poenicke, "The Invisible Hand."

BIBLIOGRAPHY

Aldrich, Lorenzo. *A Journal of the Overland Route to California*. Lansingburgh, N.Y.: n.p., 1851.

Atwood, Wallace W. *The Physiographic Provinces of North America*. New York: Ginn and Co., 1940.

Auden, W. H. "Ode to Terminus." *New York Review,* 11 July 1968.

Babbit, Irving. *Rousseau and Romanticism*. New York: Houghton Mifflin, 1919.

Ball, John. *Autobiography*. 1874. Grand Rapids, Mich.: Dean Hicks Co., 1925.

——. "Remarks upon the Geology, and Physical Features of the Country West of the Rocky Mountains, with Misc. Facts." *American Journal of Science and Arts* 28, no. 1 (April 1835).

Bennet, Edward, et al. *Journal of Neurobiology* 3 (1972): 47.

Bidwell, John. *A Journey to California with Observations About Country, Climate, and the Route to This Country.* 1841. San Francisco: John Henry Nash, 1937.

Bord, Janet. *Mazes and Labyrinths of the World*. New York: E. P. Dutton, 1975.

Born, Wolfgang. *American Landscape Painting*. New Haven: Yale University Press, 1948.

Boyden, Stephen, ed. *Impact of Civilization on the Biology of Man*. Toronto: University of Toronto Press, 1968.

Brown, John Evans. In *Memoirs of an American Gold Seeker*. Ed. Mrs. Katie E. Blood. New Haven: Association of Publishers of American Records, 1907.

Bruff, J. Goldsborough. *Gold Rush*. Ed. Georgia Willis Read and Ruth Games [Gaines]. New York: Columbia University Press, 1944.

Bryant, Edwin. *What I Saw in California, Being the journal of a Tour by the Emigrant Route and South Pass of the Rocky Mountains, Across the Continent of North America, the Great Desert Basin and Through California, in the Years 1846, 1847.* New York: D. Appleton and Co., 1848.

Bryant, William Cullen. "The Prairies." In *Poems*. Boston: Russell, Odiorne, and Metcalf, 1834.

Campbell, Joseph. *The Masks of God: Primitive Mythology*. New York: Viking Press, 1959.

Castaneda, Carlos. *The Teachings of Don Juan: A Jaqui Way of Knowledge*. Los Angeles: University of California Press, 1968.

Catlin, George. *Letters and Notes on the North American Indians in 1832*. Vol. 1. London: Tosswill and Myers, 1841.

"Catlin's Gallery (The Wigwam)." *New England Farmer and Gardener's Journal* 15, no. 47 (May 30, 1838). Reprinted from the *National Intelligencer*.

Clyman, James. *Journal*. Ed. Charles L. Camp. California Historical Society, 1928.

Cobb, Edith. "The Ecology of Imagination in Childhood." *Daedalus* 88, no. 3 (1959): 537–48.

——. *The Ecology of Imagination in Childhood*. New York: Columbia University Press, 1977.

Collier, John. *On the Gleaming Way*. Denver: Alan Swallow, 1962.

Cook, Roger. *The Tree of Life, Image for the Cosmos*. New York: Thames and Hudson, 1988.

Cooper, James Fenimore. *The Prairie*. London: Henry Colburn and Richard Bentley, 1832.

Cornish, Vaughan. *Scenery and the Sense of Sight*. Cambridge: Cambridge University Press, 1933.

Crawford, Medorem. "With the Oregon Pioneers of 1842." Journal of Medorem Crawford. Ed. F. G. Young. *Sources of the History of Oregon* 1, no. 1 (1897): 39.

Delano, A. *Life on the Plains and Among the Diggings Being Scenes and Adventures of an Overland Journey to California with Particular Incidents of the Route, Mistakes and Sufferings of the Emigrants, the Indian Tribes, the Present and the Future of the Great West*. Auburn and Buffalo: Miller, Orton, and Mulligan, 1854.

De Smet, Jean P. *Letters and Sketches*. In *Early Western Travels*, ed. Reuben Gold Thwaites. Cleveland: Arthur H. Clark, 1906.

De Voto, Bernard. *Across the Wide Missouri*. Boston: Houghton Mifflin, 1947.

Douglas, Mary. *Purity and Danger*. New York: Praeger, 1966.

Downing, A. J. "How to Choose a Site for a Country Seat." In *Rural Essays*. New York: n.p., 1857.

Drew, Wayland. "Wilderness and Limitation." *Canada Forum* 52 (1973): 625.

Dundass, Samuel Rutherford. *Journal of Samuel Rutherford Dundass, Formerly auditor of Jefferson County, Ohio, Including His Entire Route to California As a Member of the Stubenville Company Bound for San Francisco in the Year 1849.* Stubenville, Ohio: n.p., 1857.

Eco, Umberto. "The Original and the Copy." In *Understanding Origins,* ed. Francisco J. Varella and Jean-Pierre Crea. Boston: Kluwer, 1992.

Ehrenfeld, David. *The Arrogance of Humanism.* New York: Oxford University Press, 1981.

Eliade, Mircea. *The Sacred and the Profane.* New York: Harcourt, Brace, 1959.

Ellis, Michael. "Play, Theory and Research." In *Environmental Design: Research and Practice,* ed. William Mitchell. Los Angeles: University of California Press, 1972.

Erikson, Erik H. *Identity, Youth and Crisis.* New York: W. W. Norton, 1968.

Farnham, Thomas J. *Travels in the Great Western Prairies, the Anahuac and Rocky Mountains, and in the Oregon Territory.* Poughkeepsie: Kelley and Lossing, 1841.

Fernandez, James. "The Mission of Metaphor in Expressive Culture." *Current Anthropology* 15, no. 2 (1974): 119–45.

Ferris, W. A. *Life in the Rocky Mountains: A Diary of Wanderings on the Sources of the Rivers Missouri, Columbia and Colorado from February, 1830, to November, 1835, by W. A. Ferris, Then in the Employ of the American Fur Company, and Supplementary Writings by Ferris, with a detailed map of the fur country, drawn by Ferris in 1836.* Ed. Paul C. Philips. Denver: F. A. Rosenstock, Old West Publishing Co., 1940.

Fisher, R. T. "New England Forest: Biological Factors." In *New England's Prospect 1933,* ed. John K. Wright. Amer. Geog. Soc. Spec. Pub. No. 16. New York: American Geographical Society, 1933.

Flax, Jane. *Thinking Fragments: Psychoanalysis, Feminism and Postmodernism in the Contemporary West.* Berkeley: University of California Press, 1990.

Foster, Hal. "Signs Taken for Wonders." *Art in America,* June 1986.

Gallegos, Eligio Stephen. *The Personal Totem Pole: Animal Imagery, the Chakras, and Psychotherapy.* Santa Fe: Moon Bear Press, 1982.

Geikie, Sir Archibald. *Landscape in History and Other Essays.* New York: Macmillan, 1905.

Ghent, W. J. *The Road to Oregon: A Chronicle of the Great Emigrant Trail.* New York: Longmans, Green, 1929.

Gray, L. C., John B. Bennett, Erich Kraemer, and W. N. Sparhawk. "The Causes: Traditional U.S. Attitudes and Institutions." In *Soils and Men.* Year Book of Agriculture. Washington, D.C.: U.S. Department of Agriculture, 1938.

Greenwood, Grace (Mrs. Sarah Jane Clark Lippincott). *New Life in New Lands.* New York: J. B. Force, 1873.

Guthrie, Tyrone. *New York Times Magazine,* 27 November 1955, 27.

Hale, Israel F. "Diary of a Trip to California in 1849." *Quarterly of Society of California Pioneers* 2, no. 2 (June 1925).

Hammerton, Philip Gilbert. *Landscape.* London: n.p., 1885.

Hastings, Loren B. "Diary of Loren B. Hastings" (1847). *Transactions of the 51st Annual Reunion of the Oregon Pioneer Association, June 21, 1923.* Portland, Ore.: n.p., 1926.

Hawkes, Jacquetta. *A Land.* With drawings by Henry Moore. London: Cresset Press, 1954.

Hockett, Charles F., and Robert C. Ascher. "The Human Revolution." *Current Anthropology* 5, no. 3 (1964): 135–68.

Hussey, Christopher. *The Picturesque: Studies in a Point of View.* London: G. P. Putnam's Sons, 1927.

Huxley, Aldous. *The Doors of Perception.* New York: Harper, 1954.

Irvine, William. *Apes, Angles, and Victorians.* New York: McGraw-Hill, 1955.

Irving, Washington. *Astoria; or Anecdotes of an Enterprize beyond the Rocky Mountains.* Ed. Richard Dilworth Rust. 1836. Boston: Twayne, 1976.

Isaac, Eric. "God's Acre." *Landscape* 14, no. 2 (1964–65).

——. "Religion, Landscape and Space." *Landscape* 9, no. 2 (1959–60).

Isham, G. S. *Guide to California, And the Mines And Return By The Isthmus With a General Description Of That Country, Compiled From A Journal Kept by Him In a Journey to That Country in 1849 and 1850.* New York: A. T. Howel, 1850.

Jackson, J. B. "The Westward Moving House." *Landscape* 23, no. 3 (1973).

Johnson, G. L. *Philosophical Transactions of the Royal Society of London* Series B, vol. 194 (1901).

——. *Proceedings of the Zoological Society of London.* 1983.

Johnson, Overton, and William H. Winter. *Route Across the Rocky Mountains, with a Description of Oregon and California, their Geographical Features, Their Resources, Soil, Climate Productions.* Lafayette, Ind.: J. B. Semans, 1846.

Jung, Carl. *Psychology and the Unconscious.* Reprint, Princeton: Princeton University Press, 1992.

Krieger, Martin H. "What's Wrong with Plastic Trees?" *Science* 179 (1973): 446–54.

Laughlin, William. "Hunting, an Integrating Biobehavioral System and Its Evolutionary Importance." In *Man the Hunter,* ed. Richard Lee and Irven DeVore. Chicago: Aldine, 1968.

Lee, Richard B. "Art, Science, or Politics? The Crisis in Hunter-Gatherer Studies." *American Anthropologist* 94 (1993): 31–54.

Lenneberg, Eric H. *The Biological Foundations of Language.* New York: Wiley, 1967.

Lévi-Strauss, Claude. *The Savage Mind.* Chicago: University of Chicago Press, 1966.

———. *Totemism.* Boston: Beacon Press, 1963.

Lewin, Bertram. *The Image and the Past.* New York: International Universities Press, 1968.

Lillard, Richard G. *The Great Forest.* New York: Knopf, 1947.

Lowenthal, David. "Is Wilderness Paradise Enow?" *Columbia University Forum,* Spring 1964.

Lugn, A. L. *The Pleistocene Geology of Nebraska.* Nebr. Geol. Survey Bull. 10, 2d ser., 1935.

Luria, A. R. *The Mind of a Mnemonist.* New York: Basic Books, 1968.

MacLeish, Archibald. "Where a Poet's From." *Saturday Review,* 2 December 1967.

McCall, A. J. *The Great Oregon Trail in 1849.* Reprinted from the *Steuben Courier,* Bath, New York, 1882.

McGinley, Phyllis. "In Praise of Diversity." *American Scholar* 23 (1954): 306.

McLuhan, Marshall. *The Mechanical Bride: Folklore of Industrial Man.* New York: Vanguard Press, 1951.

Mitchell, John F. *The Earth Spirit: Its Ways, Shrines, and Mysteries.* New York: Avon, 1975.

Modell, Arthur. *Object Love and Reality.* New York: International Universities Press, 1968.

Monk, Samuel H. *The Sublime.* New York: Modern Language Association, 1935.

Neel, James V. "Lessons from a 'Primitive People.'" *Science* 170 (1970): 815.

Newcomb, Robert M. "Beckett's Road." *Landscape* 13, no. 1 (1963).

Newton, Grant, and Seymour Levine, eds. *Early Experience and Behavior.* Springfield, Ill.: C. C. Thomas, 1968.

Nicolson, Marjorie. *Mountain Gloom and Mountain Glory: The Development of the Aesthetics of the Infinite.* Ithaca, N.Y.: Cornel University Press, 1959.

Palmer, Joel. *Journal of Travels Over the Rocky Mountains to the Mouth of the Columbia River Made During the Year 1845 and 1846.* Cincinnati: S. A. and V. P. James, 1847.

Parker, Samuel. *Journal of an Exploring Tour Beyond the Rocky Mountains under the Direction of the ABCFM Performed in the Years 1835, 36, and 37 Containing a Description of the Geography, Geology, Climate, and Productions; and the number, Manners, and Custom of the Natives, with a map of Oregon Territory.* Ithaca, N.Y.: n.p., 1837.

Parkman, Francis. *The Oregon Trail: Sketches of Prairie and Rocky-Mountain Life.* Franklin Center, Pa.: Franklin Library, 1983.

Patch, Harold Rollin. *The Other World According to Descriptions in Medieval Literature.* Cambridge: Harvard University Press, 1950.

Pearce, Joseph Chilton. *The Magical Child*. New York: E. P. Dutton, 1977.

Perry, Thomas Sargeant. "Mountains of Literature." *Atlantic Monthly* 44 (September 1879): 302.

Poenicke, Klaus. "The Invisible Hand." In *Crisis of Modernity*, ed. Gunter H. Lenz and Kurt L. Shell. Boulder: Westview Press, 1986.

Price, Uvedale. *Essays on the Picturesque*. Vol. 2. London: n.p., 1810.

Rapoport, Amos. "Australian Aborigines and the Definition of Place." In *Environmental Design: Research Practice*, ed. William Mitchell. Los Angeles: University of California Press, 1972.

Reading, Pierson Barton. "Journal of Pierson Barton Reading in His Journey of One Hundred Twenty-three Days Across from Westport on the Missouri River, 450 miles Above St. Louis, to Monterey, California on the Pacific Ocean, in 1843." *Quarterly of Society of California Pioneers* 7, no. 3 (September 1930).

Repton, Humphry. *The Landscape Gardening and Landscape Architecture of the Late Humphry Repton, Esq.* Ed. J. C. Loudon. London: Longman and Co., 1811.

Root, Riley. *Journal of Travels from St. Joseph to Oregon, with Observations of that Country, Together with a Description of California, Its Agricultural Interests, and a Full Description of its Gold Mines*. Galesburg, Ill.: n.p., 1850.

Ruskin, John. "Arrows of the Chace." In *Deucalion: Collected Studies of the Lapse of Waves, and Life of Stones*. Orpington: George Allen, 1879.

Sage, Rufous B. *Scenes in the Rocky Mountains and the Oregon, California, New Mexico, Texas, and the Grand Prairies of Notes by the Way, During an Excursion of Three Years, with a Description of the Countries passed Through, Including their Geography, Geology, Resources, Present Condition, and the Different Nations Inhabiting Them*. 2d rev. ed. Philadelphia: Carey and Hart, 1847.

Sandburg, Carl. *Selected Poems*. Ed. Rebecca West. New York: Harcourt, Brace, 1926.

Santayana, George. *The Sense of Beauty*. New York: Scribner's, 1896.

Scully, Vincent. *The Earth, the Temple, and the Gods*. New Haven: Yale University Press, 1962.

Searles, Harold F. *The Nonhuman Environment*. New York: International Universities Press, 1960.

Sedgby, Joseph. *Overland to California in 1849*. Oakland: Butler and Bowman, 1877.

Sewell, Elizabeth. *The Orphic Voice*. New Haven: Yale University Press, 1960.

Sharmann, H. B. *Sharmann's Overland Journey to California*. Trans. Margaret Hoff Aummerman and Erich W. Zimmerman. N.p., n.d.

Shengold, Leonard. "The Metaphor of the Journey in 'The Interpretation of Dreams.'" *American Imago* 23 (1966): 316.

Shepard, Paul. "The American West." In *Man in the Landscape*. College Station: Texas A&M University Press, 1991.

———. *The Tender Carnivore and the Sacred Game*. New York: Scribner's, 1972.

———. "The Wilderness as Nature." *Atlantic Naturalist,* January–March 1965.

Smith, Henry Nash. *Virgin Land*. Cambridge: Harvard University Press, 1950.

Snider, Jacob R. *The Diary of Jacob Snider. Quarterly of the Society of California Pioneers* 7, no. 4 (1845): 237.

Sontag, Susan. *On Photography*. New York: Dell, 1977.

Sorkin, Michael. "See You in Disneyland." In *Variations on a Theme Park,* ed. Michael Sorkin. New York: Hill and Wang, 1992.

Spaulding, Rev. H. H. "Early Oregon Missions. Their importance in Securing the Country to Americans." Newspaper clippings from *State Rights Democrat* (Albany, Oregon), ed. M. H. Abbott, 7, no. 14 (November 17, 1866): 30.

Spivak, Mayer. "Archetypal Place." *Forum,* October 1973.

Spretnak, Charlene. *States of Grace*. San Francisco: Harper, 1991.

Staples, David Jackson. "The Journal of David Jackson Staples." Ed. Harold F. Taggert. *California Historical Society Quarterly* 22, no. 2 (June 1943): 119–51.

Thornton, J. Quinn. *Oregon and California in 1848*. New York: Harper and Bros., 1849.

Townsend, John K. *Journey Across the Rocky Mountains*. Philadelphia: Henry Perkins, 1839.

Truesdael, C. "Letter from Sutter's Mills, Calif." *Western Reserve Chronicle* 24, no. 1736 (October 24, 1849).

Varella, Francisco J., and Jean-Pierre Dupuy Crea, eds. *Understanding Origins*. Boston: Kluwer, 1992.

Vick, Roger. "Artificial Nature, the Synthetic Landscape of the Future." *The Futurist,* July–August 1989.

Vivante, Paolo. *The Homeric Imagination: A Study of Homer's Poetic Perception of Reality*. Bloomington: Indiana University Press, 1970.

Walsh, Kevin. *The Representation of the Past: Museums and Heritage in the Post-modern World*. London: Routledge, 1992.

Watson, William J. *Journal of an Overland Journey to Oregon, Made in the Year 1849; With a Full and Accurate Account of the Route, Its Distances, scenery, plains, Streams, Mountains, Game and the Everything of Use of Interest Which Meets the Traveller in the Overland Route to Oregon and California*. Jacksonville: n.p., 1851.

Watts, May. *Reading the Landscape*. New York: Macmillan, 1957.

Webster, Kimball. *The Gold Seeker of '49*. Manchester, N.H.: Standard Book Co., 1917.

White, Burton. *Human Infants: Experience and Psychological Development.* New York: Prentice-Hall, 1971.

Wilkes, George. *History of Oregon.* New York: Wm. H. Colyer, 1845.

Williams, Joseph. *Narrative of a Tour From the State of Indiana to the Oregon Territory in the years 1841–2.* Cincinnati: J. B. Wilson, 1843.

Witkin, Herman. "Development of the Body Concept and Psychological Differentiation." In *The Body Percept,* ed. Seymour Wapner. New York: Random House, 1965.

Wyeth, Nathanial J. *Correspondence and Journals* (1832). *Sources of the History of Oregon* 1, nos. 3–6.

ACKNOWLEDGMENTS

"Paintings of the New England Landscape" was first published by the College Art Association in the *College Art Journal,* 17, no. 1 (1957).

"The Cross Valley Syndrome" was previously published in *Landscape* 10, no. 3 (1961).

"Ugly Is Better" was previously published in the *Pitzer Participant* (1975) and in Paul Shepard, *Encounters with Nature* (Washington, D.C./Covelo, Calif.: Island Press/Shearwater Books, 1999).

"Five Green Thoughts" was previously published in the *Massachusetts Review* 21, no. 2 (summer 1980) and in Shepard, *Encounters with Nature.*

"Place in American Culture" was previously published in the *North American Review* (fall 1977) and in Paul Shepard, *Traces of an Omnivore* (Washington, D.C./Covelo, Calif.: Island Press/Shearwater Books, 1996).

"Place and Human Development" was previously published in the Proceedings of the *Symposium on Children, Nature, and the Urban Environment* (Washington, D.C.: United States Forest Service and the Pinchot Institute, 1977) and is reprinted by permission of the Pinchot Institute for Conservation, 2002.

"An Ecstasy of Admiration" was a chapter in Paul Shepard's 1954 Yale University doctoral dissertation, *American Attitudes towards the Landscape in New England and the West, 1830–1870,* later edited by Paul Shepard.

"The Nature of Tourism" was previously published in *Landscape* (summer 1955): 29–33 and in Shepard, *Encounters with Nature.*

"They Painted What They Saw" was previously published in *Landscape* (1953).

"Dead Cities in the American West" was previously published in *Landscape* 6, no. 2 (1956).

"English Reaction to the New Zealand Landscape before 1850" was previously published by Pacific Viewpoint as Monograph No. 4, 1969.

243

"The Garden as Objets Trouvés" was previously published in *The Meaning of Gardens,* ed. Mark Francis and T. Hester (Cambridge, Mass.: MIT Press, 1990), 148–53.

"Phyto-resonance of the True Self" was previously published in Shepard, *Traces of an Omnivore,* 27–32. Reprinted by permission of Island Press.

"Virtually Hunting Reality in the Forests of Simulacra" was previously published in *Reinventing Nature,* ed. Michael E. Soulé and Gary Lease (Washington, D.C./ Covelo, Calif.: Island Press/Shearwater Books, 1995). Reprinted by permission of Island Press.

INDEX

Townsend, John K., 95, 111, 177

trappers, 100

travel industry. *See* tourism

travel literature, 194; cross valley in, 21; geology in, 14; guidebooks, 122, 129; about North American grasslands, 48–49; Oregon Trail, 23–26; Watts's guidebooks, 71–72; Yosemite Valley, 28

trees: on prairie, 96, 105, 135–36, 140; and solitude, 118–19

Truesdael, C., 106–7

Trumbull, John, 167–68

unconscious, 76

Van Diest, Adrian, 194

Victoria (New Zealand), 195

Victoria and Albert Museum (London), 204

View of the Round-Top in the Catskill Mountains (Cole), 67–68

View of the White Mountains (Cole), 10

Vince, Dr., 103

Virgil, 44, 46

virtual reality, 219, 221

Vivante, Paolo, 41

wagons, covered, 116, 117, 152–53

Waimate station (New Zealand), 195

Wakefield, E. J., 197

walkabout, 74

Walsh, Kevin, 219–20

Wanganui (New Zealand), 189, 195

water gaps. *See* cross valleys

Watson, William, 179

Watts, May, 71–72

Wellington, New Zealand, 185

Wells, H. G., 223

West, mythology of the, 89–90, 182

West, Rebecca, 72–73, 73–74

West Point, view from, 15–17

West Point from Fort Putnam (D. Johnson), 17

Whangaroa Harbour, 195

White, Burton, 64

Whitehead, Alfred North, 217

White Mountains, 4, 157; as America's Alps, 10; Crawford Notch, 22–23; Franconia Notch, 22–23

Whorf, Benjamin, 214

Wildcat Ridge, 175, 179–80, 181

Wilder, Thornton, 69–70

wilderness: artistic evaluation of, 165; as escape, 5; immorality of, 99–101, 152, 186–89; nineteenth-century perceptions of, 12–13; preservation of, 28; and tourism, 156–57; as virtuous, 189–90

Williams, Henry Smith, 124

Williams, Joseph, 100–101

Wind River Mountains, 105, 110, 142

Winter, William, 176

Wolf, Roy, 158, 159

Wordsworth, William, 33, 47, 118, 156, 190

Wyeth, Captain Nathaniel, 147

Wyoming, 92; human litter in, 129; Laramie Range, 137; and volcanism, 103, 107

Yates, William, 190

Yellowstone, 157, 160

Yosemite Valley, 160; Greenwood's comment upon, 163; preservation, 28, 157; tourist's comment, 156

Young, J. Z., 181